I0795656

IMAGES
of America

RIDGEFIELD PARK

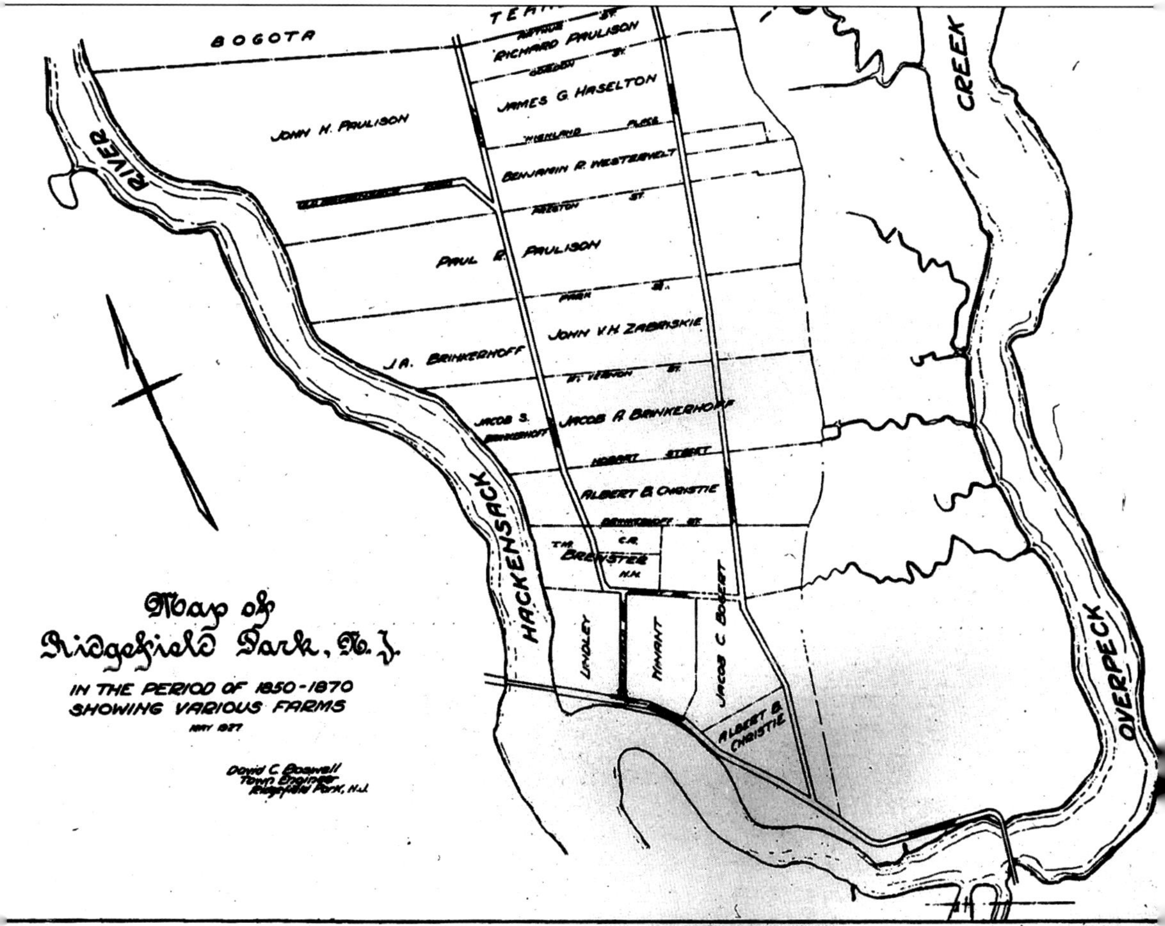

Before Ridgefield Park Was Divided Into Lots

e—The boundary lines of these farms and land holdings are shown according to the names of the streets as they are ay. In many instances the actual lines of these farms were from 100 to 250 feet either side of the streets named on the ma the exception of Main Street or Old Hackensack Road.

An 1870 Map of Farms. This map shows land holdings and farms from 1850 to 1870. Only a handful of families occupied the village property before it was divided into lots.

IMAGES
of America

RIDGEFIELD PARK

Donna E. Rose-McEntee

ARCADIA
PUBLISHING

ISBN 978-0-7385-1223-5

Published by Arcadia Publishing
Charleston, South Carolina

Printed in the United States of America

Library of Congress Catalog Card Number: 2003104306

For all general information, contact Arcadia Publishing:
Telephone 843-853-2070
Fax 843-853-0044
E-mail sales@arcadiapublishing.com
For customer service and orders:
Toll-Free 1-888-313-2665

Visit us on the Internet at www.arcadiapublishing.com

Contents

ACKNOWLEDGMENTS

Compiling information for a book like this is rarely a solo effort. I would like to thank the Ridgefield Park Public Library's board of trustees and staff for granting me unlimited access to the archives. The numerous articles within those archives have been generously donated by many village residents. I regret not being able to thank each and every person who has donated materials to the library, but I would like to mention Frank Romano, Frances Fishbach, the Persich family, and the late "Hip" Murphy for the numerous photographs and postcards they contributed.

I would especially like to express thanks to Doris Conley for her tireless efforts in helping to preserve the archives of our local history. Recognition must also be given to the Tercentennial Committee for the tremendous job done on the 300th anniversary journal. It was because of their excellent publication in 1985 that I first became enthralled with the history of our village. I learned so much from their efforts.

This list would not be complete without extending my heartfelt appreciation to my husband Phil and daughter Daina Scheideler for their encouragement and faith in my ability to complete this project.

INTRODUCTION

The village, as it is affectionately known by longtime residents, is rich with history. Volumes can be written about the history of this town and its people. This book offers but a glimpse into the past of small-town America and the development of the village, honoring the people who helped to make Ridgefield Park a thriving community.

Native Americans were the first inhabitants of this area. Legend tells us that Sarah Roelphs Kiersted acted as an interpreter between Dutch settlers and Chief Oratam, head of the Lenni Lenape tribe. In return, she was given more than 200 acres of land, which included today's Ridgefield Park, Bogota, and Teaneck. Hendrick Brinkerhoff purchased land along the Hackensack River in 1685 and became the first European to inhabit the land now known as Ridgefield Park. More settlers came to the area to farm the lands. Eventually, city dwellers were drawn to Ridgefield Park by the woods and greenery along the Hackensack River, often spending the summer. Farms soon gave way to developments, and a community was born. Originally a part of Hackensack, this area became the township of Ridgefield. In 1892, the village was officially incorporated. This change came about through the efforts of local citizens who were tired of the political control imposed on them and desired a form of self-government. It is this spirit that still remains in Ridgefield Park. Citizens are active in all aspects of the community. Many residents choose to stay in the village their entire lives, making their homes, raising families, and seeking work within the community. Generations remain within the village borders, and many names from the past still ring familiar.

Traditions abound in a small community like Ridgefield Park, and Independence Day is a perfect example. The Fourth of July celebrations are not taken lightly in Ridgefield Park. Dating back to the 1890s, and proudly recognized as featuring the nation's oldest continuously running parade, the celebration draws large crowds. Spectators line the parade route, often setting out chairs to save a place, and families gather each year in the same spot. The day starts with a bomb blast in the early morning, signaling the beginning of the festivities. The annual inspection of the fire department is the first event. A children's parade is held in the morning. Families work diligently for weeks, often in secrecy, to prepare elaborate costumes and floats in an effort to garner a trophy. The main parade, led by the board of commissioners, is held midday and includes marching bands, floats, members of the village volunteer services, and other local groups. Visitors are often amazed at the elaborate decorations that adorn homes throughout the village. Baseball games, concerts, and barbeques are held. People from all over the New York metropolitan area flood the village to attend the concert and fireworks in Veterans Park. The Fourth of July in Ridgefield Park continues to be a celebration of gratitude for the freedoms enjoyed in this great nation.

Religious freedom has been the foundation of many communities since the birth of the country. Ridgefield Park is a fine example of such freedom. Although considered a small community that stretches just over one mile square, the village has been home to churches of almost every faith. It is this diversity and acceptance that has made Ridgefield Park what it is today.

Education has always been a top priority in the village. As more people settled in town and raised families, the need for schools grew from the first one-room schoolhouse to the network of schools present today. Ridgefield Park currently boasts three elementary schools and a public high school. The high school also serves students of neighboring Little Ferry. A parochial school educates students from kindergarten through eighth grade. As times change, the village adapts. Nowhere is this more evident than in the numerous day-care facilities and preschools that have opened in the village. With the dedication of the local board of education and the concern of citizens, education will always be in the forefront.

Early settlers were drawn by the green meadows that bordered the waters surrounding Ridgefield Park. The Hackensack River and the Overpeck Creek have long been a source of recreation, transportation, and sustenance. In years gone by, these waters drew visitors to what was once considered a vacation playland. While most of us cannot imagine swimming in these waters today, efforts to clean up the environment are evident. Wildlife is returning, water quality has improved, and once again residents are looking at the river and creek as places to enjoy Mother Nature and her bounties.

Leisure activities, competitive sports, and community involvement have been a mainstay in the village for many years. Water sports, baseball, football, and tennis are a part of the history. A strong sports program in the village schools and town-sponsored recreational activities continue to offer the lessons of discipline and healthy competition to local children. Ridgefield Park proudly boasts of championship teams in every sport.

From the modest fieldstone houses built by the first settlers to the grand homes of prominent citizens, Ridgefield Park offers a variety of architecture. As the village grew and farms gave way to developments, more streets were added. Gone are yesterday's dirt roads and wooden sidewalks. Horse and pedestrian traffic have given way to automobile traffic jams along Main Street. The village has grown tremendously in the last century, and many of the older homes are gone or have been remodeled. However, it is interesting to see how many still stand. Take the time to look through these photographs and see if you recognize any of the scenes. Your imagination will transport you back to a simpler time.

Commerce is always the fulfillment of a need. When the village was young, these needs were different than they are today. Hotels and stables served travelers who stopped along a weary journey. Small stores functioned as meeting places for locals and also served as schools and churches. In many aspects, Ridgefield Park remains the same small town. Although the population has grown and transportation has made travel easier, many village residents still do their shopping on Main Street and patronize local businesses. In turn, these businesses continue to give back to the community, not only by providing their services, but by their generous contributions to local schools, organizations, and volunteer services. It is this mindset that helps to keep Ridgefield Park a caring and close-knit community.

If one factor can be credited with the growth of Ridgefield Park, it would be the railroad. Mortimer Smith and Peter Kenny found the three-mile walk to the nearest station in Leonia to be too much. It was through their efforts that the first station was built in the village. Eventually, there were three stations, the main station at the foot of Mount Vernon Street, West View at the foot of Central Avenue, and Little Ferry at Bergen Turnpike. The ease of commuting to New York City helped to draw people to the village and make homes here. At one time, Ridgefield Park had more commuters than any other location along the New York Central System except White Plains, New York. It is a possibility that a commuter system will serve this area again. This would certainly help reduce traffic and pollution and ease daily commutes for residents.

The safety of its people was the catalyst for the formation of the local police and fire departments. As the population expanded, the Ridgefield Park Protective and Improvement Association was formed. Considered constables, the first lawmen (1889) protected citizens against "thieves and marauders." It was not until 1907 that the first uniformed police department was formed. Necessity was indeed the mother of invention when referring to our volunteer fire department. In the 1800s, it was not unusual for entire buildings to be lost because of the lack of equipment and manpower. Citizens formed fire companies throughout the village to ensure adequate coverage. Equipment was often housed in local barns until firehouses were built. Using true manpower, volunteers often pulled carts of fire apparatus when no horses were available.

This project evolved as a way to raise money for the expansion of the public library and make this information available to the public. It is hoped that you will enjoy this collection and perhaps learn a thing or two. Readers are encouraged to continue the journey down memory lane by visiting the public library, where a wealth of information can be found.

One

MAPS AND MISCELLANY

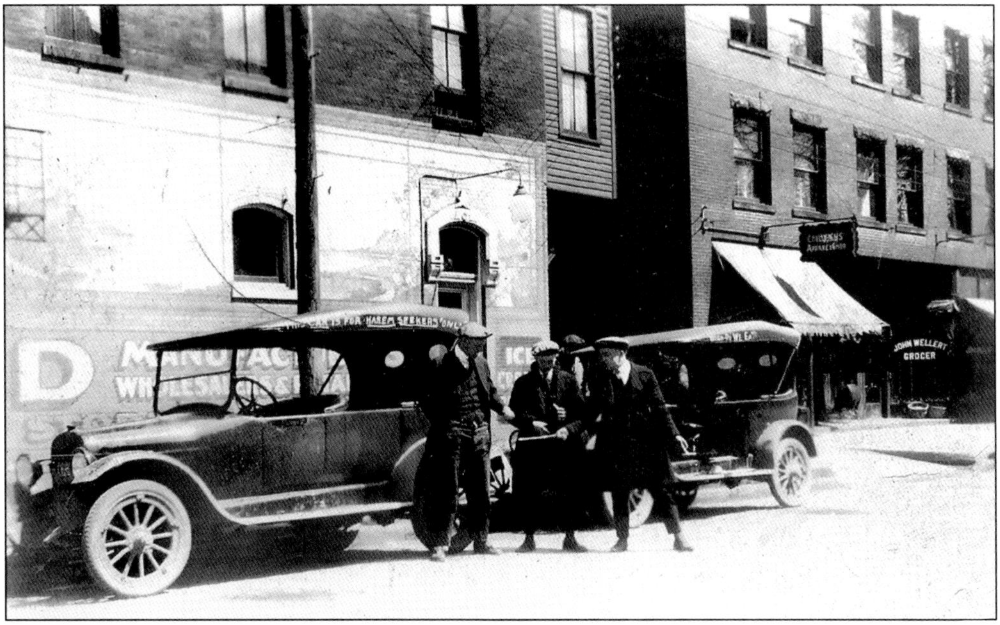

A ROAD TRIP FROM DETROIT. In 1919, Louis Eucker and friends traveled to Detroit to pick up this car, a 1919 Maxwell. A bit of humor is evident as a handwritten sign on the roof's edge states, "This Car is for Harem Seekers 'Only.'"

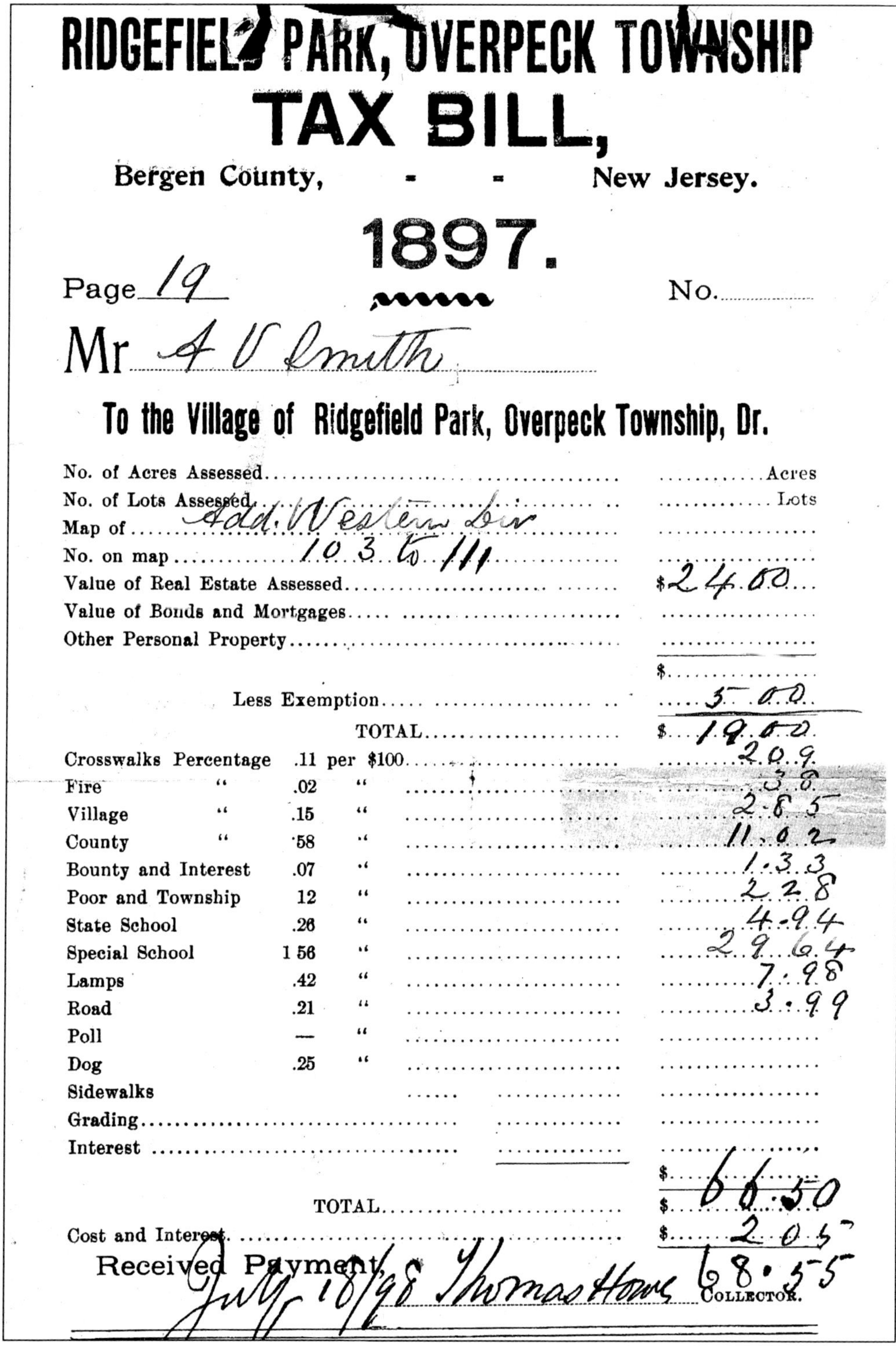

RIDGEFIELD PARK, OVERPECK TOWNSHIP

TAX BILL,

Bergen County, - - New Jersey.

1897.

Page 19 No.

Mr A V Smith

To the Village of Ridgefield Park, Overpeck Township, Dr.

No. of Acres Assessed		Acres
No. of Lots Assessed		Lots
Map of	Add. Western Div	
No. on map	103 to 111	
Value of Real Estate Assessed		$24.00
Value of Bonds and Mortgages		
Other Personal Property		
		$
Less Exemption		5.00
TOTAL		$19.00
Crosswalks Percentage	.11 per $100	2.09
Fire "	.02 "	.38
Village "	.15 "	2.85
County "	.58 "	11.02
Bounty and Interest	.07 "	1.33
Poor and Township	12 "	2.28
State School	.26 "	4.94
Special School	1 56 "	29.64
Lamps	.42 "	7.98
Road	.21 "	3.99
Poll	— "	
Dog	.25 "	
Sidewalks		
Grading		
Interest		
		$
TOTAL		$66.50
Cost and Interest		$2.05

Received Payment July 18/98 Thomas Howe 68.55 Collector.

A Tax Bill. In 1897, A.V. Smith paid $68.55 for his yearly property tax. At that time, his home was valued at $24 according to this document.

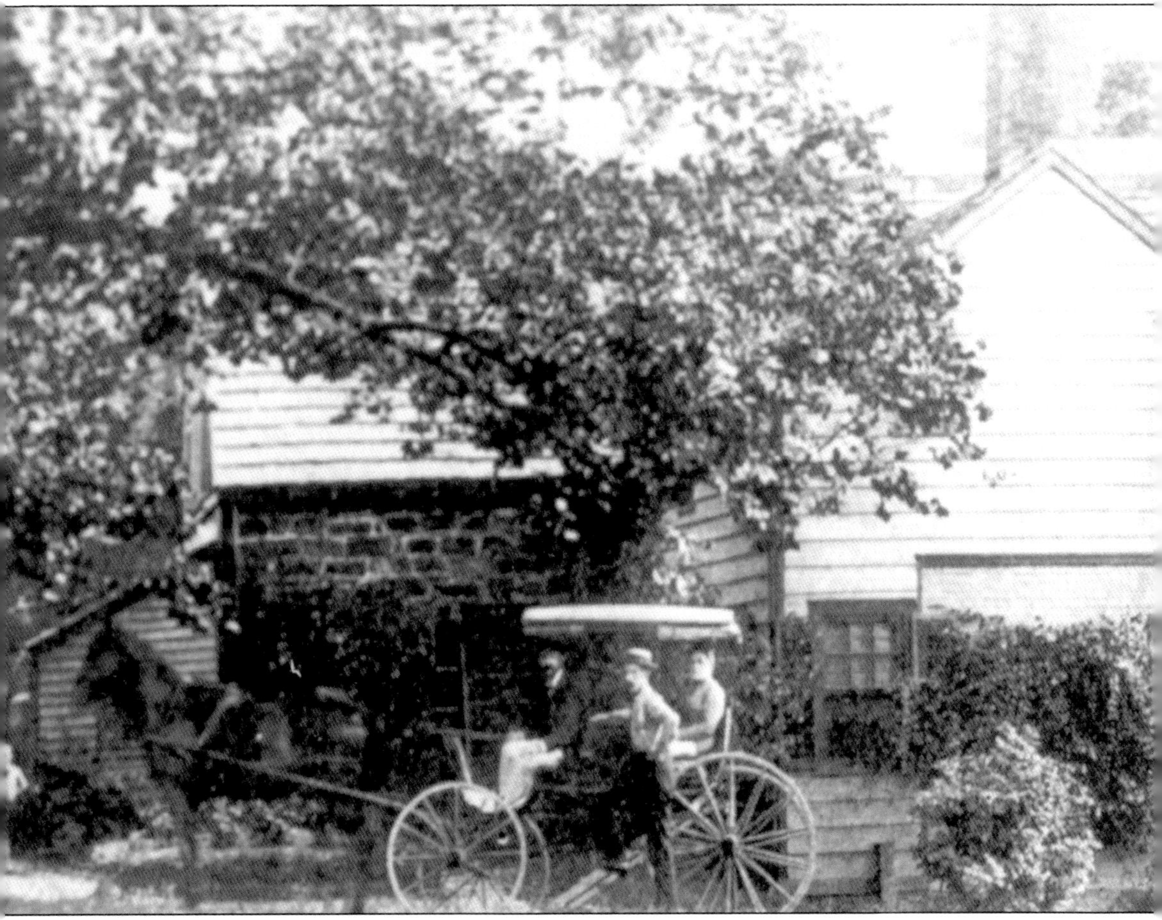

THE PAULISON-CHRISTIE HOUSE. This picture was taken when the Christie family still lived in the home. James Christie is standing beside the carriage.

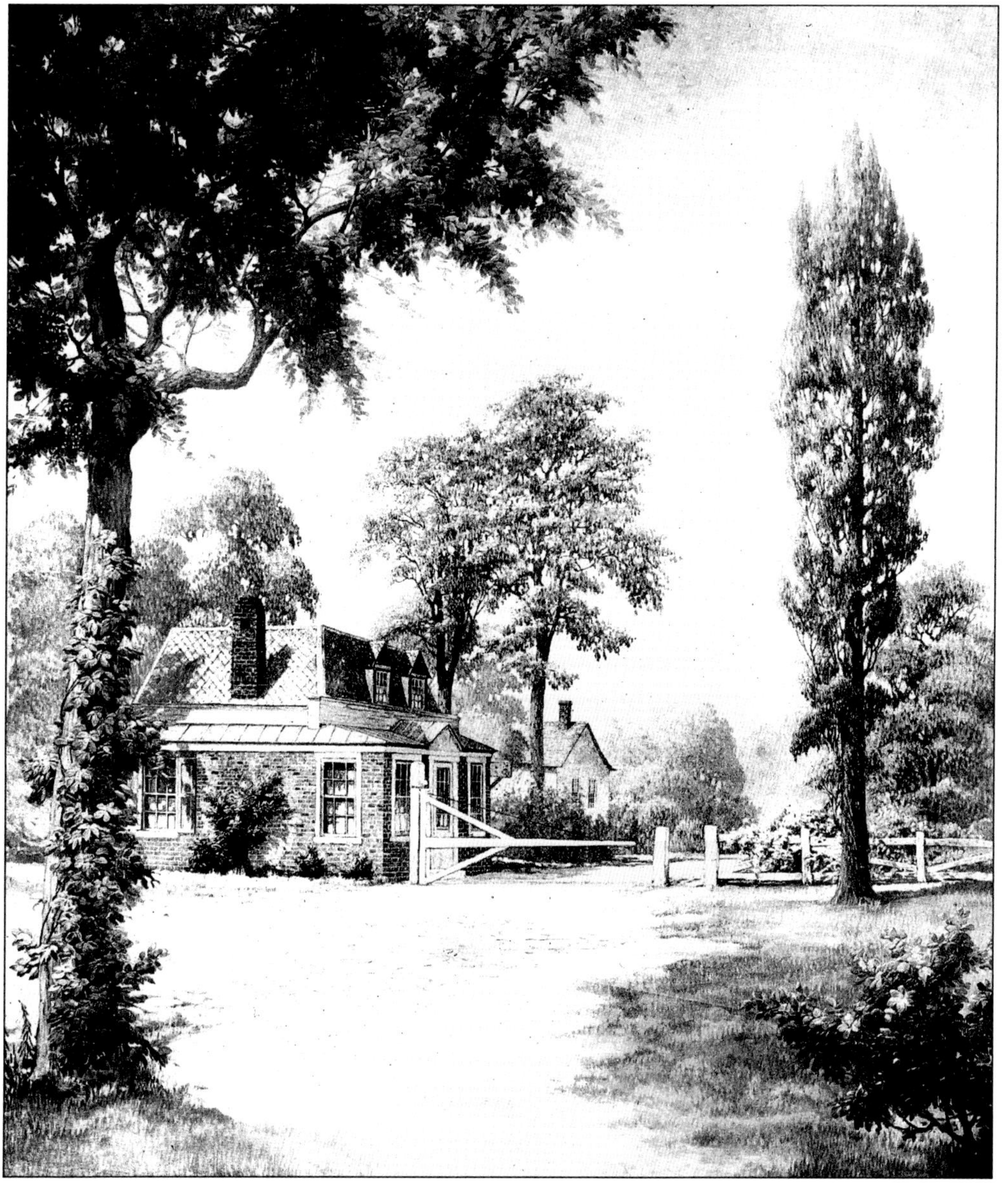

A TOLLGATE. This is an example of one of the tollgates along the Bergen Turnpike. It was in the area of the Overpeck Creek. Tolls were collected until 1915.

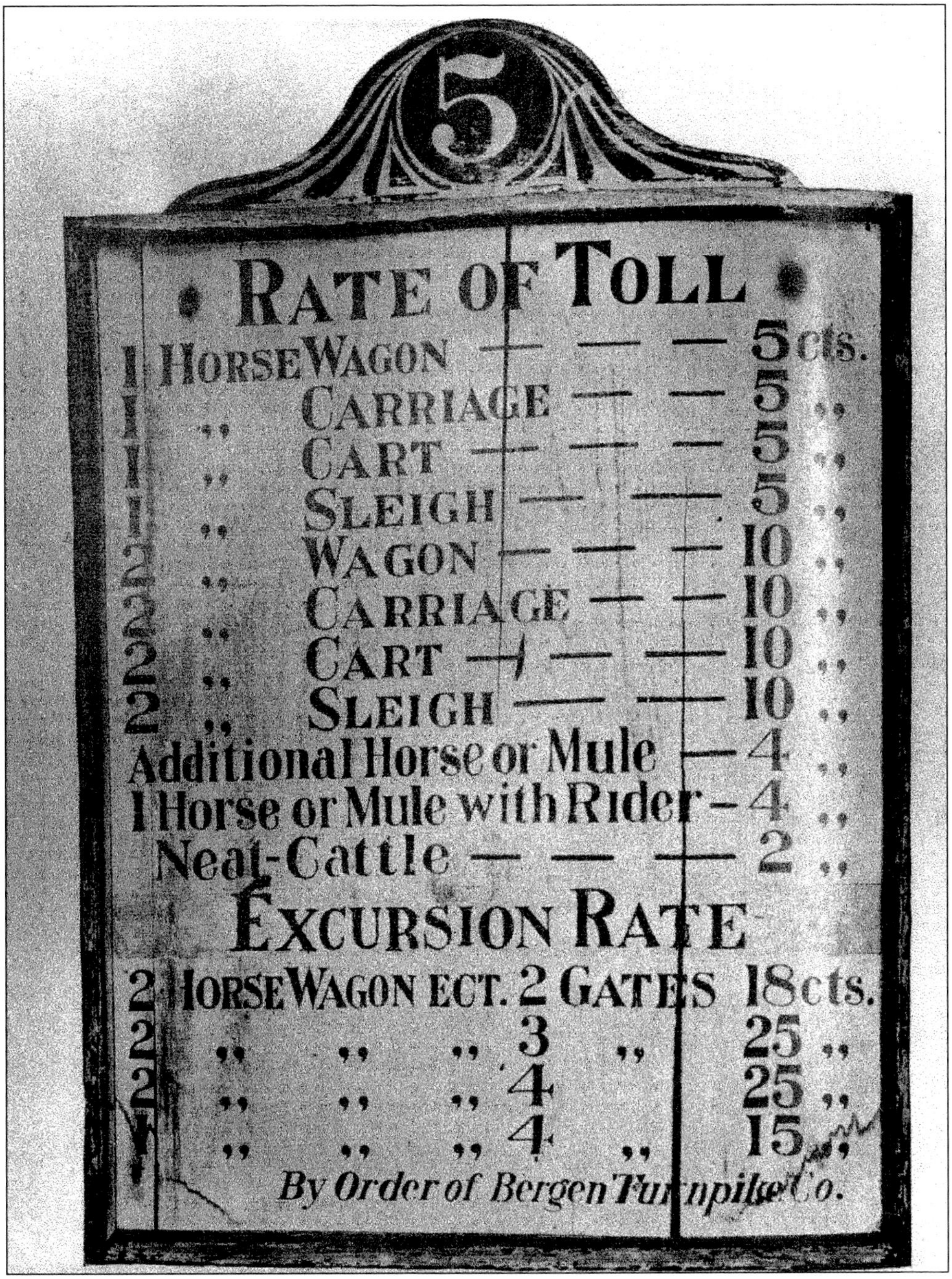

TURNPIKE FEES. This sign was posted along the Bergen Turnpike, which was private. Fees were charged to pass through one of four different tollgates along the route. Farmers from this area brought their goods to the New York markets via this thoroughfare.

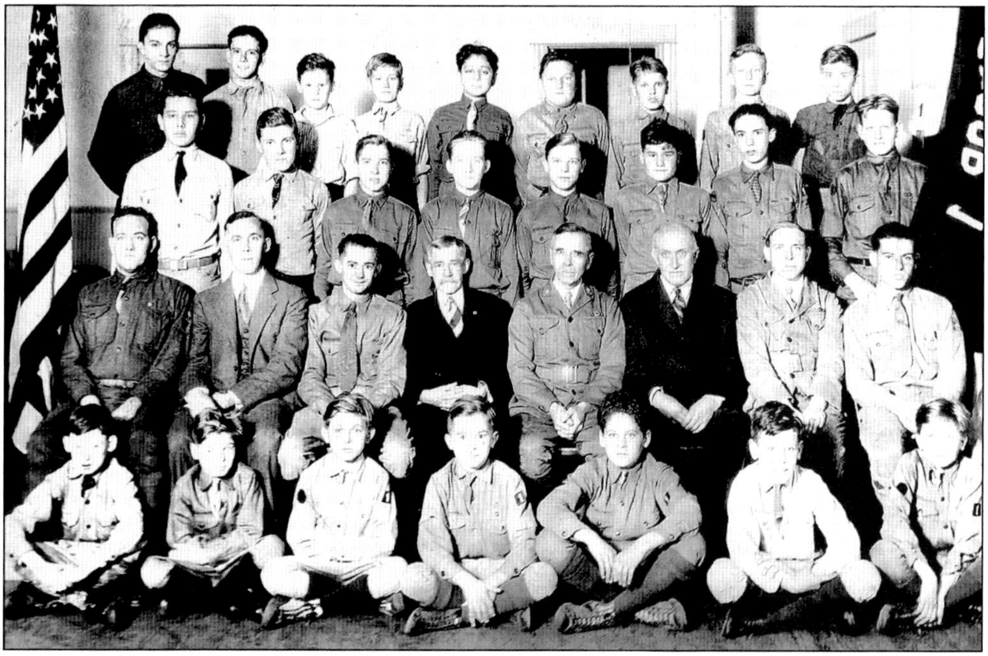

TROOP NO. 1. Boy Scouts from Troop No. 1 gather for a photograph in 1929. Troop No. 1 is the oldest Boy Scout troop in the country and still meets at the Baptist church on Euclid Avenue.

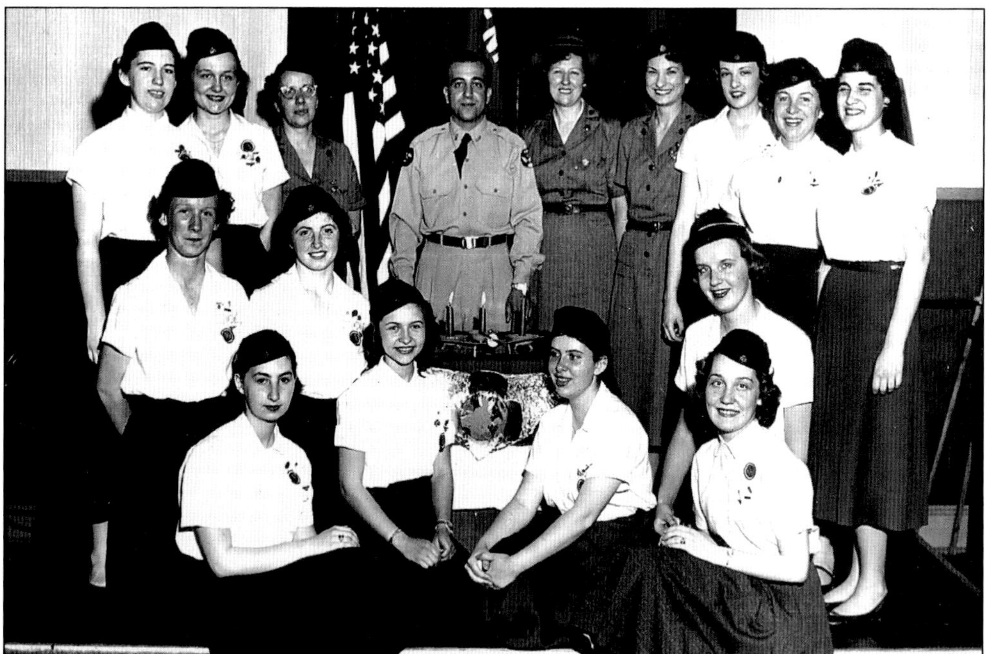

THE SILVER FALCONS. In June 1955, the Girl Scout Troop No. 18 gathered for the presentation of silver wings. Seen here are, from left to right, (front row) Annette Kraut, Joyce Jacobi, Rose Muller, and Carol-Jo Schroeder; (middle row) Mary Ellen Grater, unidentified, and Arlene Bock; (back row) Diane Brown, Jane Ollermann, ? Bracia, Carl Hansen, unidentified, Lucile Spin, Carolyn Zammit, Rosalie Mocco, and Emily Brancia.

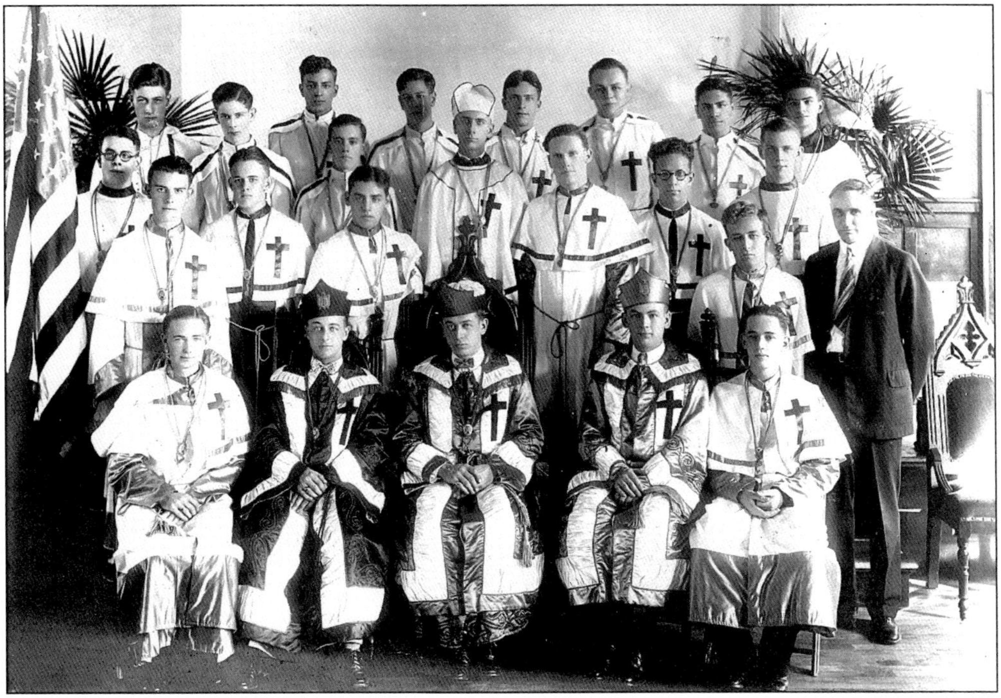

THE DEMOLAY. Seen here is the Nathan Hale chapter of the DeMolay in 1927. Monthly meetings were held at the Masonic temple.

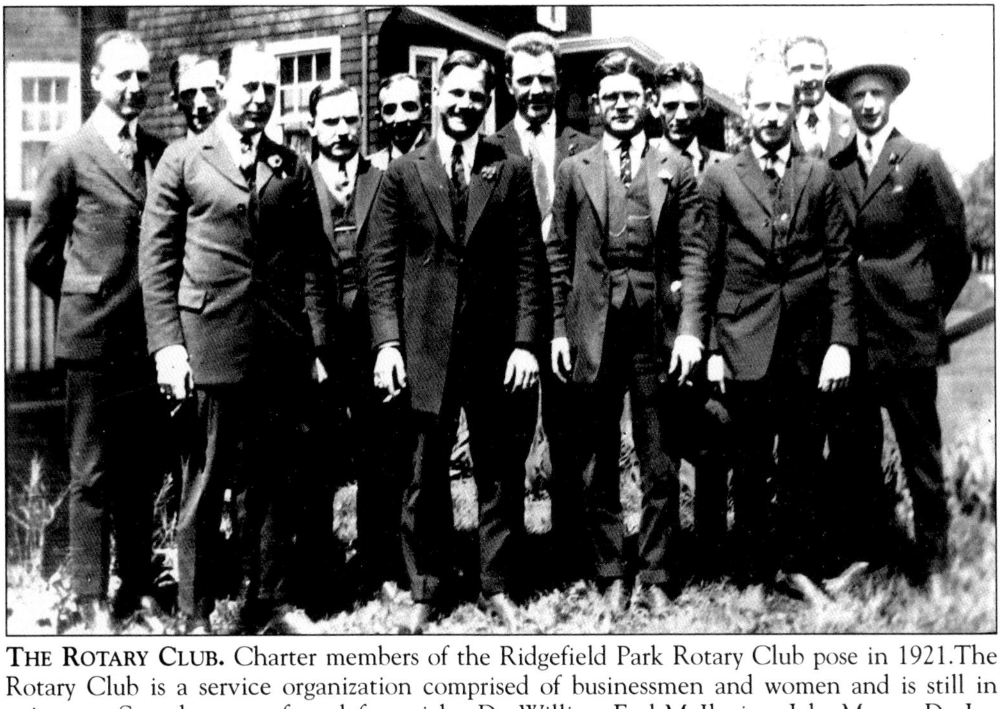

THE ROTARY CLUB. Charter members of the Ridgefield Park Rotary Club pose in 1921.The Rotary Club is a service organization comprised of businessmen and women and is still in existence. Seen here are, from left to right, Dr. William Earl McIlvaine, Jake Mavus, Dr. Joe Hamilton, Frank Morrison, Tom Taranto, Bill Stieh, Gordon Lees, Frank Smith, Francis Lloyd, Dr. John Morrison, Fred Brewster, and Bernie Diekman.

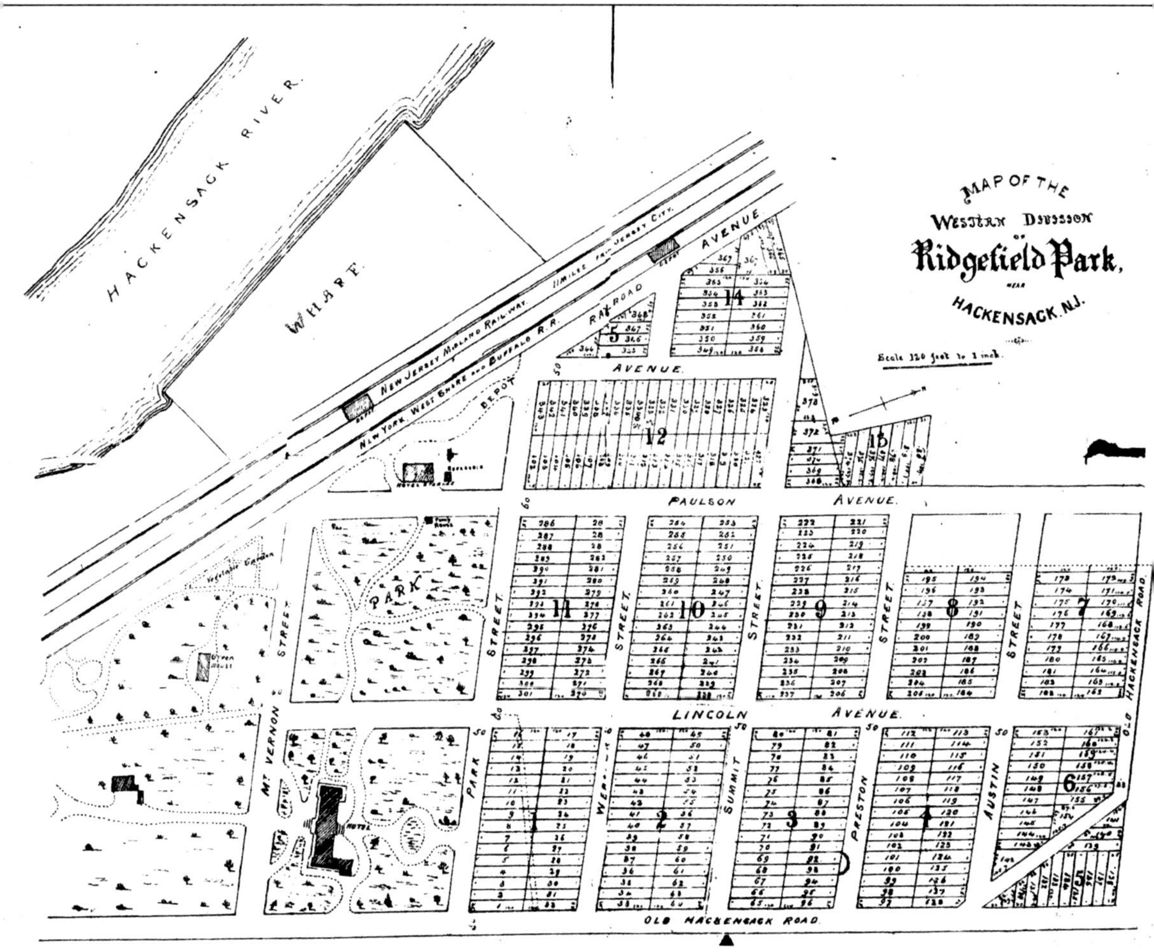

A Map of the Western Division of Ridgefield Park. This map shows the property lot divisions of Ridgefield Park, along with other interesting things in the village. Note the wharf along the Hackensack River, the Ridgefield Park Hotel on Mount Vernon Street, and the hotel stables on Paulison Avenue near Mount Vernon Street.

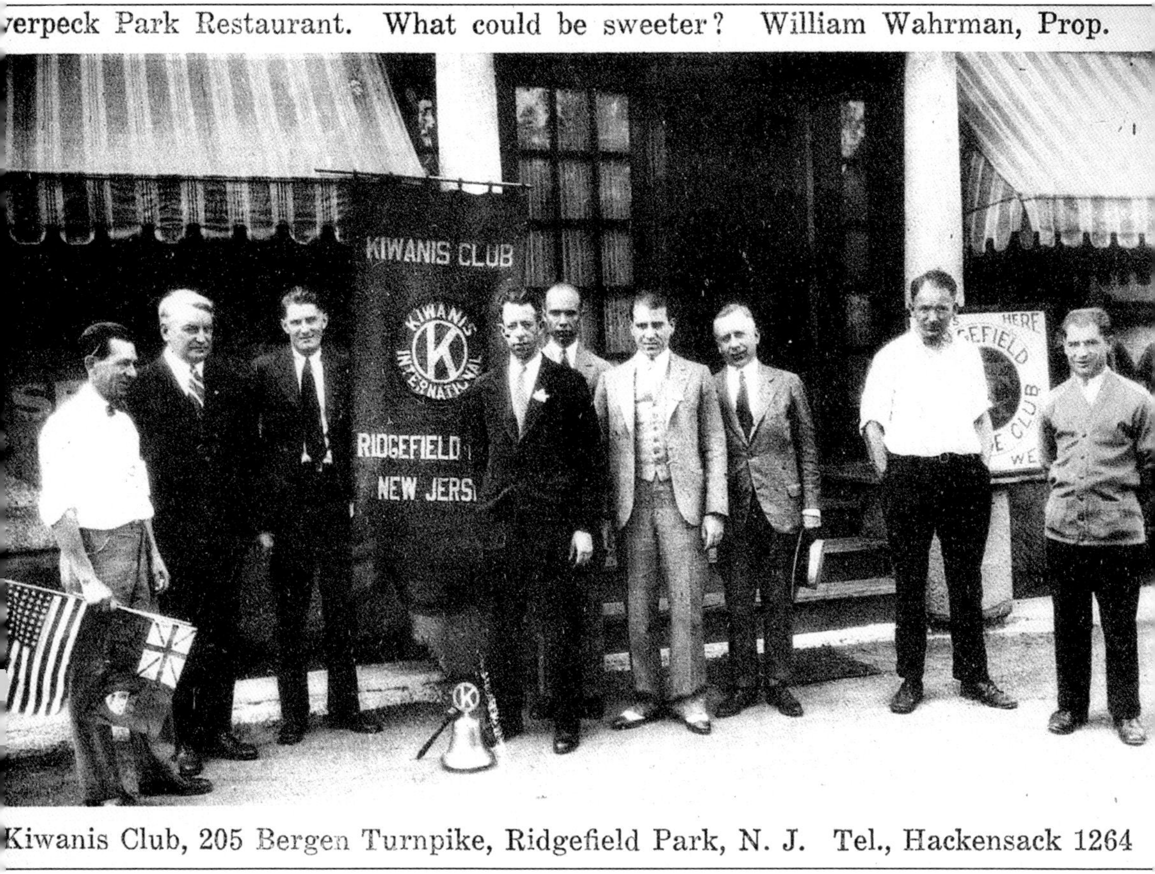

THE KIWANIS CLUB. Meetings of this service organization were held at Wahrman's Overpeck Park Restaurant.

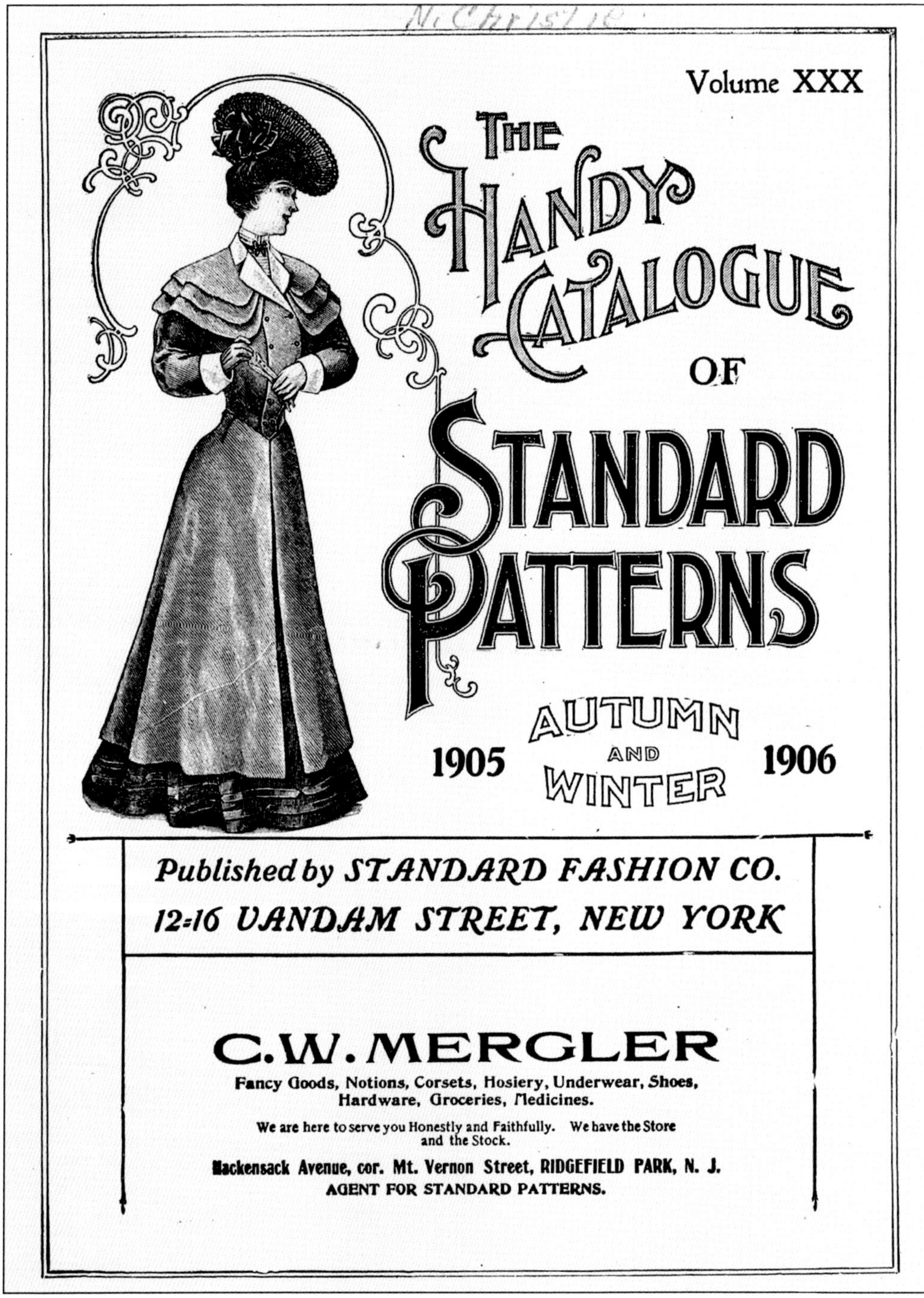

STANDARD PATTERNS. In 1905 and 1906, pattern books were available at Mergler's Corner Store. Women could purchase patterns for 10¢ to 20¢ and sew garments or hire a seamstress.

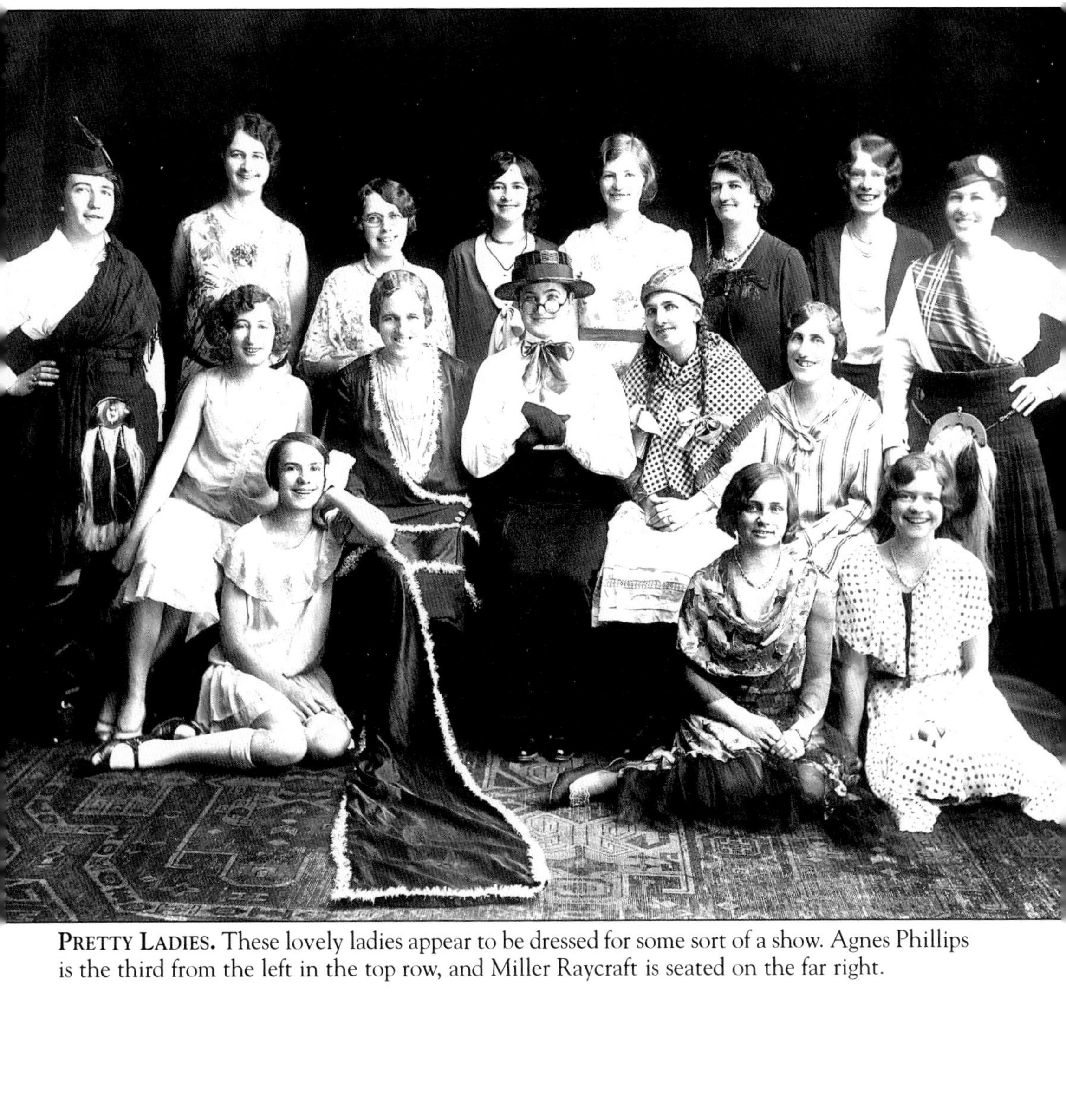

PRETTY LADIES. These lovely ladies appear to be dressed for some sort of a show. Agnes Phillips is the third from the left in the top row, and Miller Raycraft is seated on the far right.

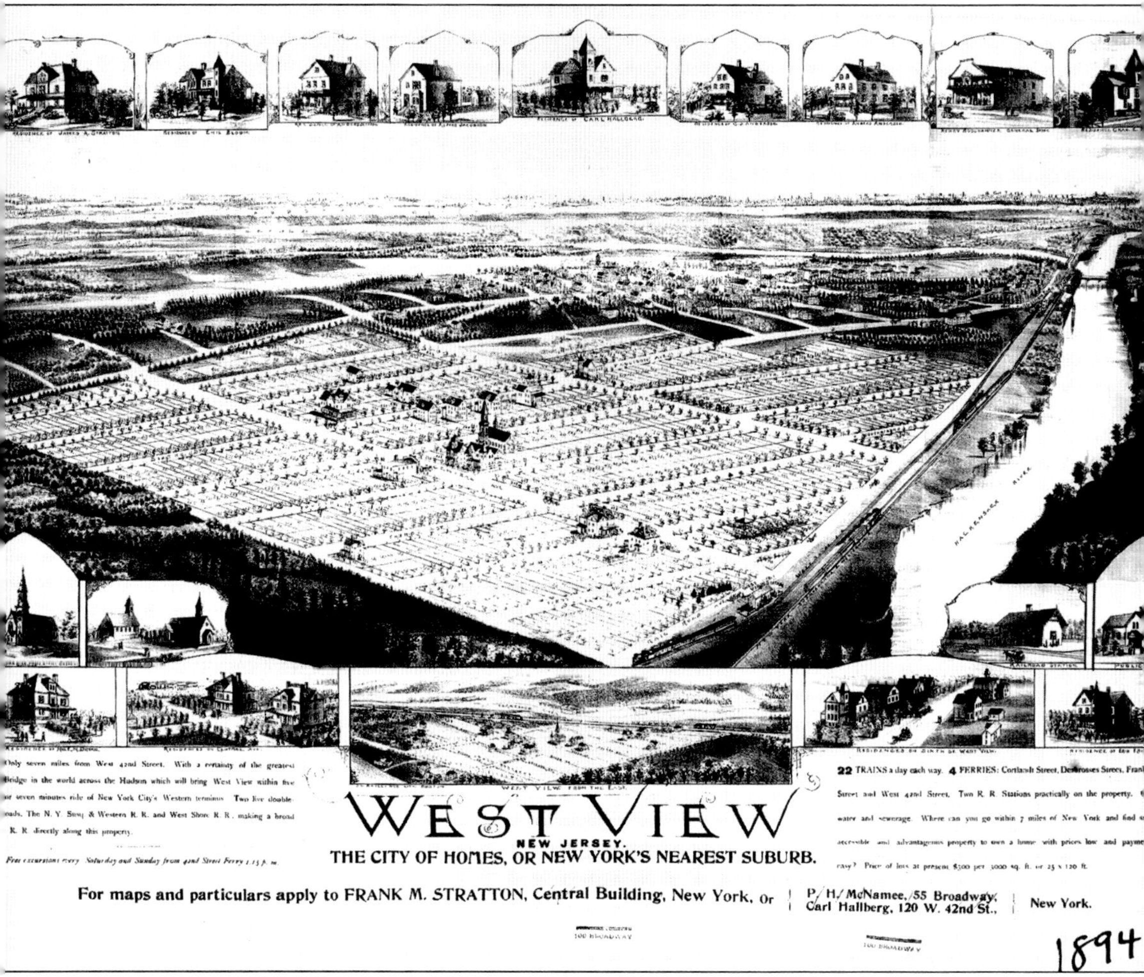

AN 1894 WEST VIEW MAP. This map was used to entice buyers to "New York's Nearest Suburb." This advertisement touted 22 trains and 4 ferries allowing easy accessibility to New York City. Lots were priced at $300 per 3,000 square feet, or 25 by 120 feet. The property was originally Paulison's Farm and was purchased by the Stratton family in 1891.

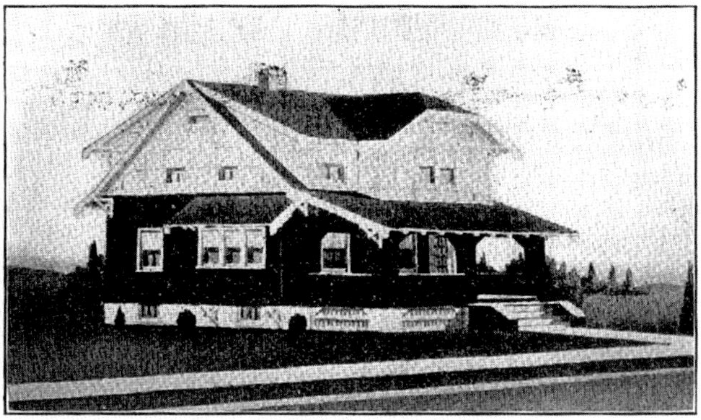

Our Homes are the Talk of the Town

One of our Handsome Moderate-Priced Houses

PRICES FROM $3,000, UP; $200 OR MORE AS FIRST PAYMENT
BALANCE LESS THAN RENT

6, 7 and 8 rooms, tiled bath, hardwood trim, parquet floors, beamed ceilings, Dutch dining rooms, open fireplaces, built-in-bookcases, china closets, large plots, gas, electricity, sewer, steam heat. Near station and schools. Title Insurance policies

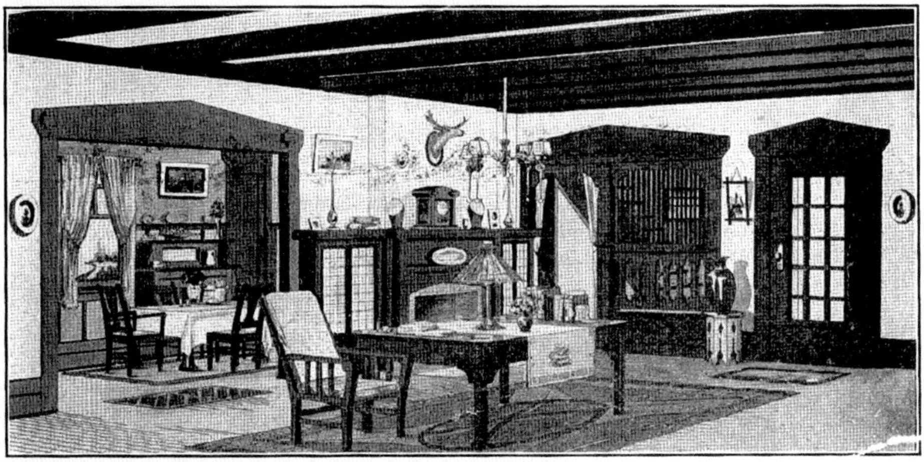

This illustration shows how Our Handsome Craftsman Homes lend themselves to Artistic Interior Decoration

Title Policies by North Jersey Title Ins. Co., of Hackensack
Guarantee Mortgage & Title Ins. Co., of Passaic

ACT QUICKLY IF YOU WANT ONE.

JOHN A. BALDWIN

OFFICE, 1 MT. VERNON STREET **OPPOSITE RAILWAY STATION**

RIDGEFIELD PARK, NEW JERSEY

NEW YORK CITY OFFICE, 80 MAIDEN LANE Telephone John 1598

Member Ridgefield Park Real Estate and Insurance Agents' Association

"OUR HOMES ARE THE TALK OF THE TOWN." This advertisement appeared in a booklet for the first annual carnival and fair in 1916. Prices of homes with six to eight rooms started at $3,000.

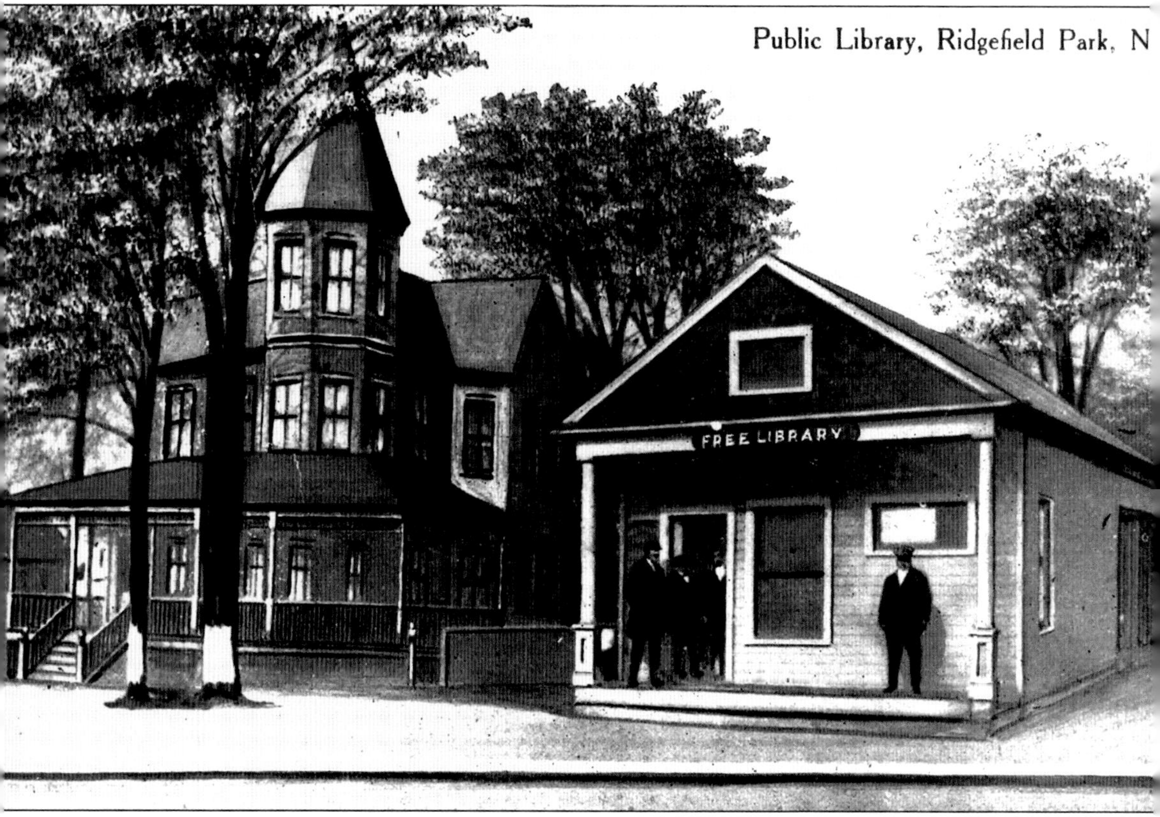

THE PUBLIC LIBRARY. First organized in 1894, with the help of Josie K. Barnes, the library was in a small building on the corner of Lincoln Avenue and Mount Vernon Street. The building was known as the Woman's Bazaar. After a fire in 1910 that destroyed the building, the library was reopened in the municipal building on Main Street. The collection of reading materials soon outgrew the space, and a store on the corner of Cedar and Main Streets became its home. Eventually outgrowing that space, the property of the old Congregational church was purchased by the town commissioners, and the home of the present library was established. Although not the original building, the library still stands on the corner of Cedar Street and Euclid Avenue. It has undergone several renovations and additions as the needs of the community have grown.

Two

THE FOURTH OF JULY

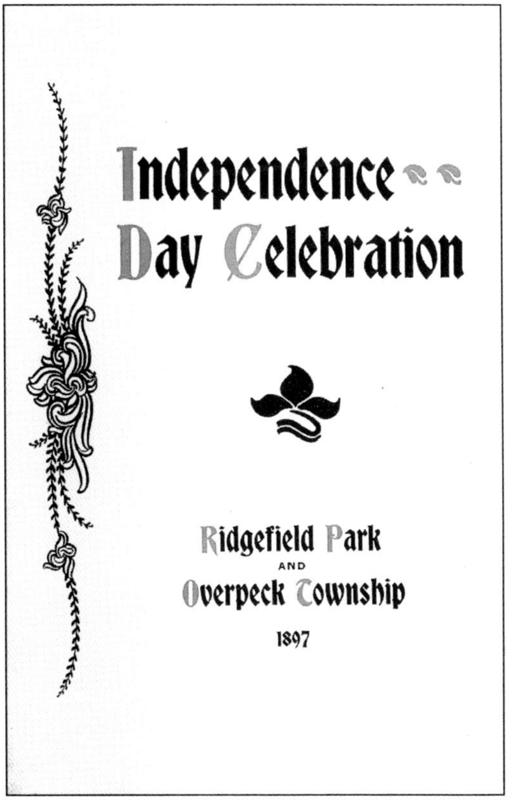

AN INDEPENDENCE DAY PROGRAM. This handout from 1897 is filled with advertisements from local businesses and the schedule of events for the day's festivities. Early Fourth of July activities included a bicycle parade, races, baseball games, water sports, a children's parade, a dance, and fireworks. Not much has changed today.

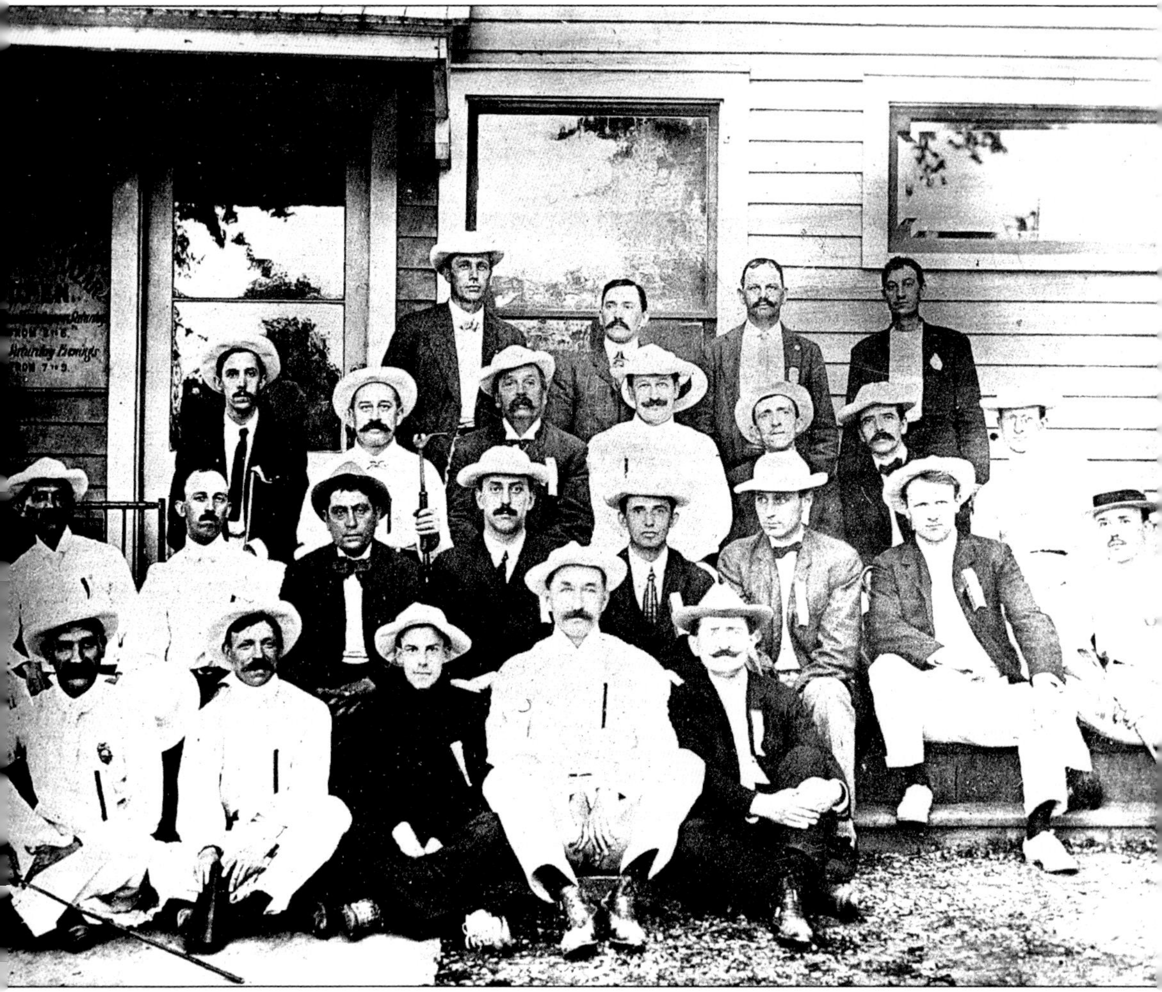

THE RIDGEFIELD PARK FOURTH OF JULY COMMITTEE. This photograph was taken between 1900 and 1905 at the northwest corner of Mount Vernon Street and Lincoln Avenue, in front of the Woman's Bazaar, home of Ridgefield Park's first library. Seen here are, from left to right, (first row) Al Price, Frank Vrooman, Samuel Shaw Jr., George Smith, and Edward F. Tukey; (second row) Frank White, William J. Morrison Jr., Fred Fleischbein, Milton Votee, Frank Lowe, Morton Brewster, Walter Townsend, and Arthur Wheatley; (third row) Burt Wheatley, C.W. Mergler, H.N. Brewster, William Squires, Harry Carpenter, Neil Monroe, and Warren Abbott; (fourth row) Henry T. Griggs, Edwin S. Ferris, Fred Rudolph, and unknown.

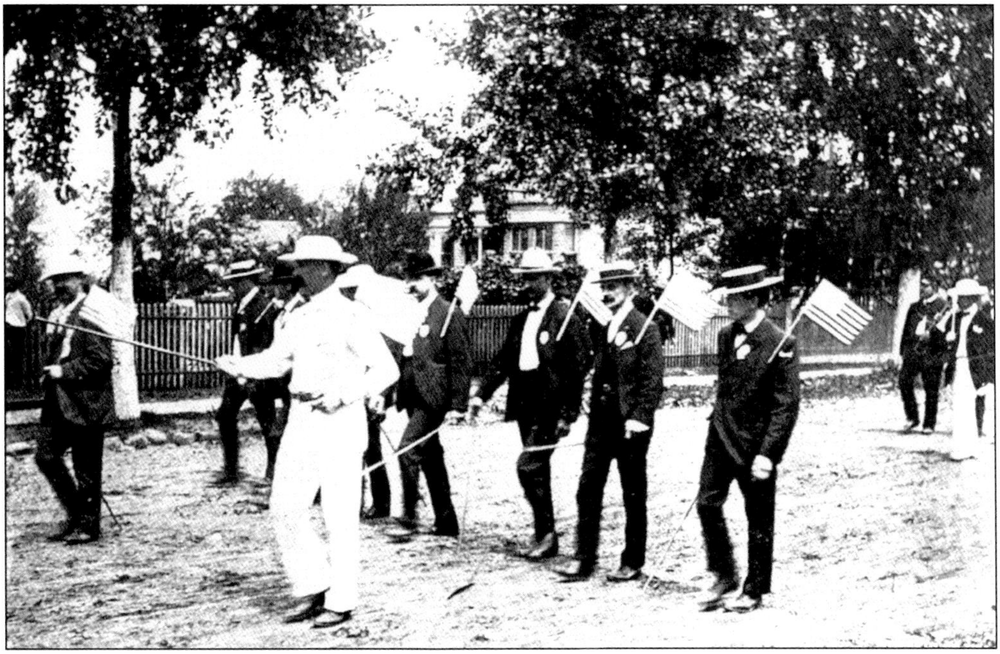

THE PARADE COMMITTEE. Members of the Fourth of July Committee march down Main Street in 1905.

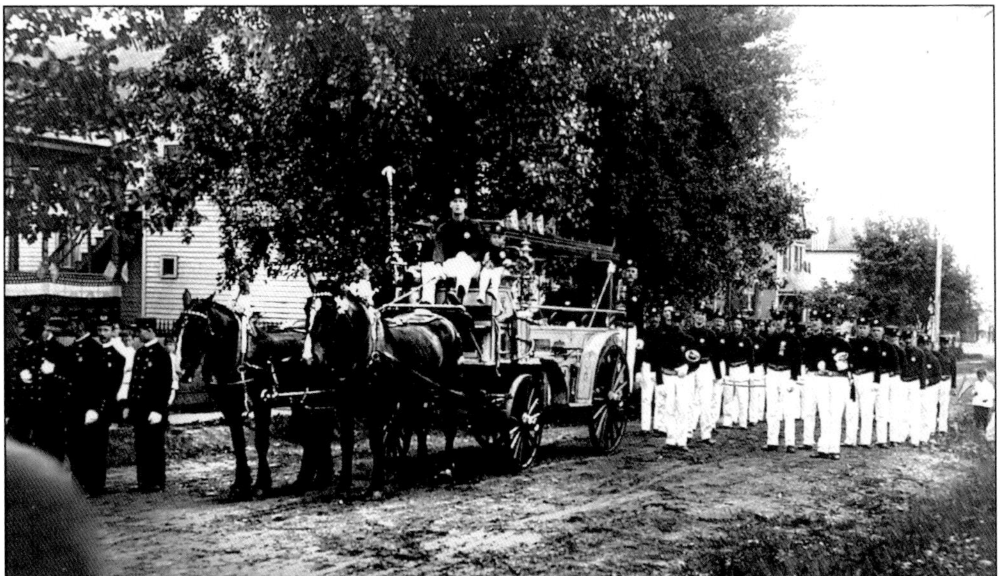

THE FIRE DEPARTMENT. Members of the village fire department gather as they prepare to march in the annual Fourth of July parade.

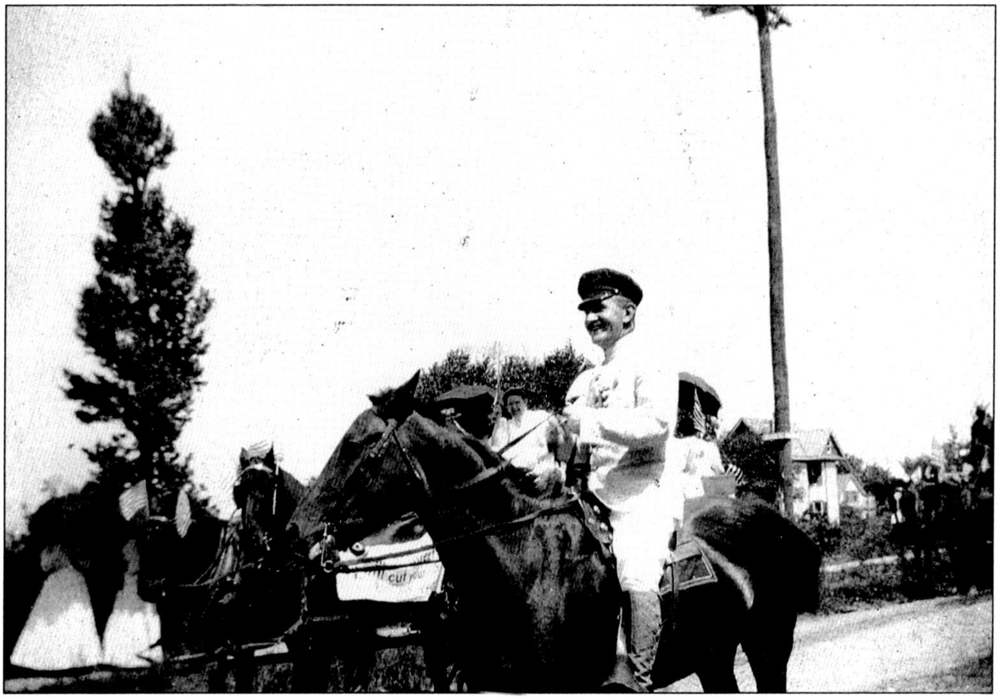

ARCHIE LEES. Archie Lees rides proudly atop a horse in the 1909 Fourth of July parade.

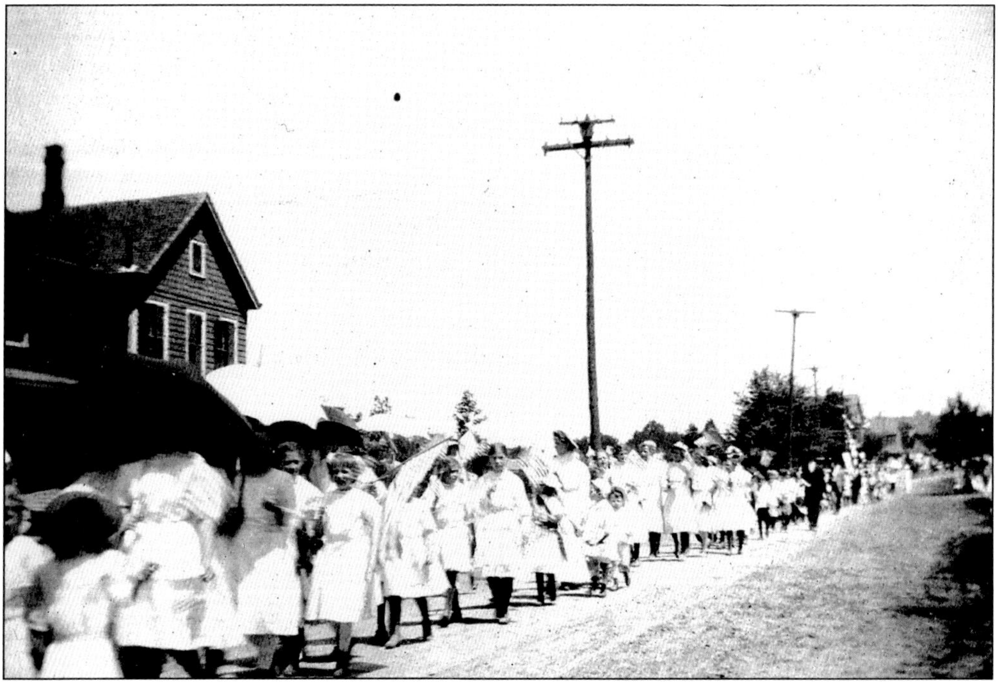

GIRLS ON PARADE. Dressed in white and carrying parasols to shade the sun, these gals march down Main Street in the 1909 Fourth of July parade.

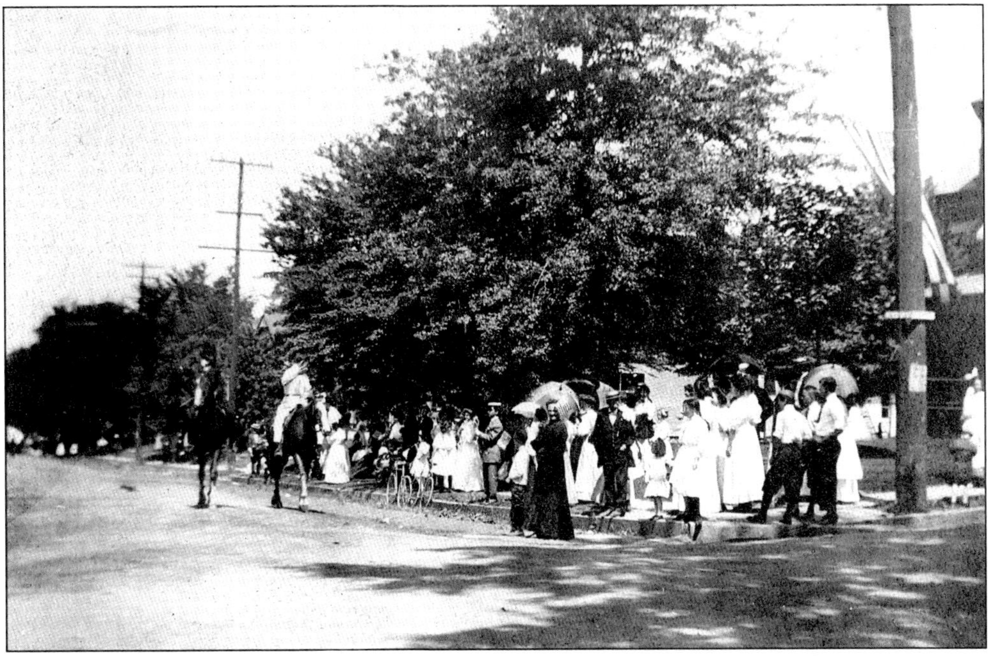

EVERYONE LOVES A PARADE. Spectators gather at the corner of Main and Mount Vernon Streets to watch the Fourth of July parade in 1909.

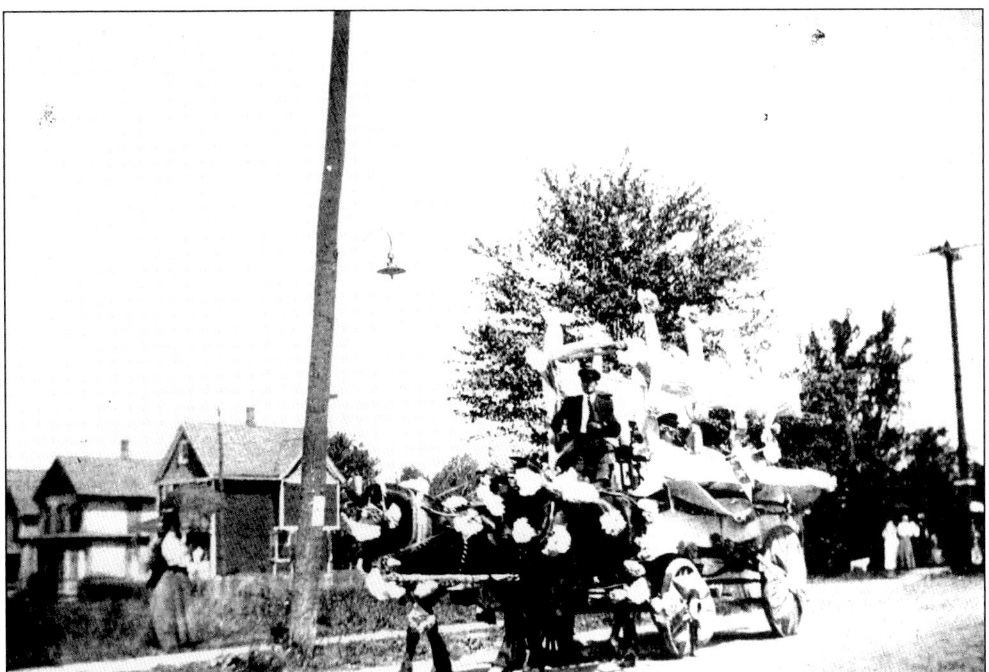

A FLOAT FROM DAYS GONE BY. A lavishly decorated horse-drawn cart makes its way down the parade route in 1909.

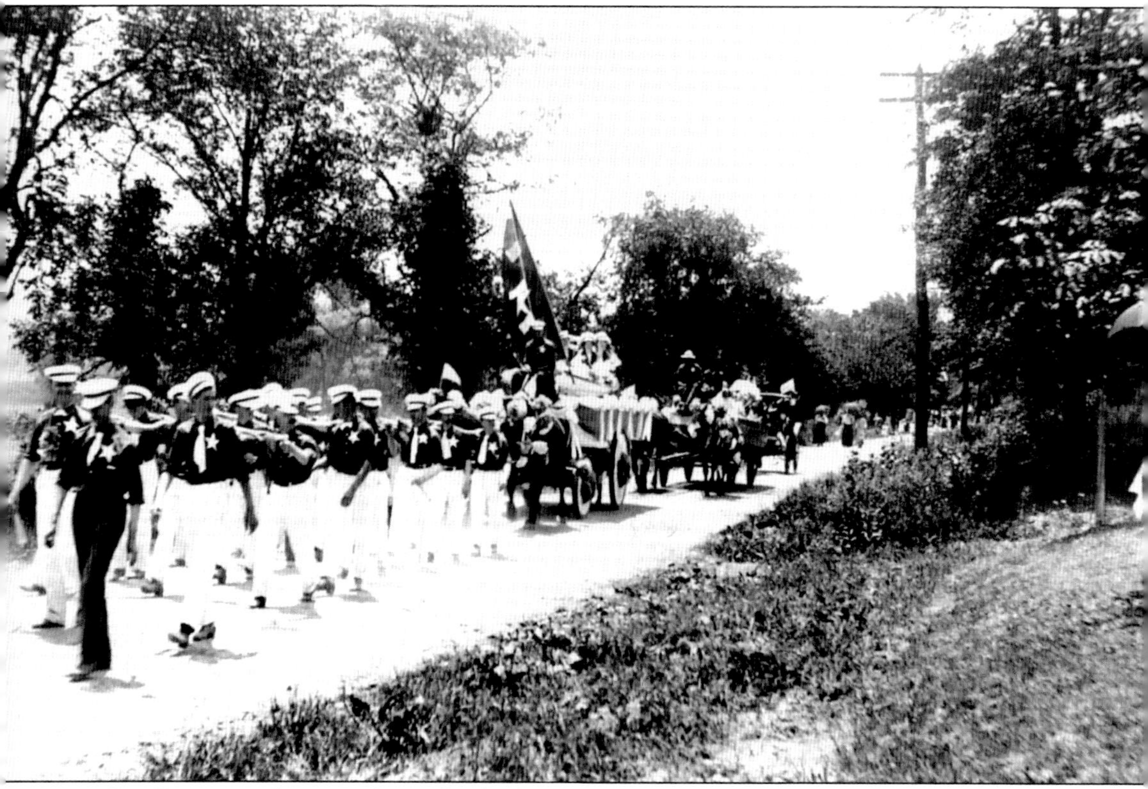

THE PARADE. The annual Fourth of July parade is the oldest continuously running parade in the nation. The first parade was held in 1894.

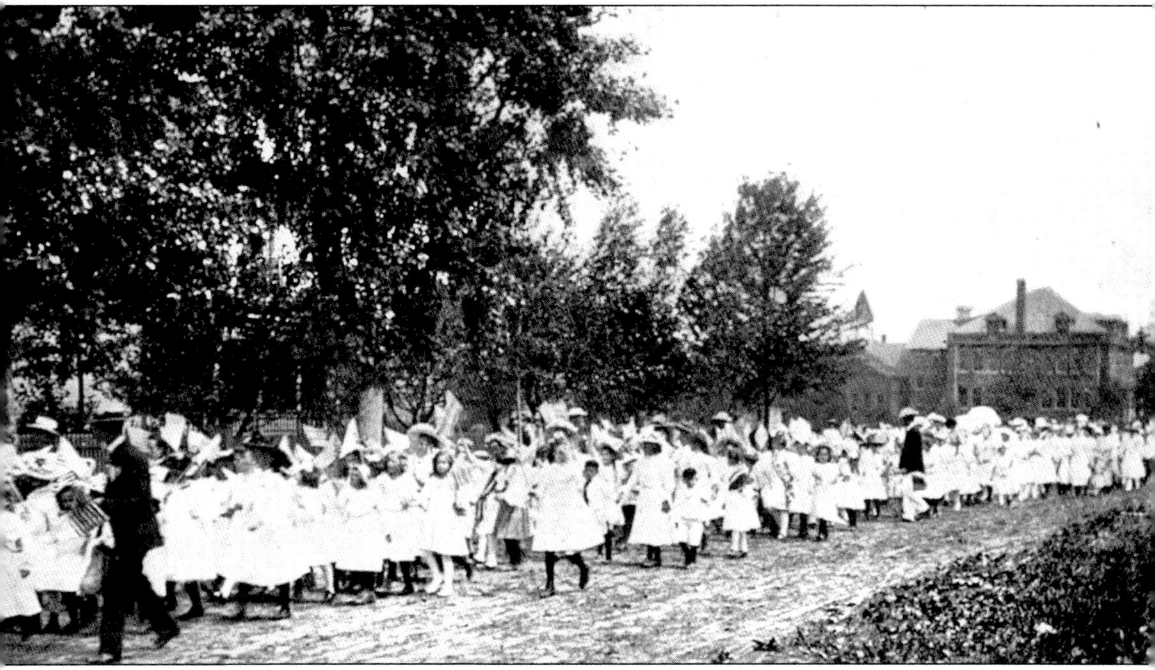

THE 1905 PARADE. Children dressed in their finest clothes make their way down Main Street in the annual Fourth of July parade.

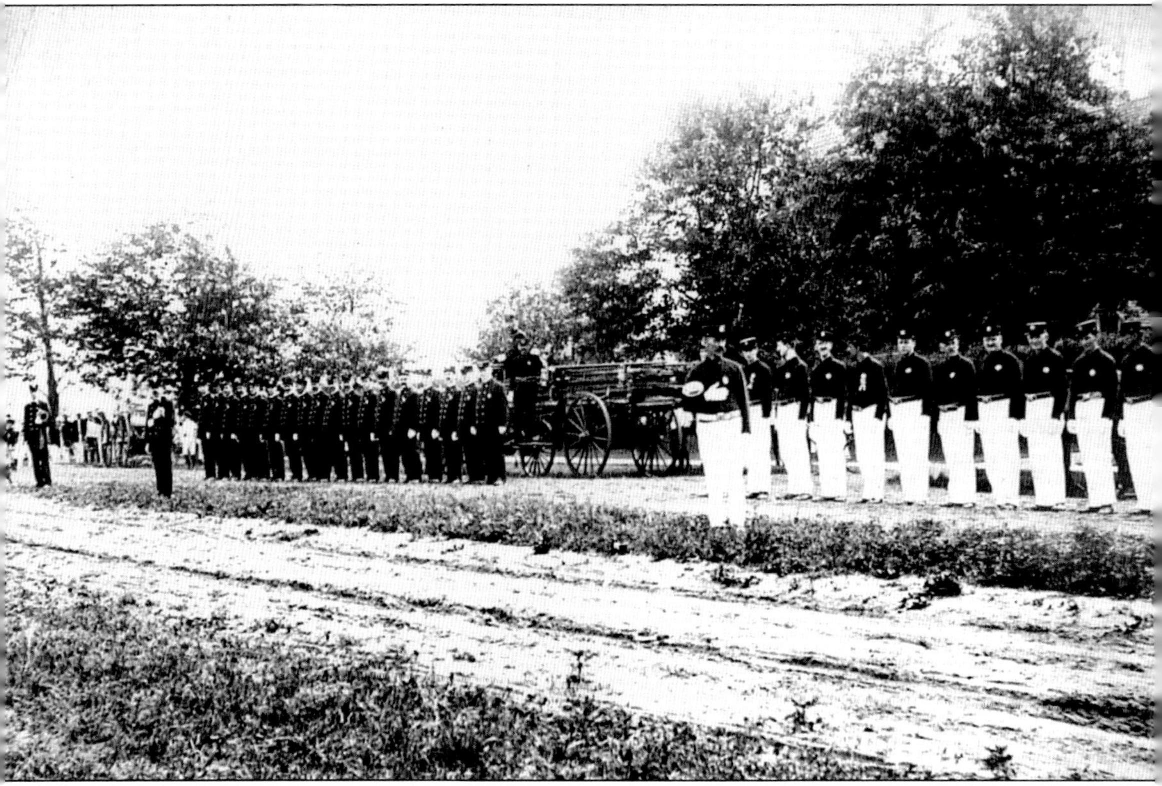

THE INSPECTION. Firemen stand at attention for the annual inspection. Awards are given each year to the company whose equipment meets the toughest scrutiny.

Three

CHURCHES

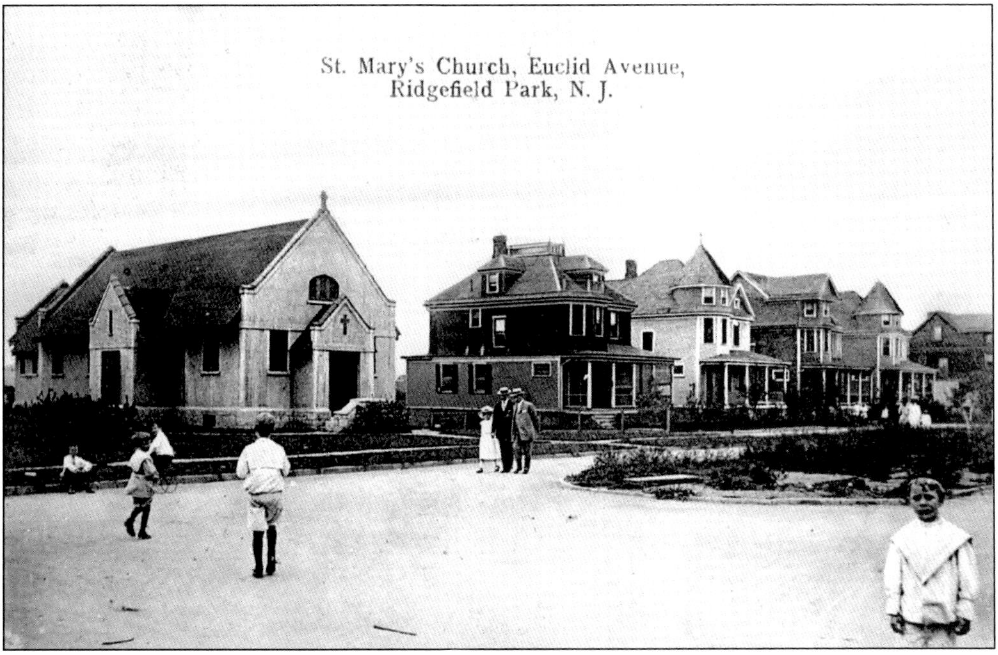

ST. MARY'S EPISCOPAL CHURCH. The original church building can still be seen at the corner of Euclid Avenue and Preston Street, although St. Mary's parish has disbanded.

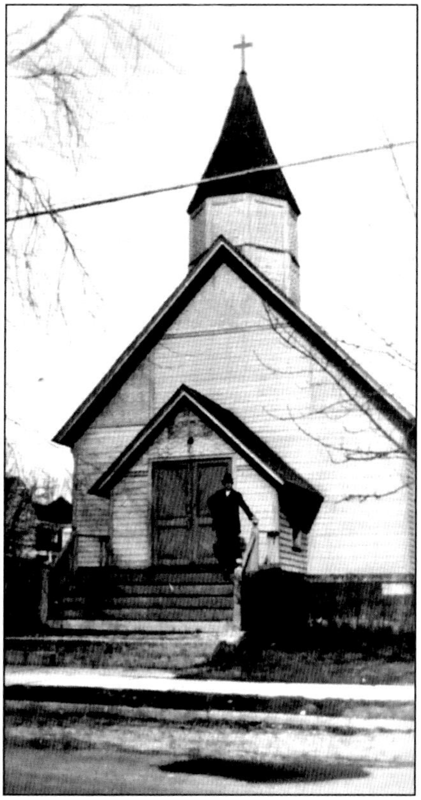

The First St. Francis Church. Built in 1890, this was the first church building erected in the village. It was heated with a pot-bellied stove, and kerosene lamps provided light. The new church was built in 1915.

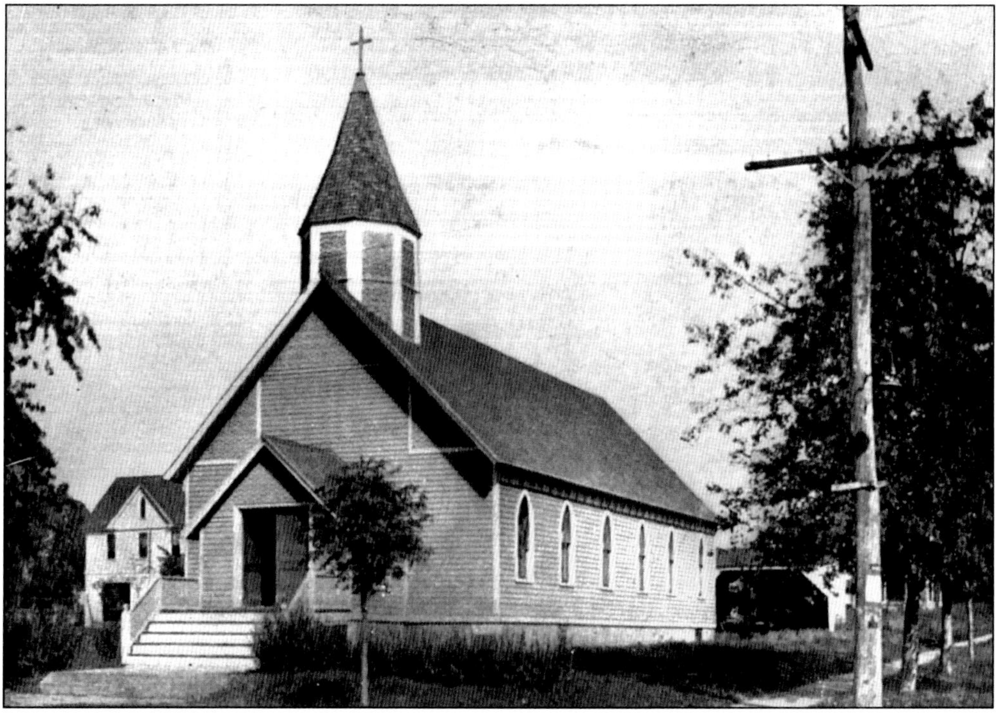

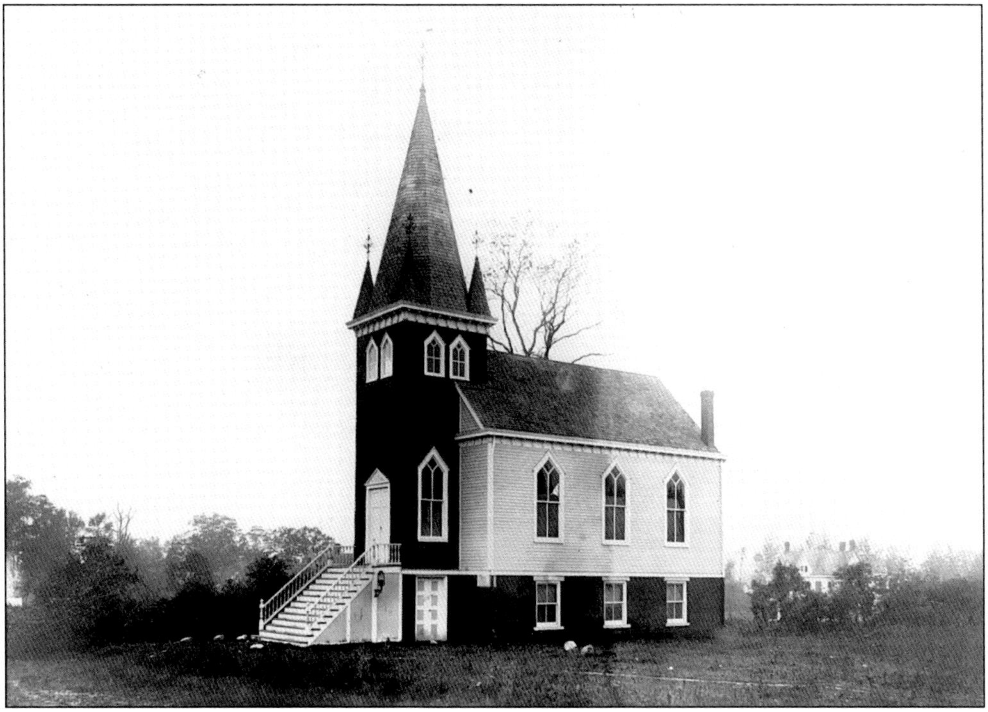

THE SCANDINAVIAN LUTHERAN CHURCH. This photograph is from 1940. The church was located on Fifth Street near Central Avenue. After settling here and completing their homes, citizens of Scandinavian decent built this house of worship.

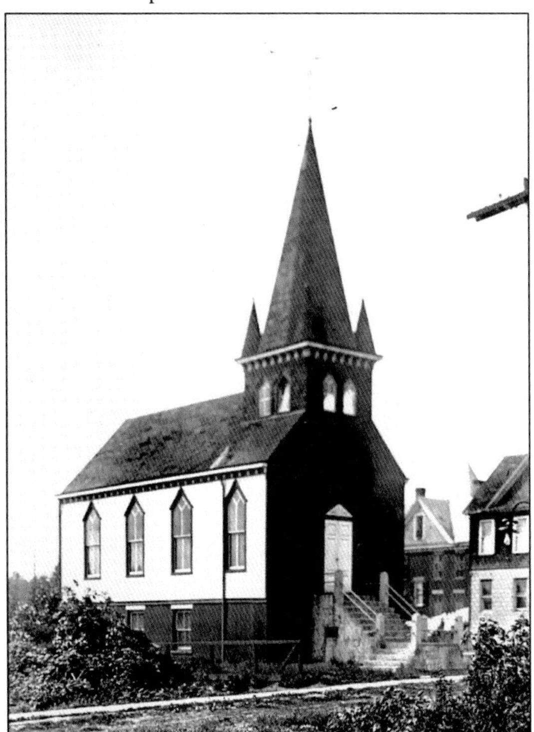

THE SCANDINAVIAN LUTHERAN CHURCH. Developers of West View showed a sketch of this proposed church to prospective buyers. The church was organized by Andrew Jeppson.

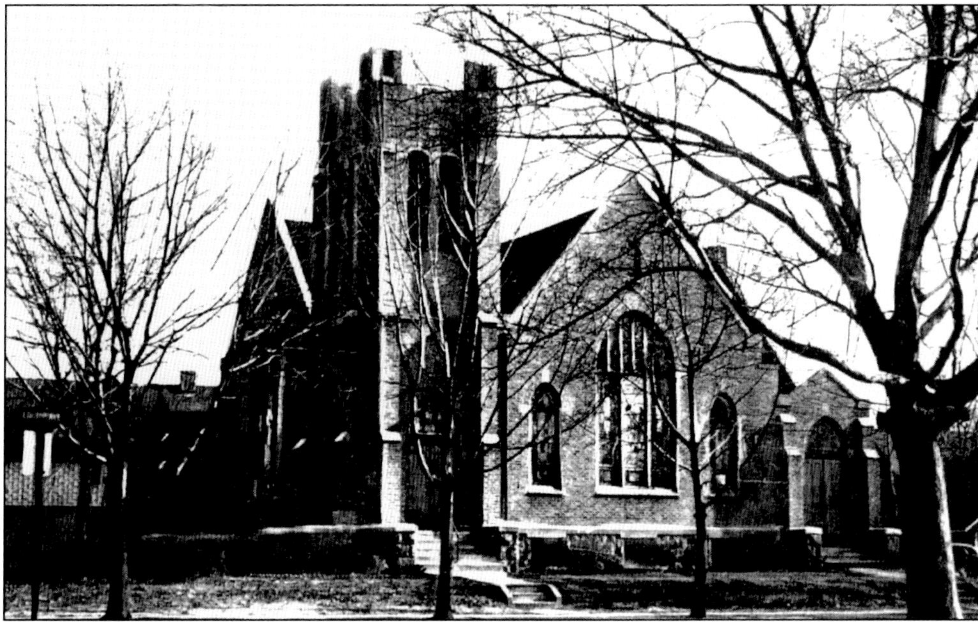

The First Baptist Church. This church sits on the corner of Euclid Avenue and Hobart Street.

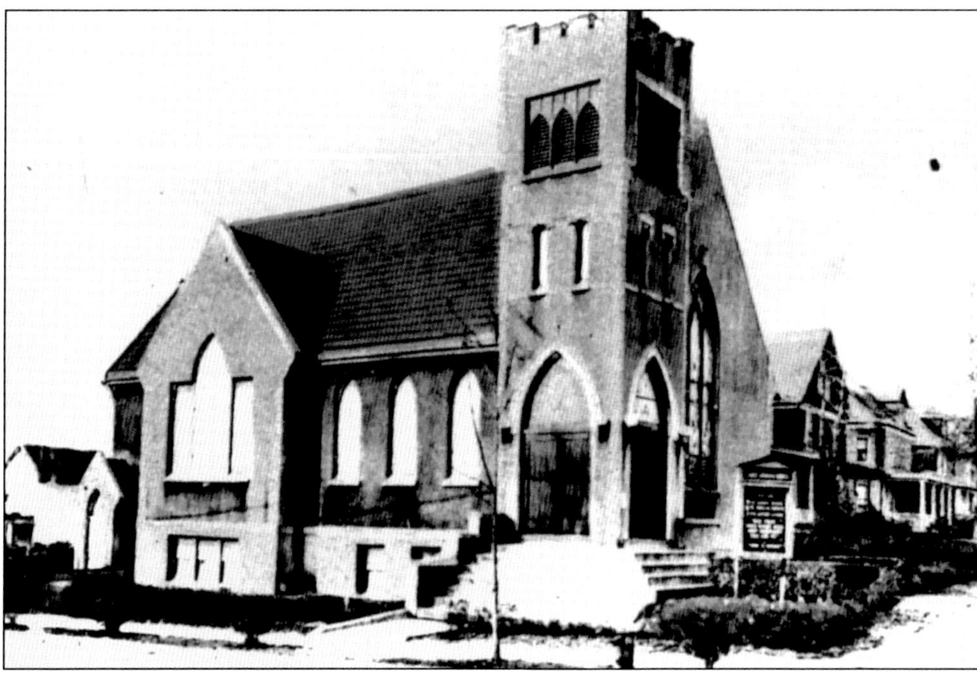

The Christ Lutheran Church. This church is located on the corner of Bergen Avenue and Mount Vernon Street.

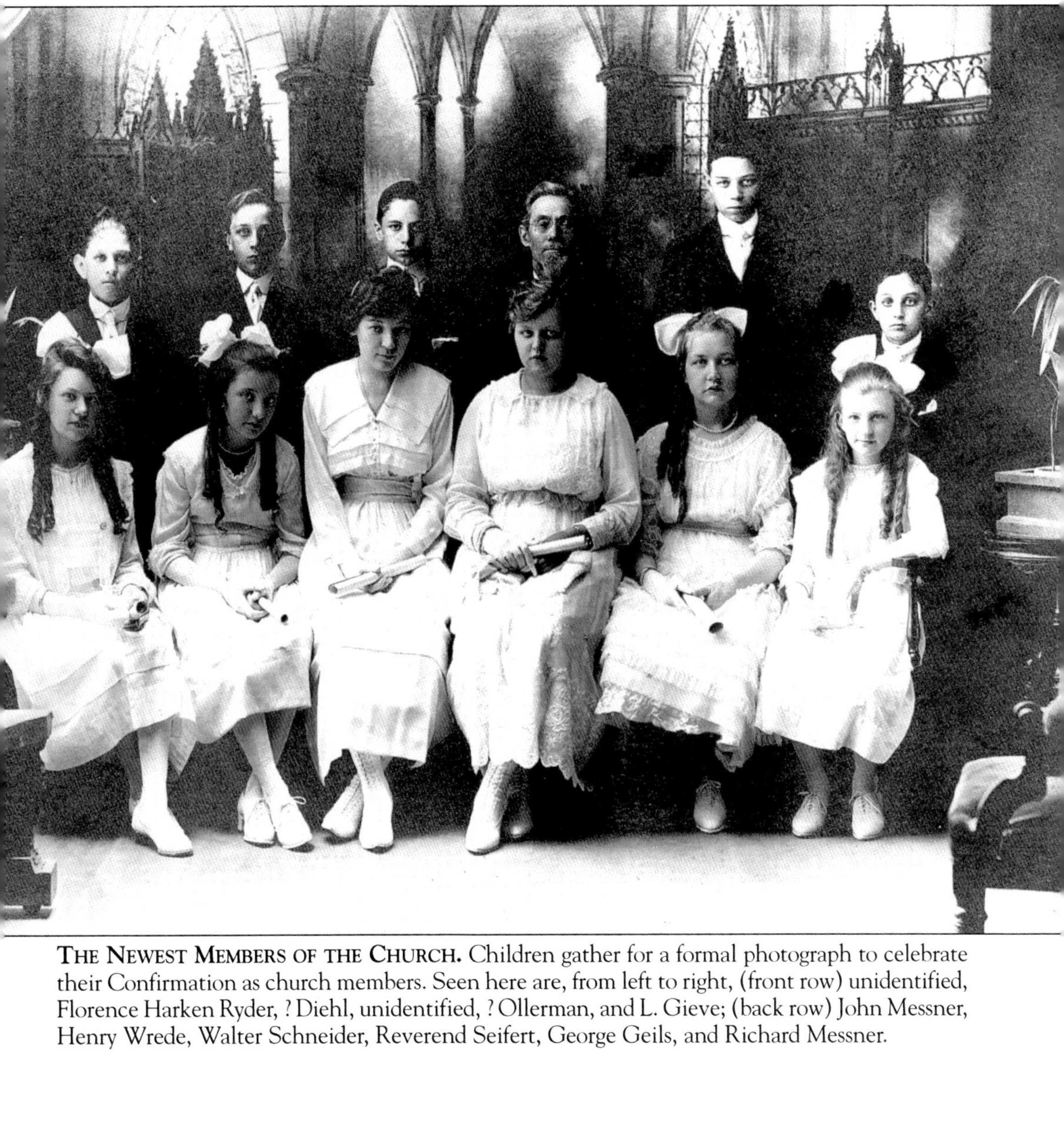

The Newest Members of the Church. Children gather for a formal photograph to celebrate their Confirmation as church members. Seen here are, from left to right, (front row) unidentified, Florence Harken Ryder, ? Diehl, unidentified, ? Ollerman, and L. Gieve; (back row) John Messner, Henry Wrede, Walter Schneider, Reverend Seifert, George Geils, and Richard Messner.

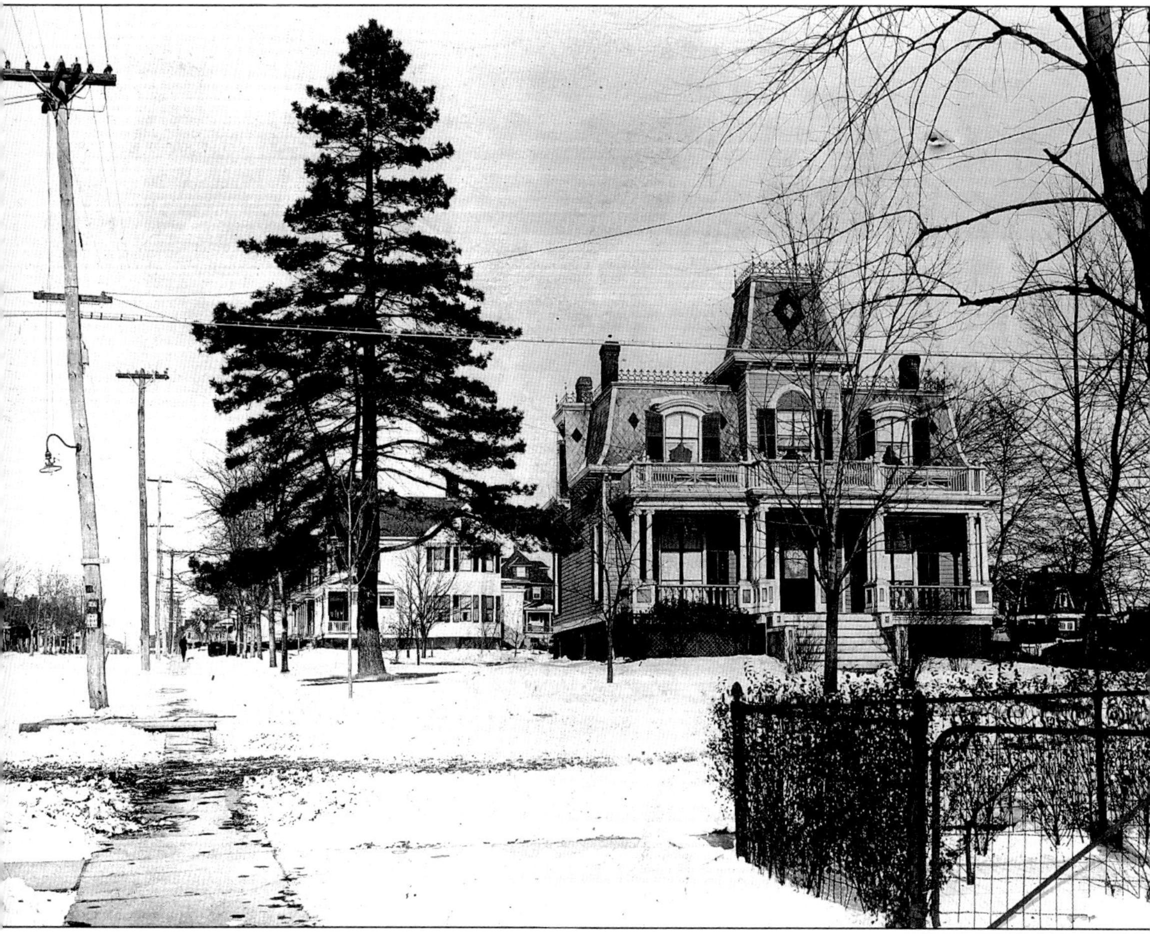

The Temple Emanuel. This building was the former home of William Donald. It was built in 1870 as a model home by the Ridgefield Park Land & Building Company. In the Panic of 1873 it was sold for $1,200. It is situated on the corner of Park Street and Bergen Avenue.

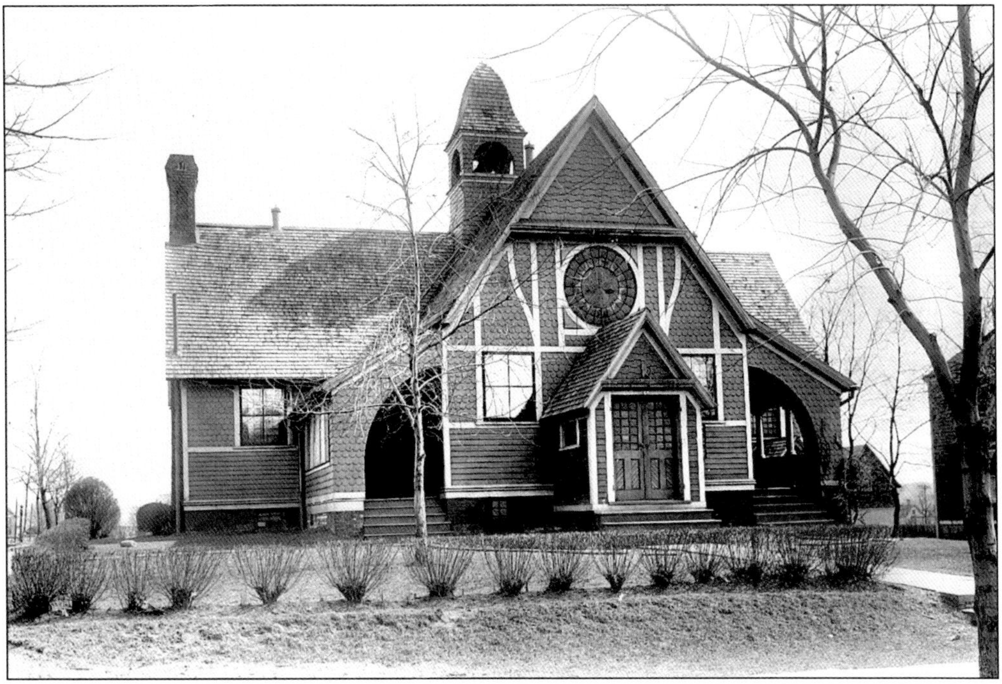

THE UNION CHURCH. In 1890, Josie Barnes and Mortimer Smith helped organize the Union Church. The building was completed in 1891. Originally facing Euclid Avenue, the building was turned to face Park Street. It has been remodeled and is now the Ridgefield Park Civic Center. The old pipe organ is still in the building.

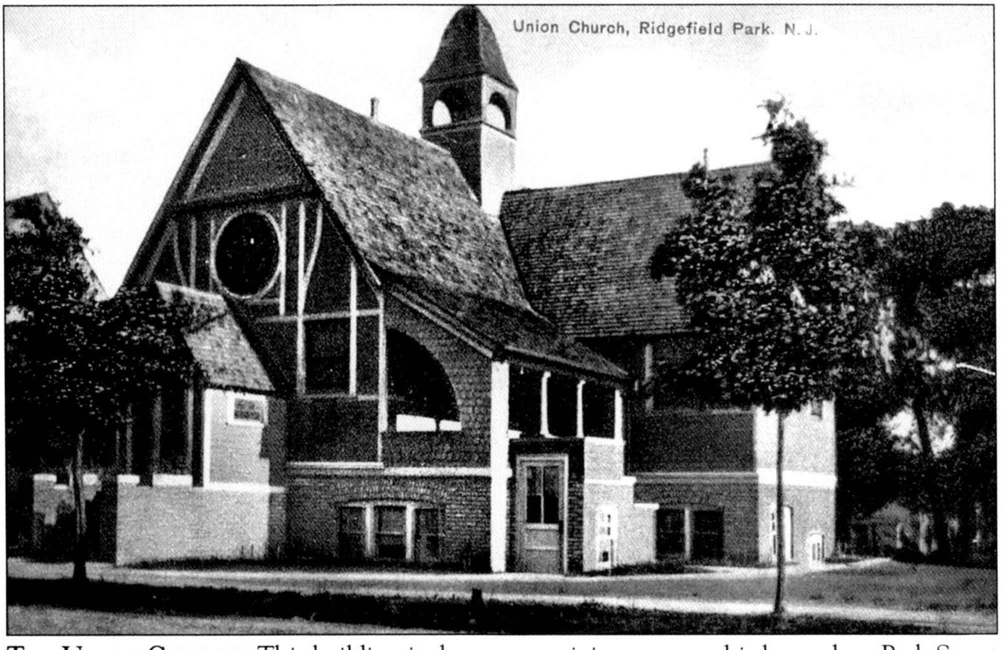

THE UNION CHURCH. This building is the current civic center and is located on Park Street near Euclid Avenue. Josie Barnes held Sunday school classes in her home, then Sheils Hall, and later a school building until this church was completed in 1891.

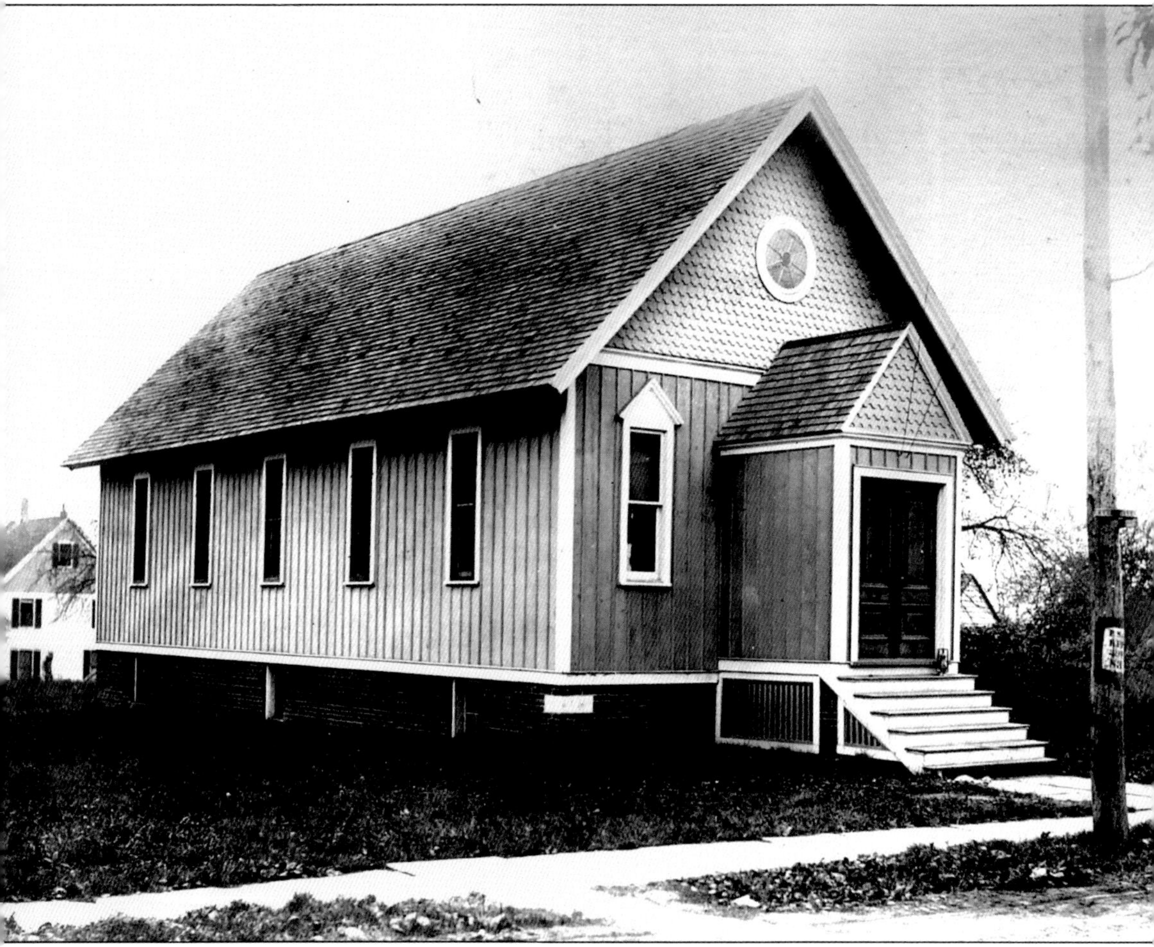

THE ORIGINAL BAPTIST CHURCH. This church building was originally located on the south side of Winant Avenue. It was eventually converted to a dwelling. The trees in the background were part of an apple orchard owned by Daniel M. Winant. "The Orchard," as it was known, was a gathering place and playground for local children.

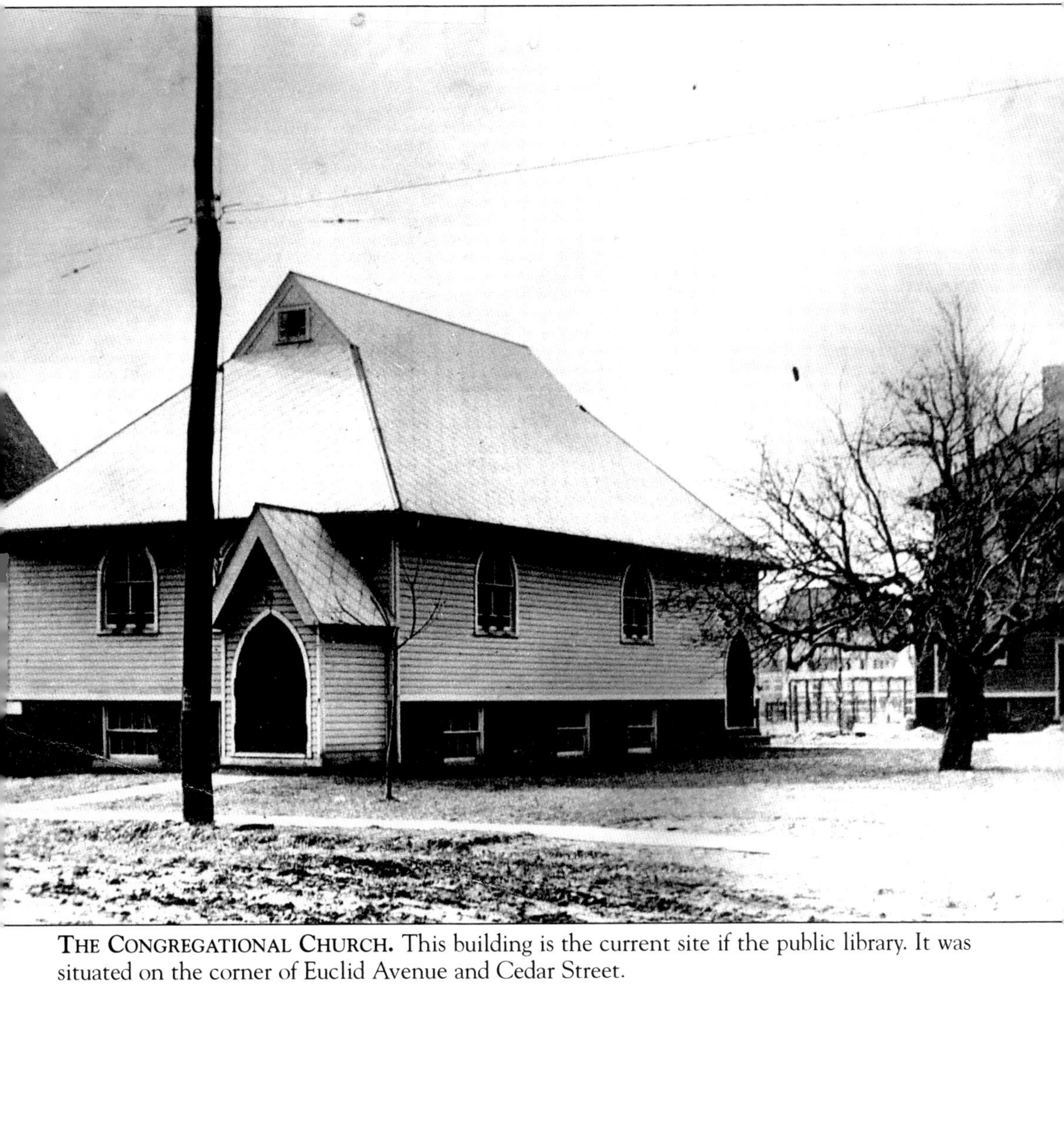

THE CONGREGATIONAL CHURCH. This building is the current site if the public library. It was situated on the corner of Euclid Avenue and Cedar Street.

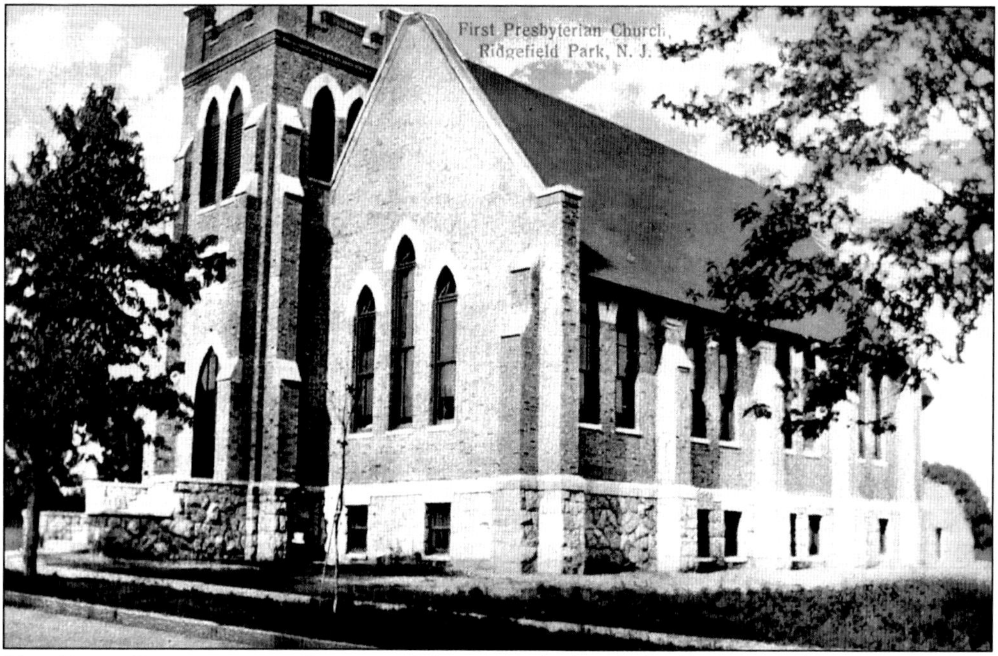

THE FIRST PRESBYTERIAN CHURCH. The original church building is still at the corner of Poplar Street and Euclid Avenue. Additions have been made to the church. It currently functions as a church and houses the local nursery school.

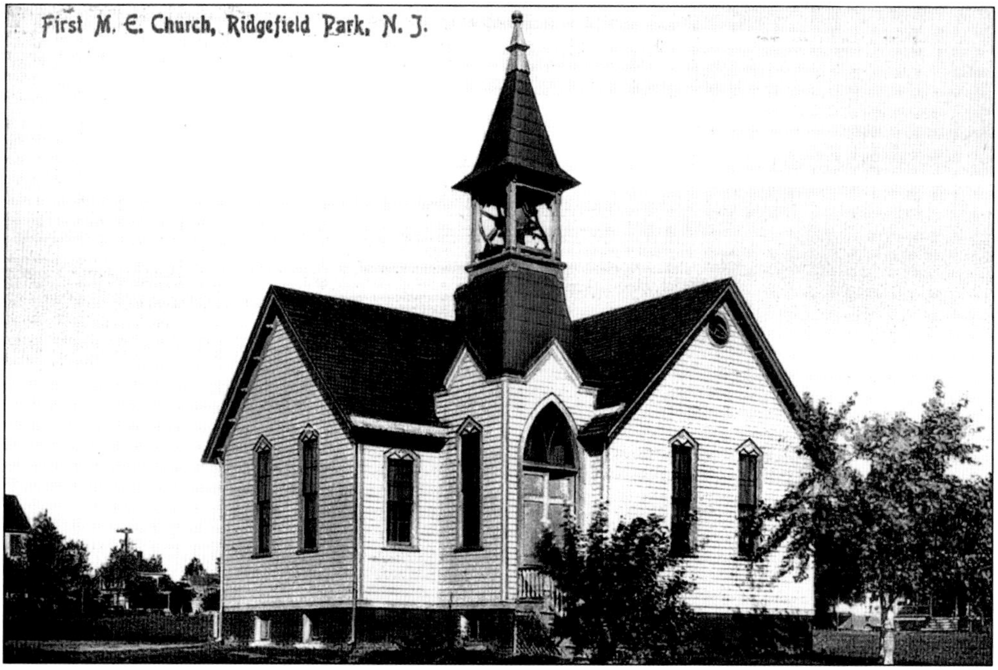

THE FIRST METHODIST EPISCOPAL CHURCH. This lovely old building still serves the community as the First United Methodist Church. Some additions have been made, but the original building is still evident.

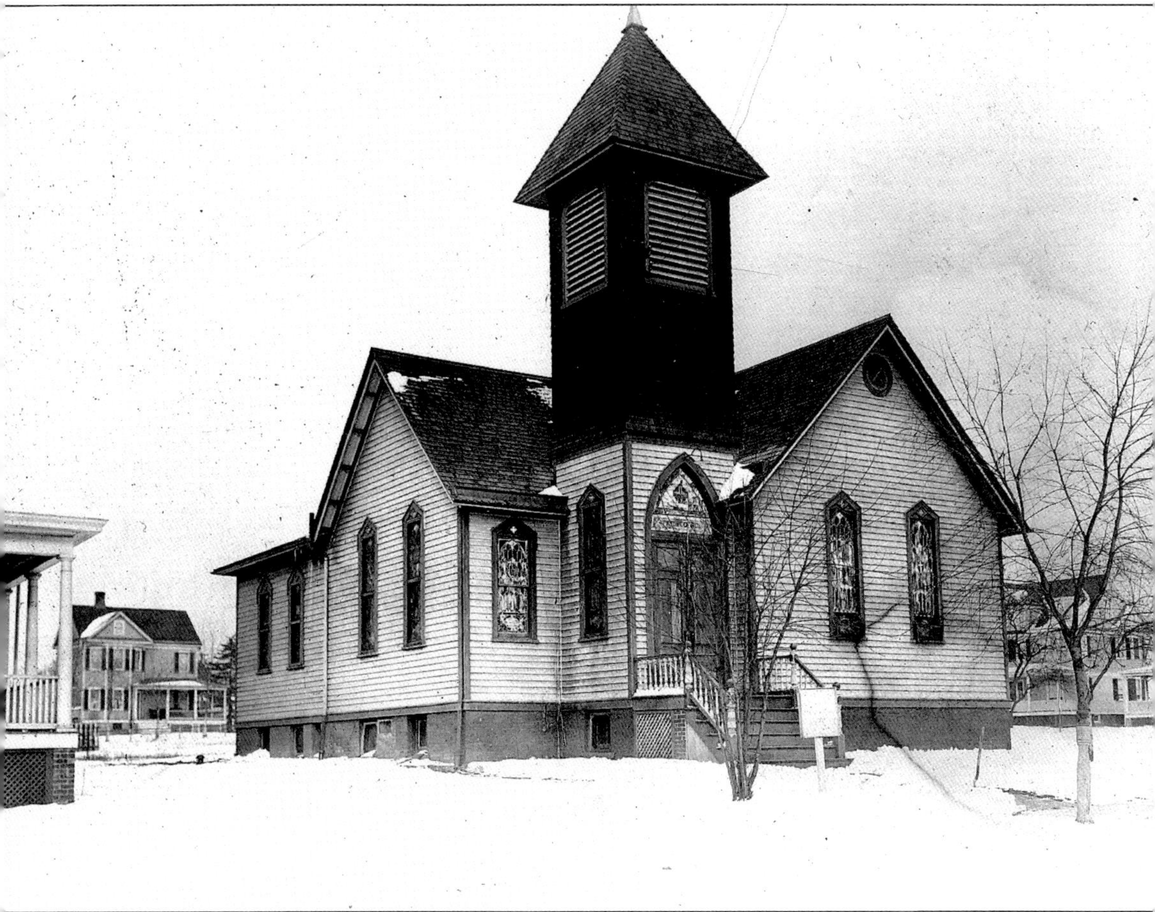

THE FIRST METHODIST EPISCOPAL CHURCH. Located at the intersection of Cedar Street and Bergen Avenue, this church was built in 1895. Before this building was completed, services were held at Sheils Hall and the town hall.

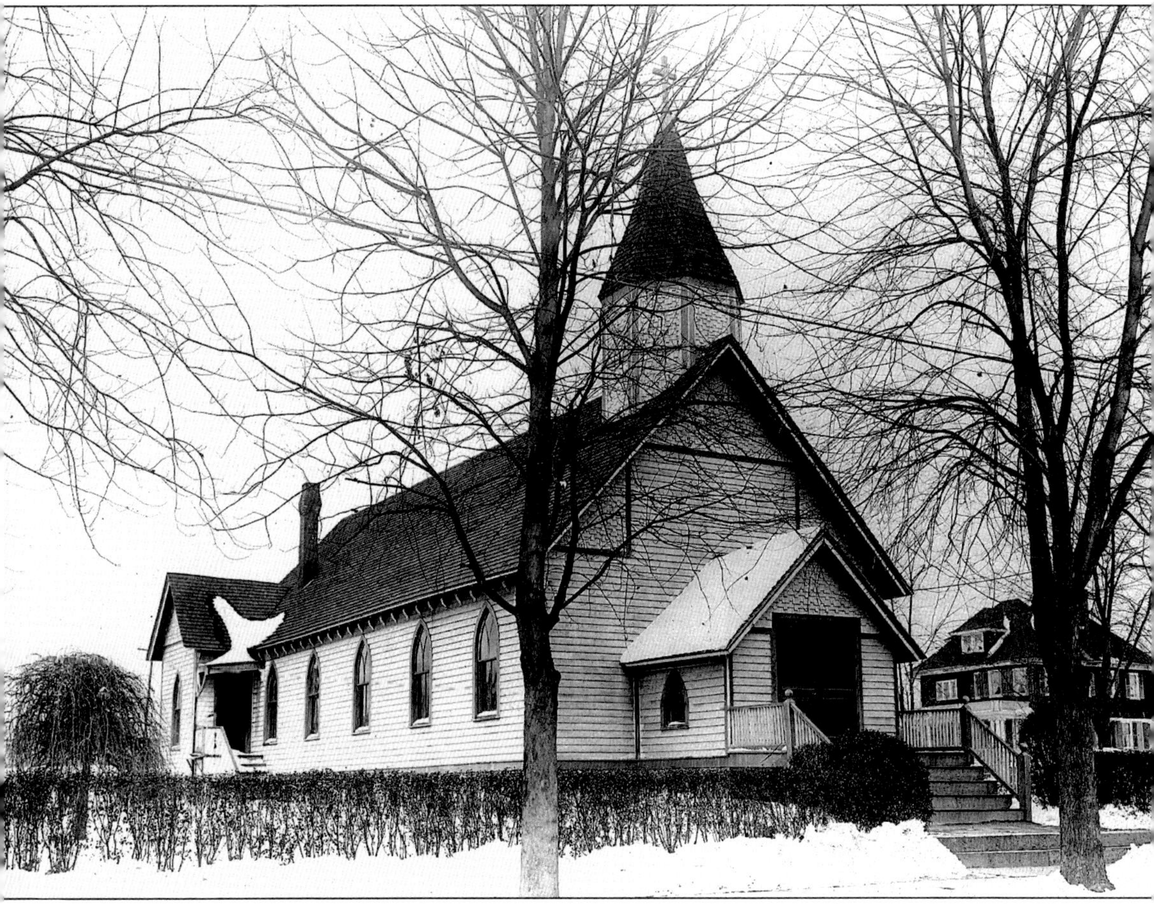

THE ORIGINAL ST. FRANCIS CHURCH. This 1910 photograph shows the St. Francis Church at Mount Vernon Street and Euclid Avenue.

Four

SCHOOLS

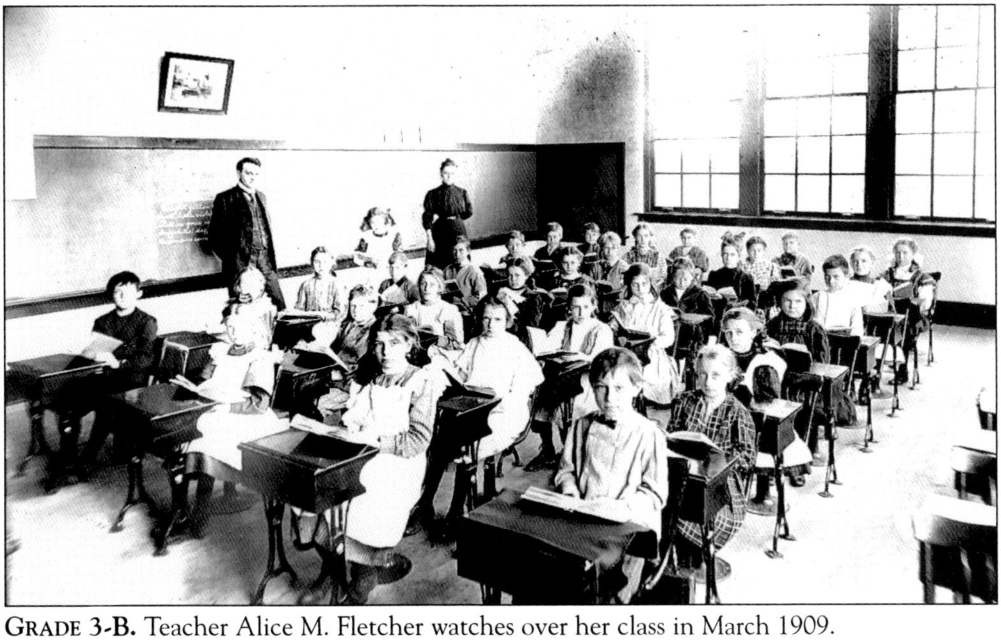

GRADE 3-B. Teacher Alice M. Fletcher watches over her class in March 1909.

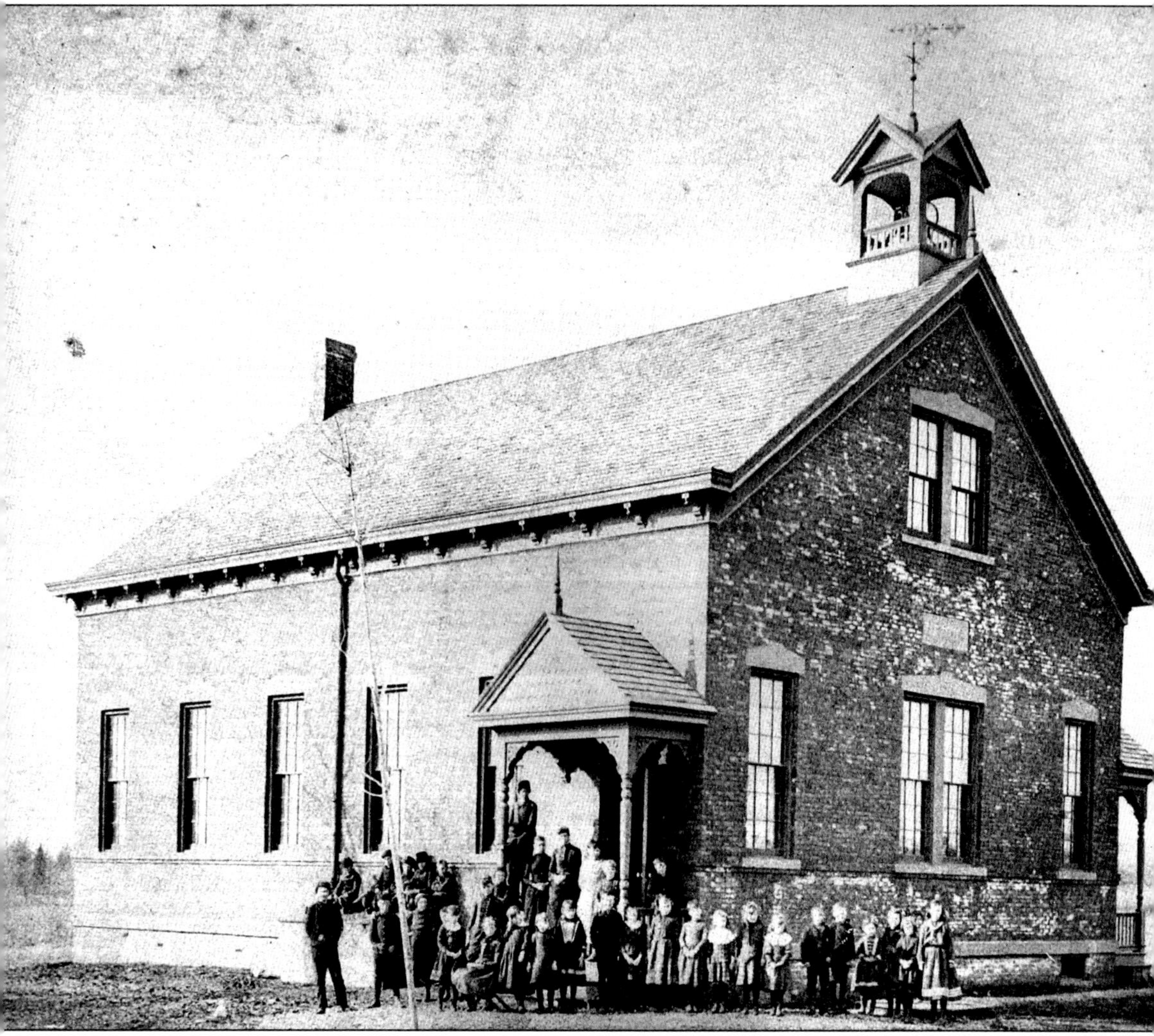

THE ORIGINAL SCHOOL NO. 1. This school served all grade levels and was built in 1886. It was located on today's Euclid Avenue and Hobart Street intersection. The school had one room and one teacher for the 20 students.

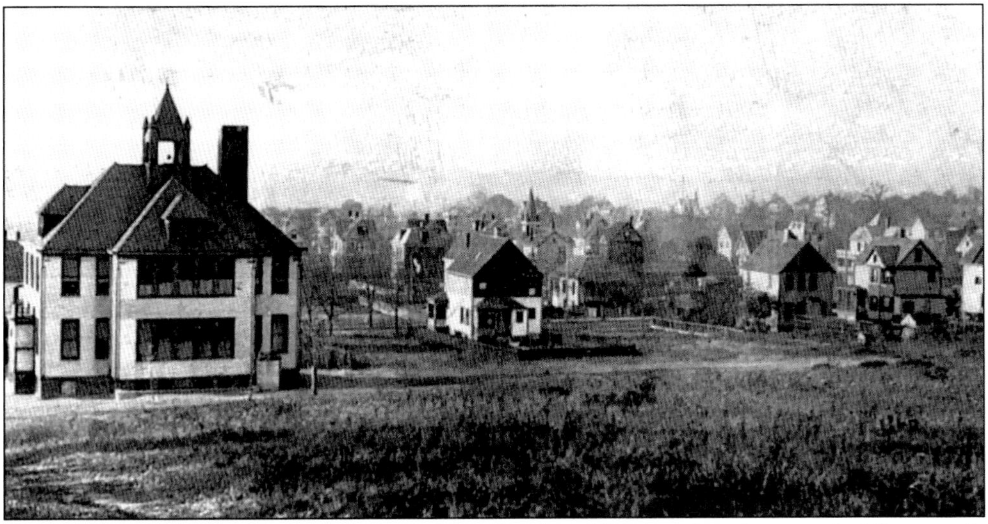

SCHOOL NO. 2. Notice the vast expanse of undeveloped land in this photograph. The steeple of the Scandinavian Lutheran Church is seen in the center of this picture.

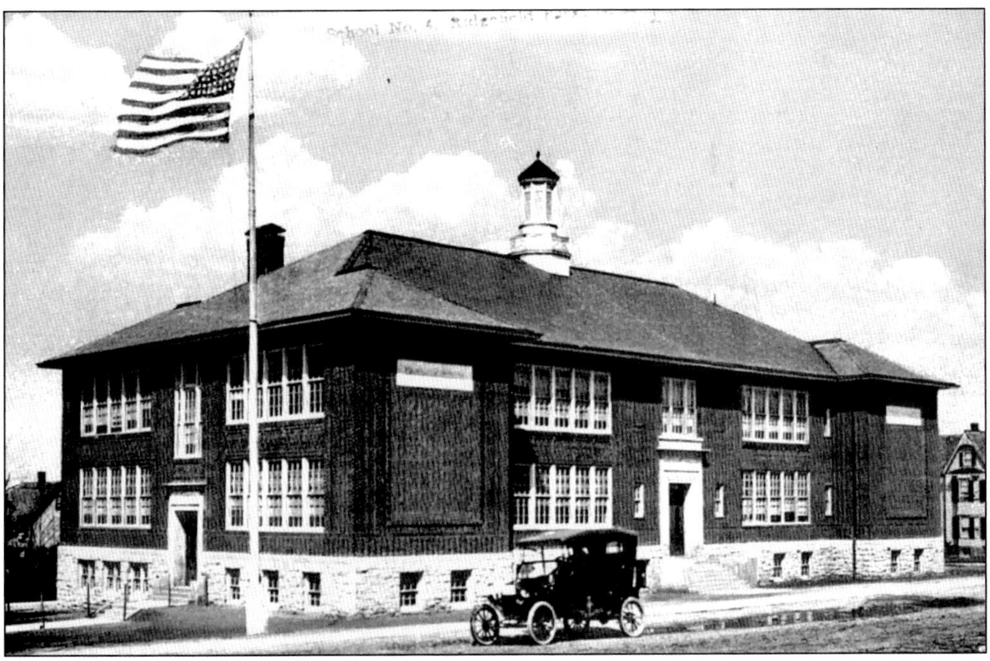

SCHOOL NO. 4. This school, known as Lincoln School, was built in 1912. It still stands between Hackensack Avenue and Austin Street on Lincoln Avenue and contains classrooms for kindergarten through sixth grade.

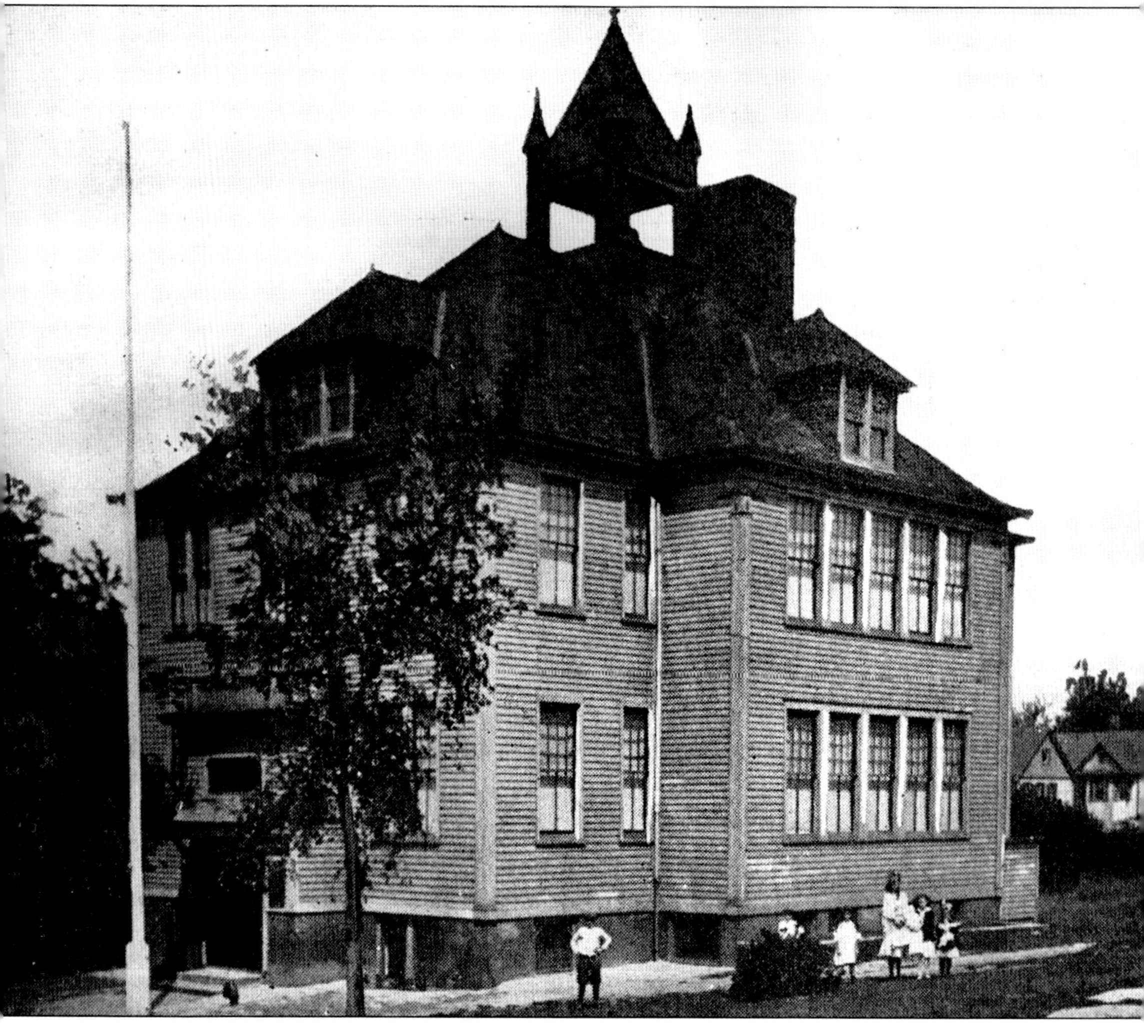

SCHOOL NO. 2. With a growing population in 1899, Ridgefield Park built its own high school, located on the corner of Eighth Street and Hackensack Avenue. Students no longer had to attend Hackensack High School. Most schools of this era had large bell towers.

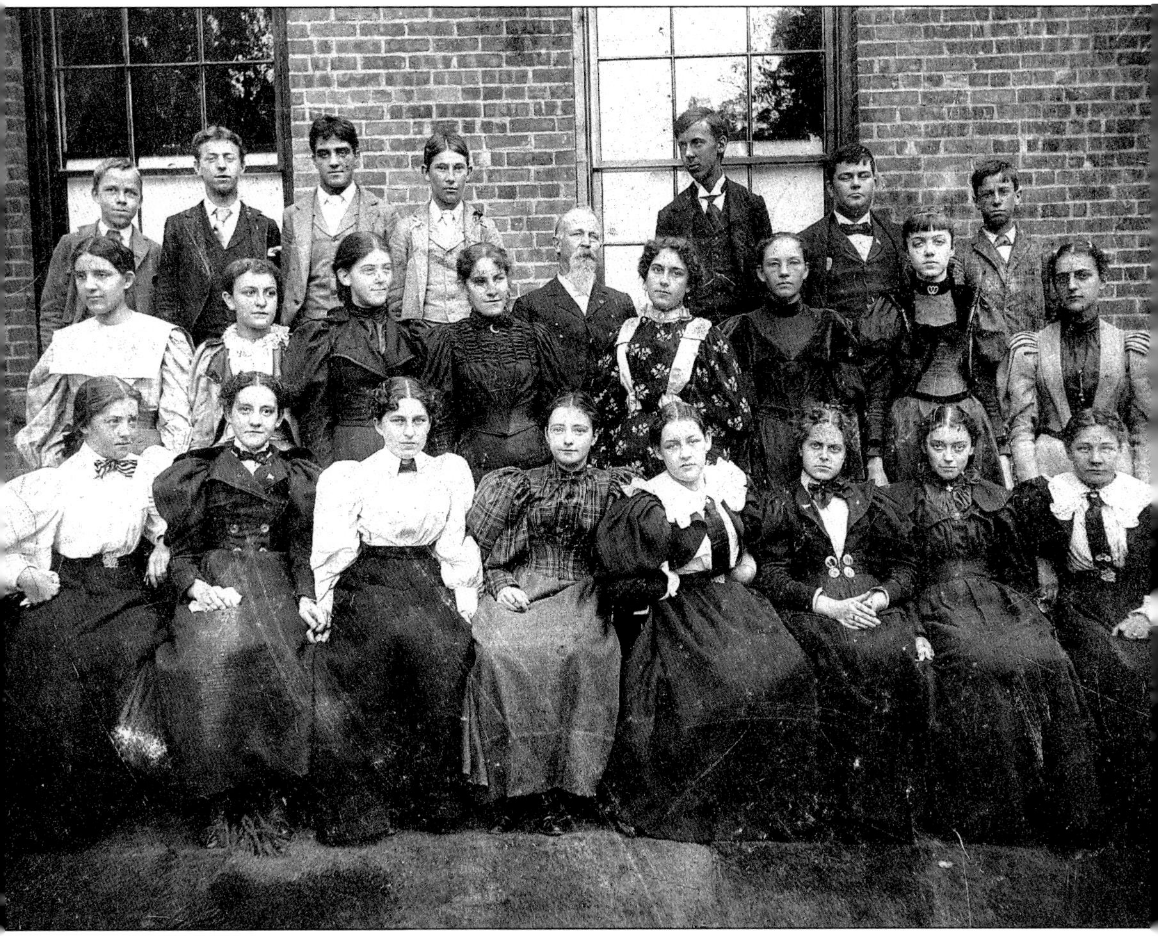

GRADUATION DAY. Before Ridgefield Park had its own high school, pupils wanting to continue their education attended Hackensack High School. There are two Ridgefield Park students in this class. They are Jessie Morrison (first row, fourth from the left) and Edith Merhof (second row, second from the left).

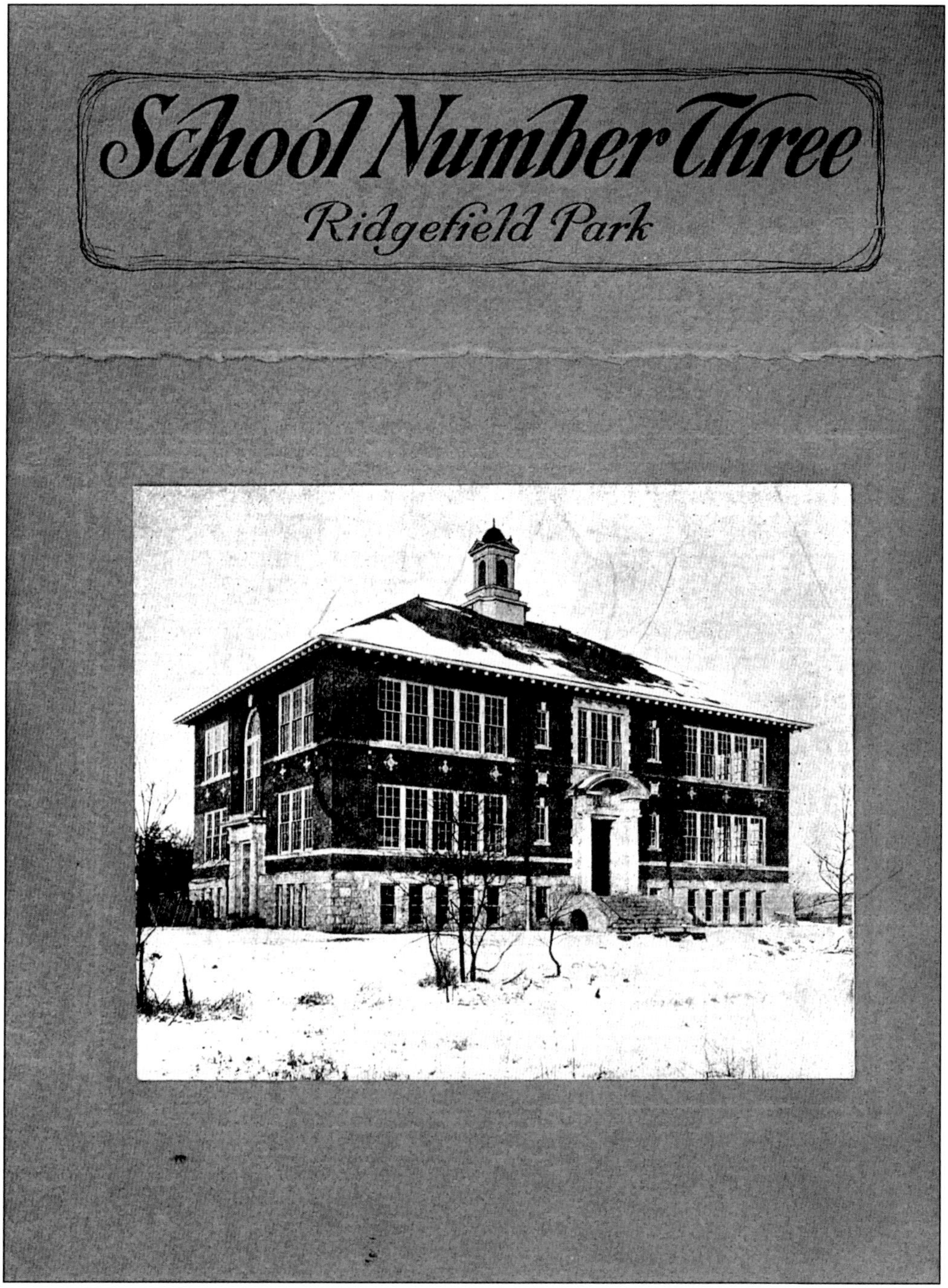

SCHOOL NO. 3. This is the cover of a program for the dedication of School No. 3 on January 30, 1909. The school was built on Teaneck Road and Henry Street. Made of Harvard brick, with limestone trim and a slate roof, the building at one time held a copper and tin bell that weighed 520 pounds. It is currently known as the Grant School and serves kindergarten through sixth grade.

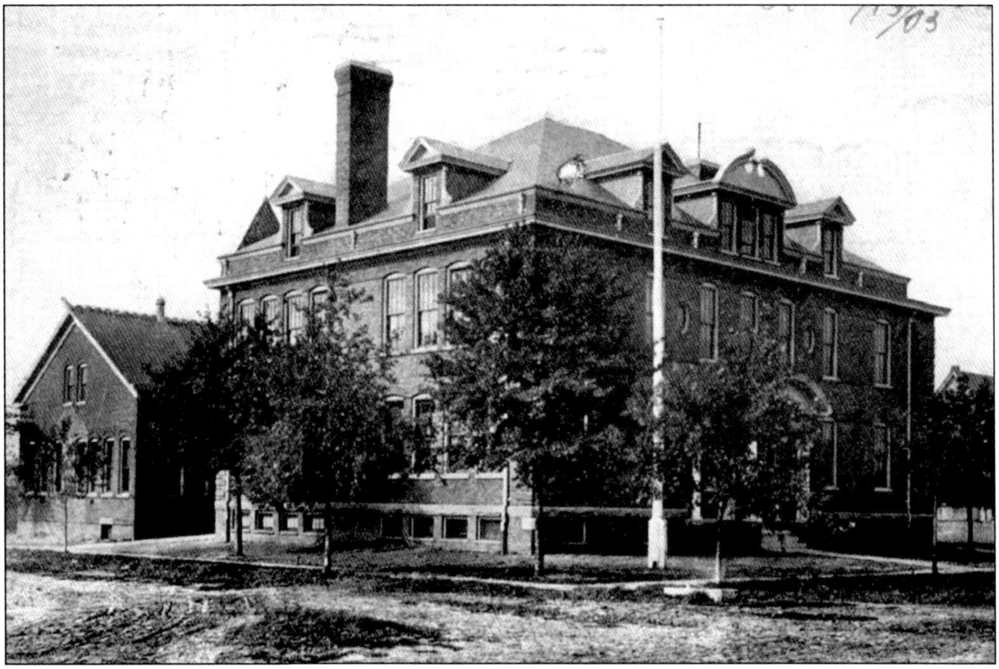

SCHOOL NO. 1. Seen here is Washington Irving School, or School No. 1, at the intersection of Euclid Avenue and Hobart Street. The school was built in 1904 and torn down in 1971. The site is now known as Fellowship Park.

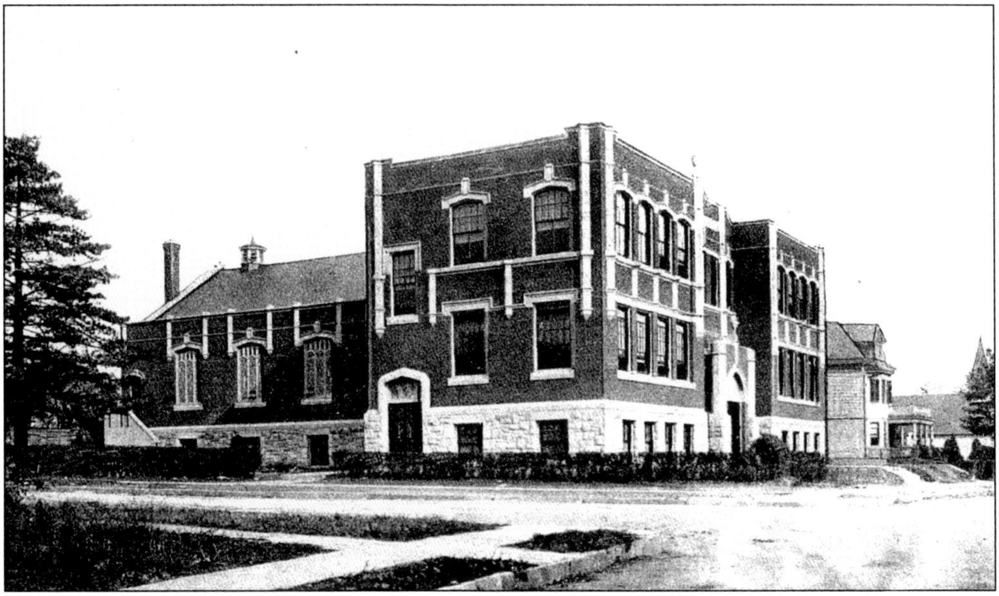

THE CATHOLIC SCHOOL. St. Francis of Assisi, a private school, is located on the corner of Bergen Avenue and Mount Vernon Street. Students in kindergarten through eighth grade attend this school, which is still in existence.

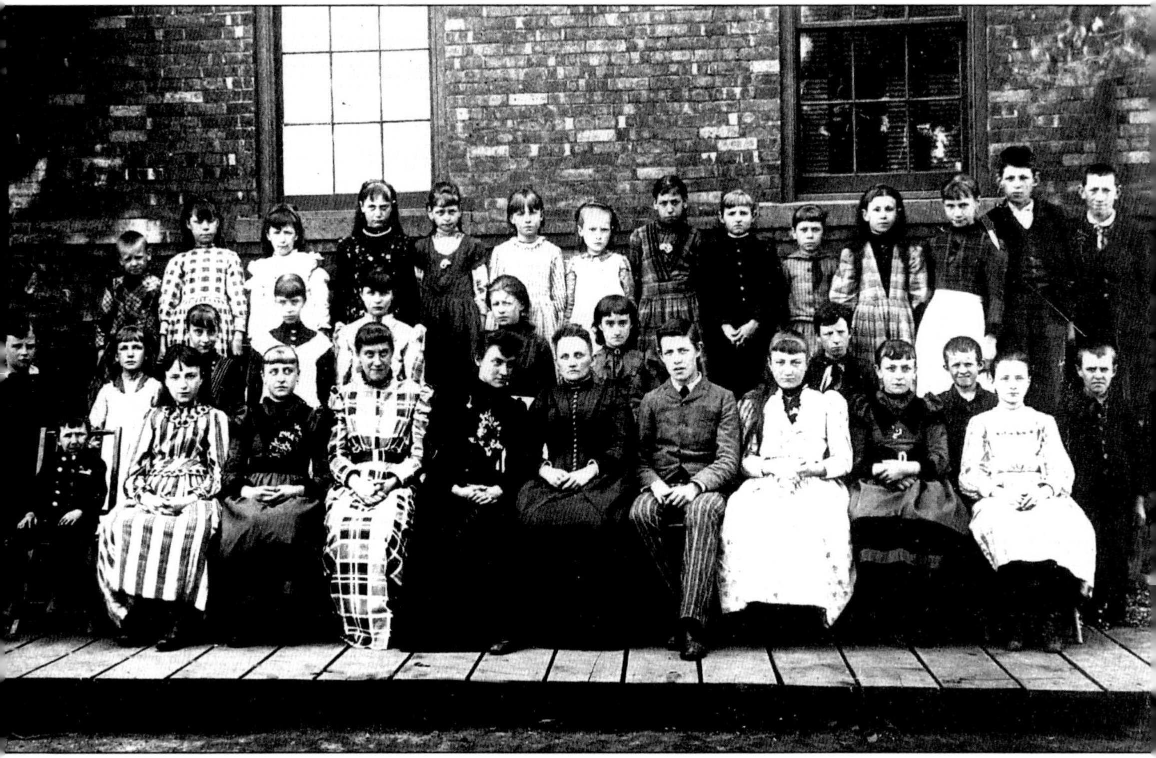

THE MIDDLE AND UPPER GRADES AT SCHOOL NO. 1. This photograph was taken in 1891. Seen here are Willie Platt, Cora Henderson, Zeo Merhof, Florence Christie, teacher Tille Meyers, teacher ? Corzine, Ernest Calloway, Edith Merhof, Jessie Morrison, Mabel Brewster, Helen Ravekes, Ricky Marns, Frances Percival, Elly Duane, James Brady, Warren Abbott, Arthur Tukey, Edgar Crandall, Alice Hunniken, Louise O'Brian, Lilly Smith, Margaret Percival, Bella Shields, Jessie Hunniken, Bertha Brewster, Mabel Brewster, Bessie Marshall, and Philip Smith.

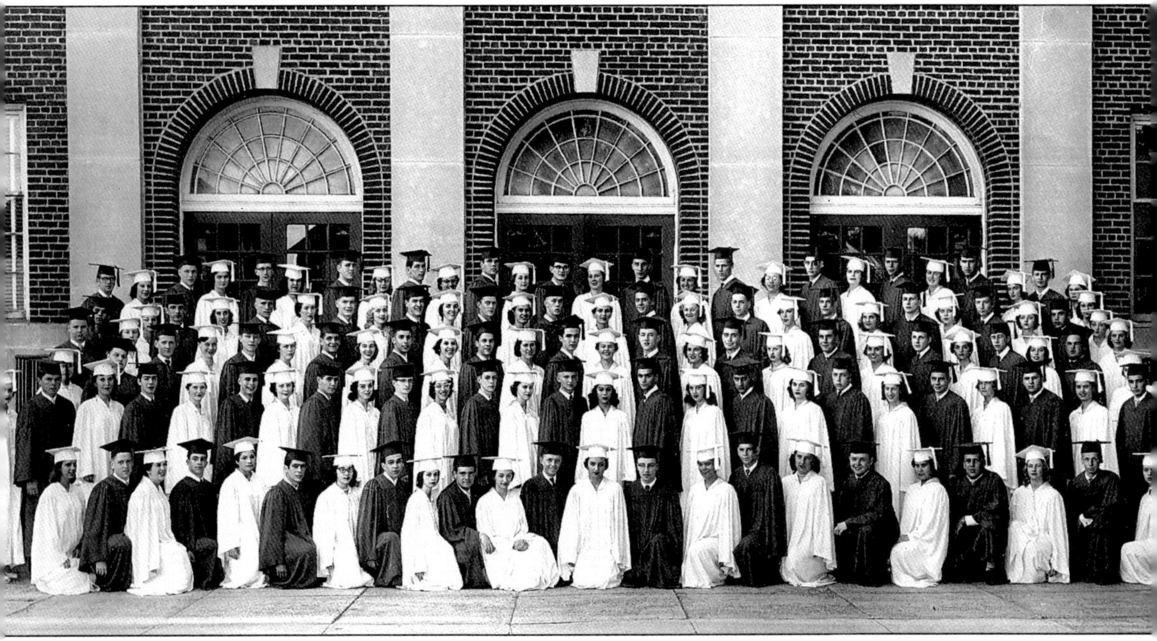

THE CLASS OF 1958. Students of the graduating class of 1958 pose for a formal photograph in front of Washington High School wearing traditional gowns of red and white.

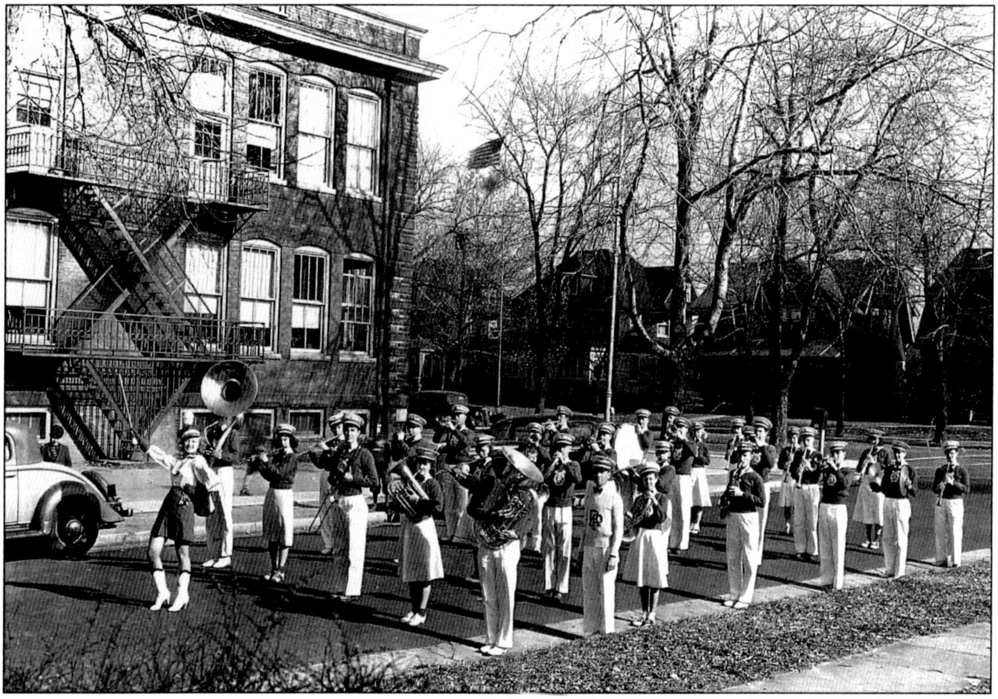

The Ridgefield Park High School Marching Band. Band members line up on Hobart Street in parade fashion in 1940.

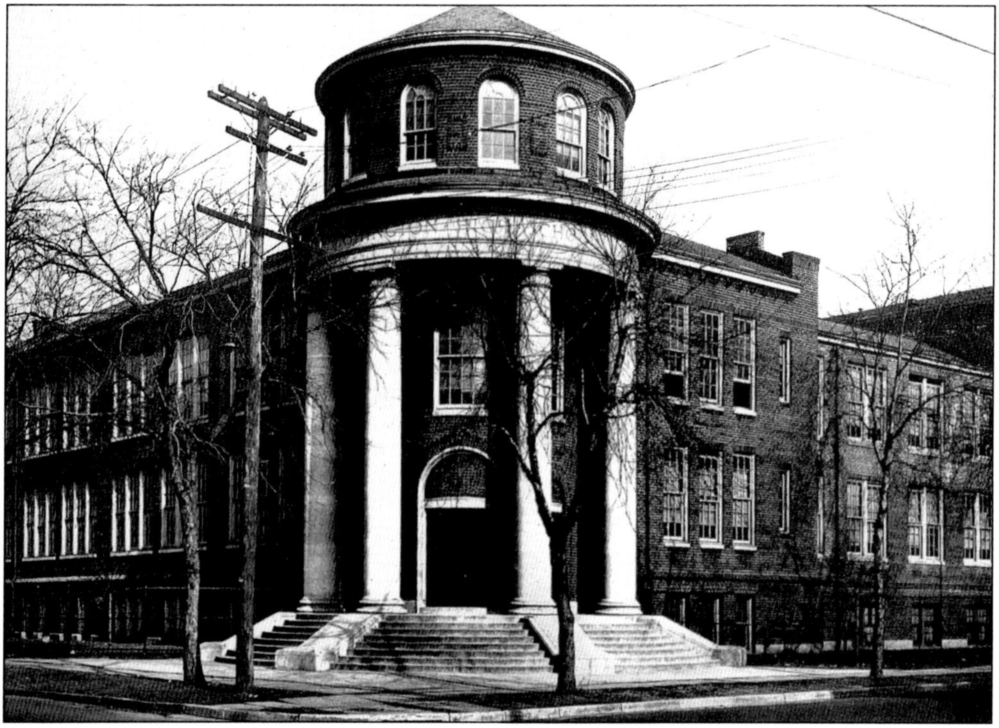

Washington High School. This building was located on the corner of Bergen Avenue and Hobart Street. It was torn down in 1971, and the property is now Fellowship Park.

Five

THE RIVER

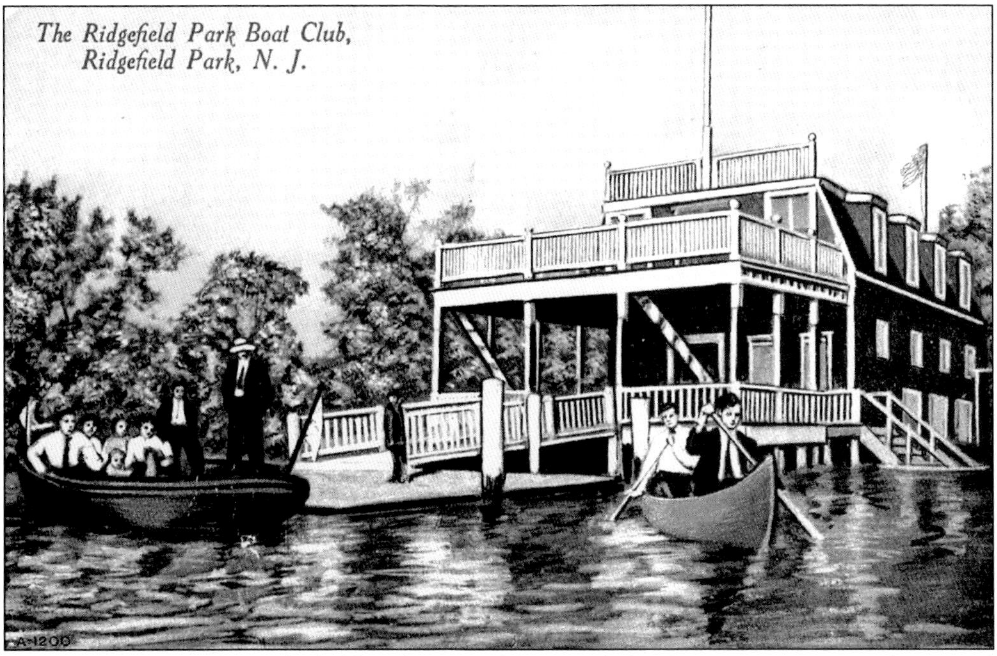

THE BOAT CLUB. The Ridgefield Park Boat Club was a hub of activity. Many people enjoyed spending time on the calm waters of the Overpeck Creek and Hackensack River. Ridgefield Park attracted many tourists. The club offered tennis and handball courts, billiard tables, and canoes to members who paid monthly dues of $1.

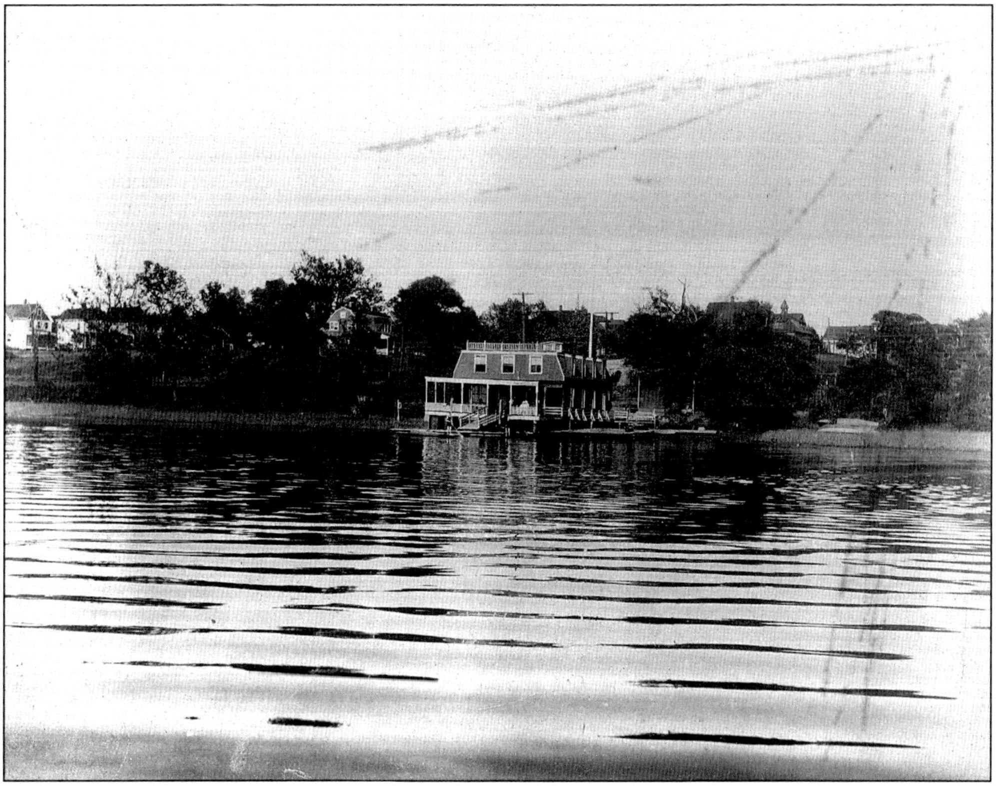

THE RIDGEFIELD PARK BOAT CLUB. The club's expansive porches allowed residents to relax and enjoy the calming waters and warm breeze of the Hackensack River. Many of the biggest social events of the year were held here.

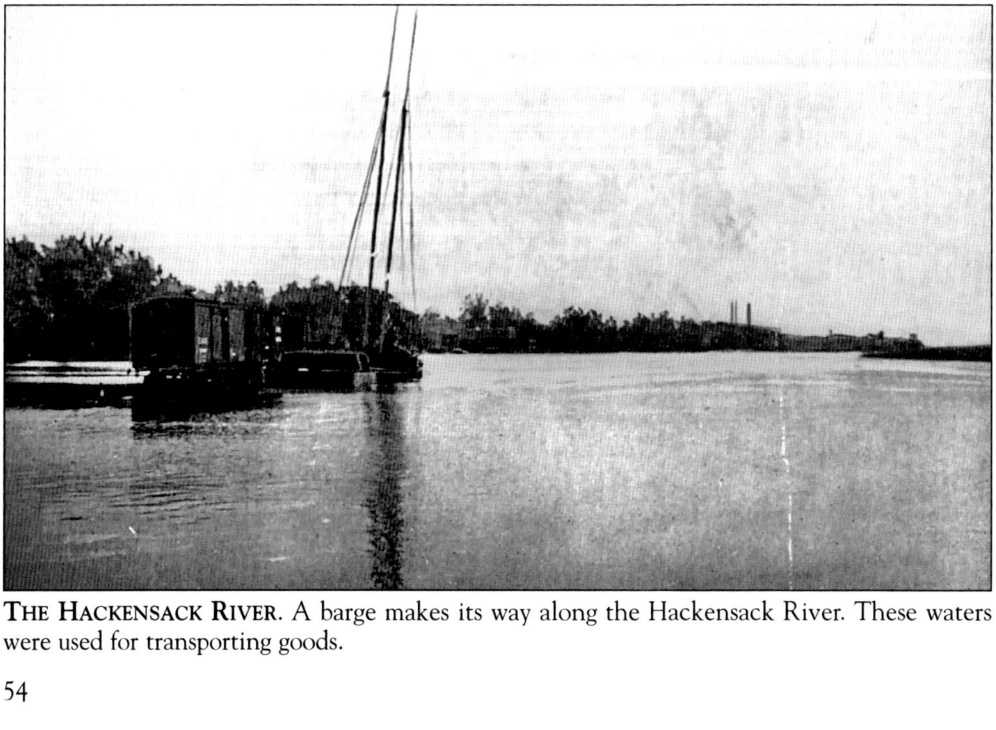

THE HACKENSACK RIVER. A barge makes its way along the Hackensack River. These waters were used for transporting goods.

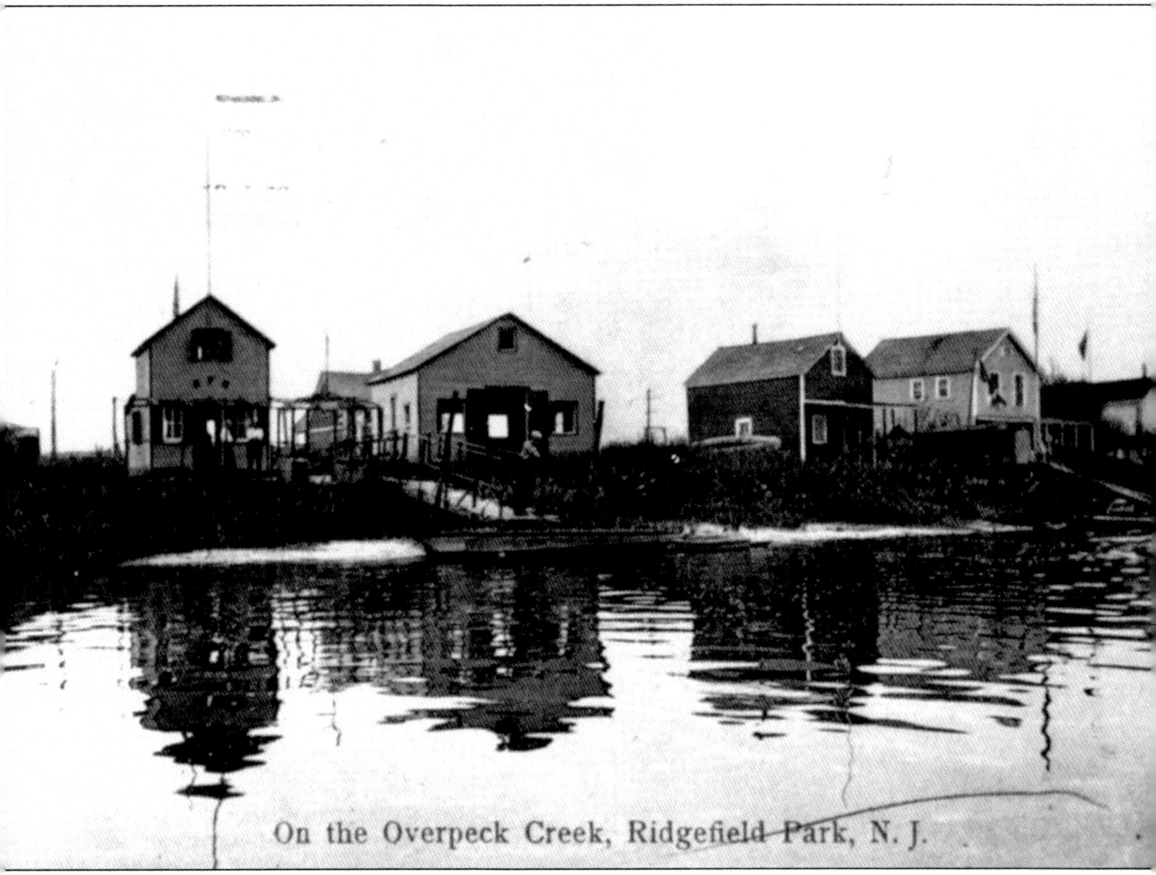

THE OVERPECK CREEK. Along the south border of Ridgefield Park runs the Overpeck Creek. This photograph shows a boathouse and dock. The creek was a popular place for boaters and swimmers at one time.

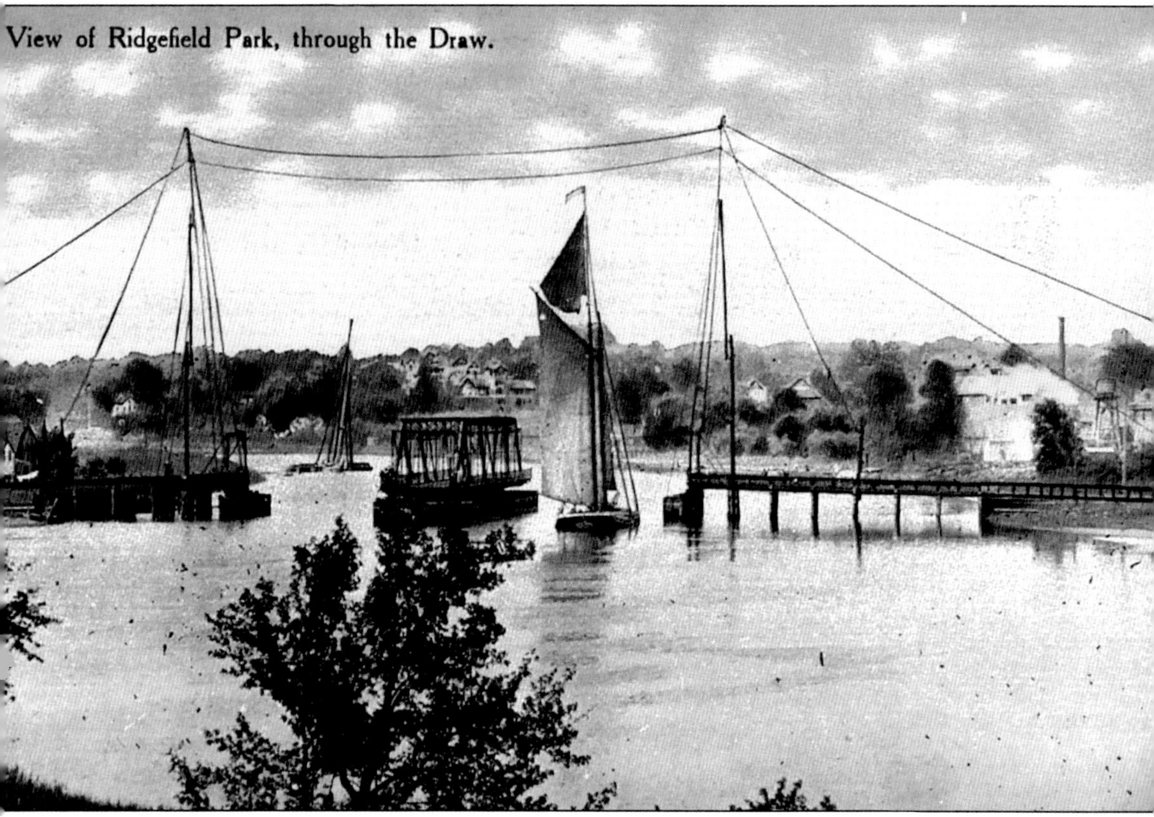

THE BRIDGE. A boat makes its way through "the draw," as the bridge at Bergen Turnpike was known.

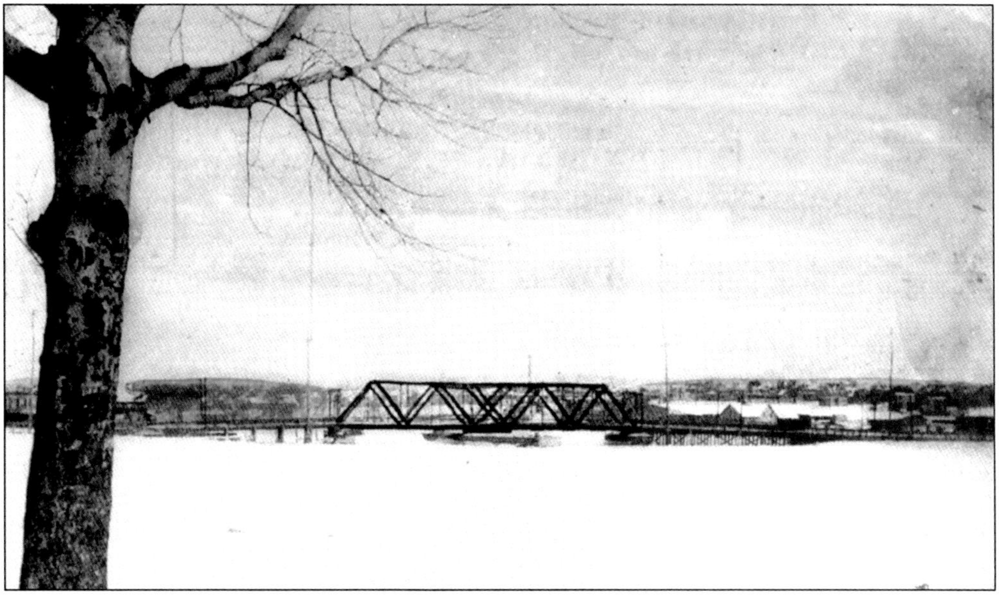

THE BRIDGE TO LITTLE FERRY. Before Route 46 was constructed, travel across the Hackensack River was by ferry or a railroad bridge that connected the Bergen Turnpike to Little Ferry.

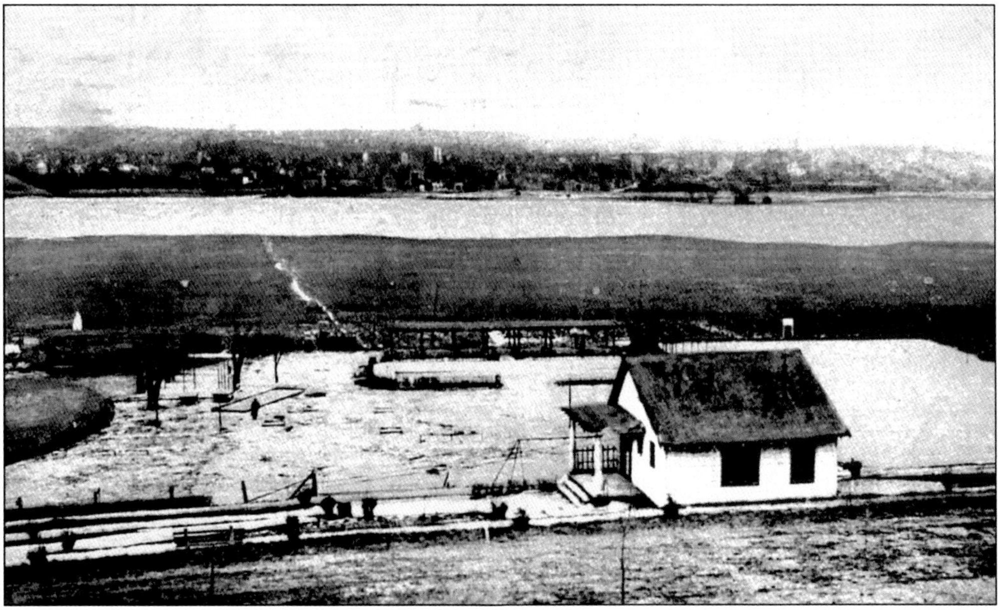

VETERANS PARK. This 1933 postcard shows the playground and pool at Veterans Park, as well as the meadows along the creek.

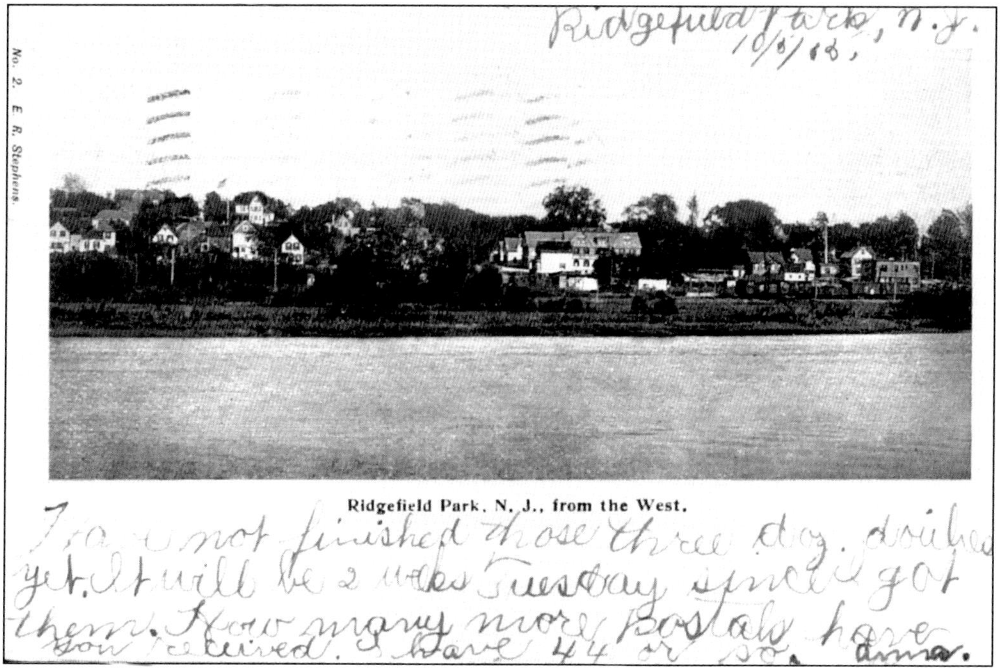

COLLECTING POSTCARDS. This 1905 postcard shows Ridgefield Park from the west. Anna, the sender, wrote, "Have not finished those three doz. doilies yet. It will be 2 weeks Tuesday since I got them. How many postals have you received. I have 44 or so."

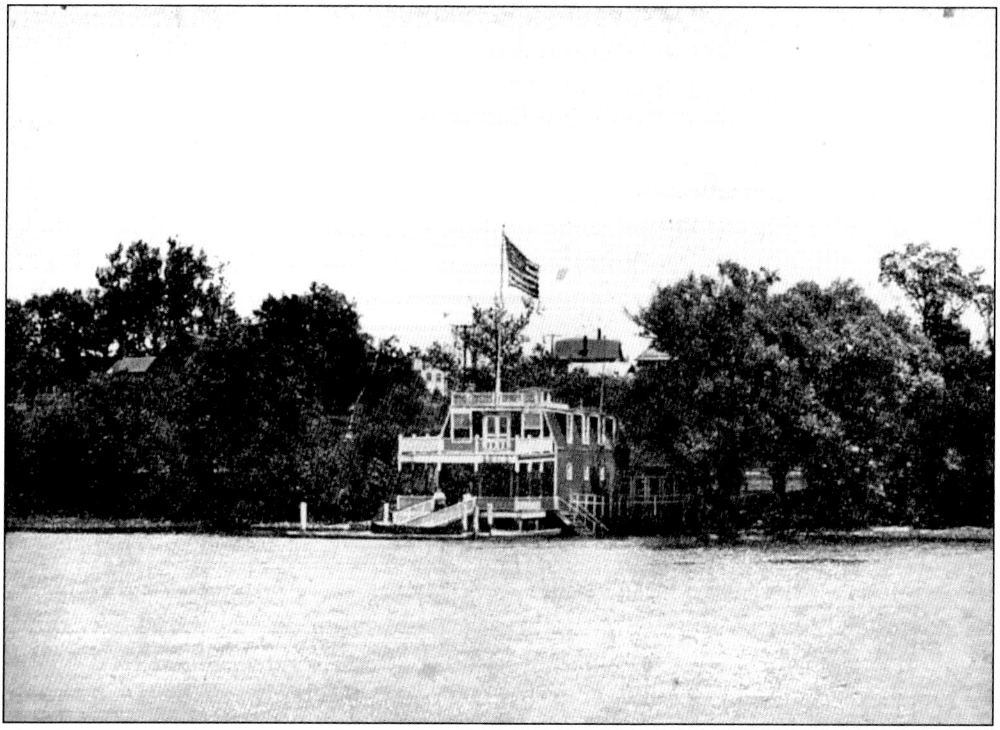

THE RIDGEFIELD PARK BOAT CLUB. This boat club was located on the Hackensack River at the foot of Brinkerhoff Street.

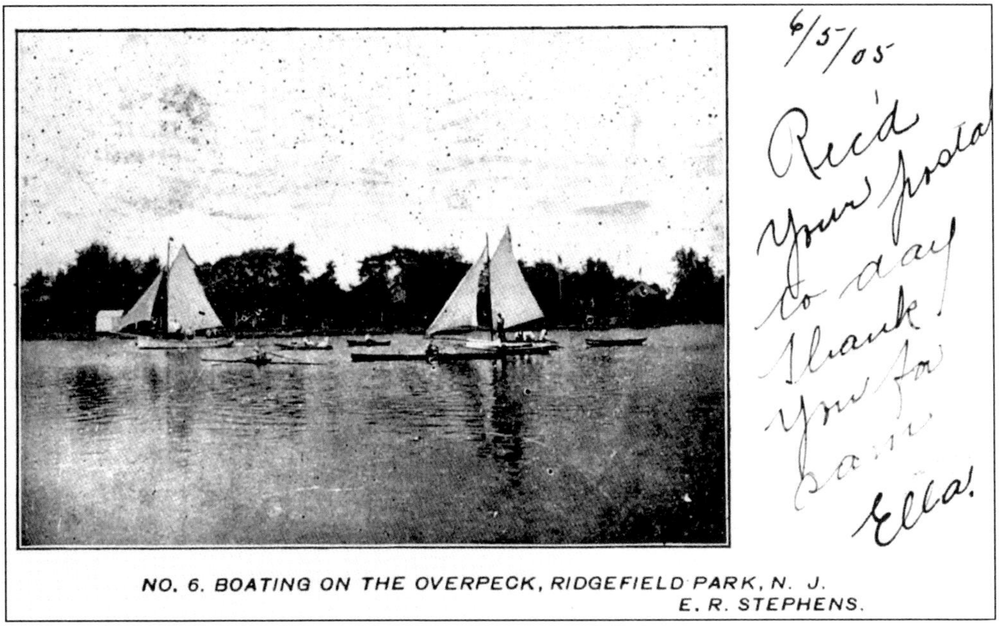

"NO. 6 BOATING ON THE OVERPECK." Many boats cruised up and down the waters surrounding Ridgefield Park. Here, sailboats, small skiffs, and rowboats create a traffic jam.

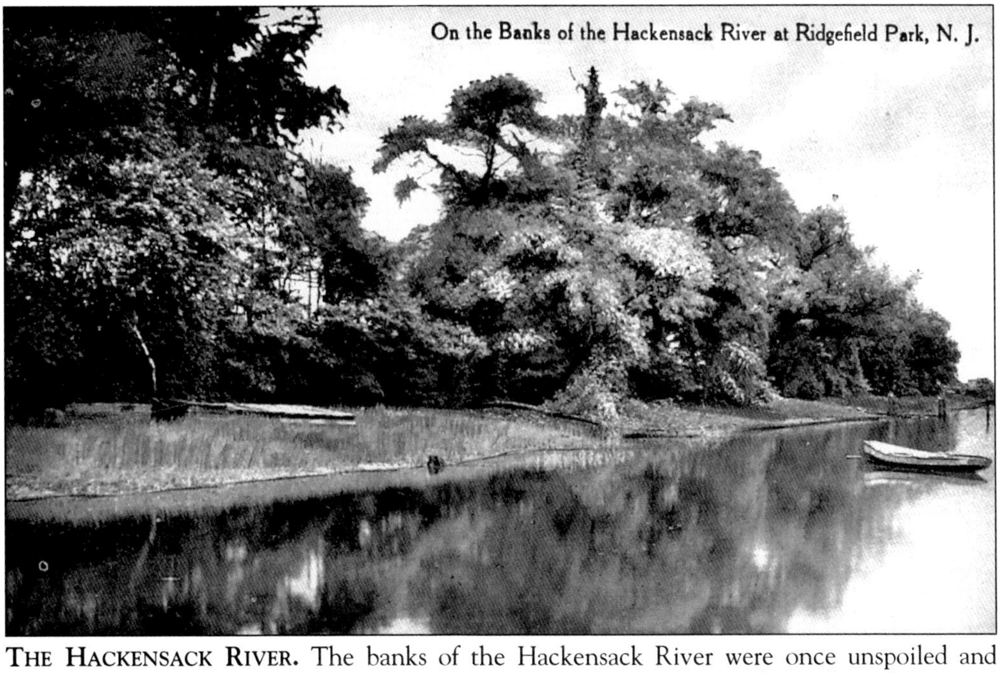

THE HACKENSACK RIVER. The banks of the Hackensack River were once unspoiled and pristine. Today, efforts are being made to clean up the waters of the Hackensack, and more and more recreational use is noticeable. This scene is a perfect example of the serene waters that drew settlers to this area.

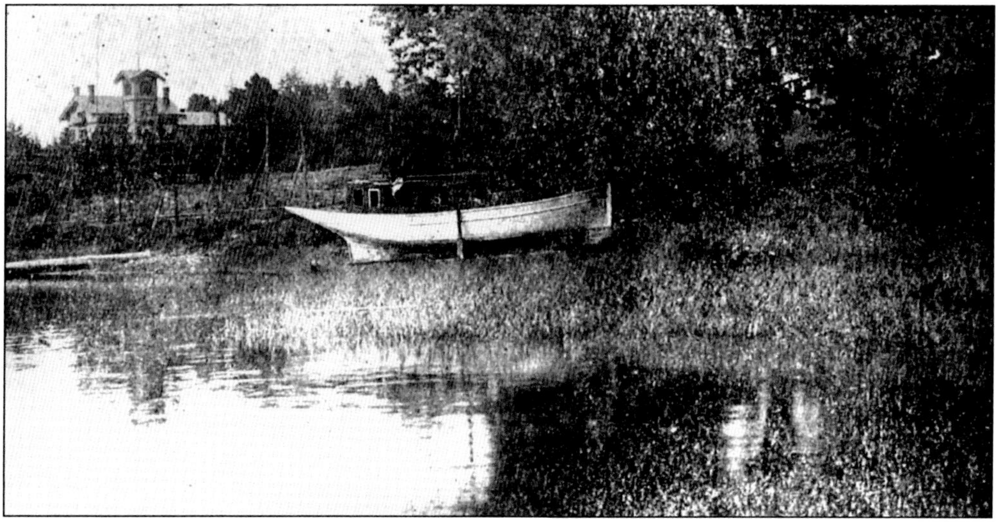

MERHOFF PARK. Land along the Hackensack River was at one time known as Merhoff Park. The Merhof Mansion, which is now the Elk's club property, is visible in the upper left.

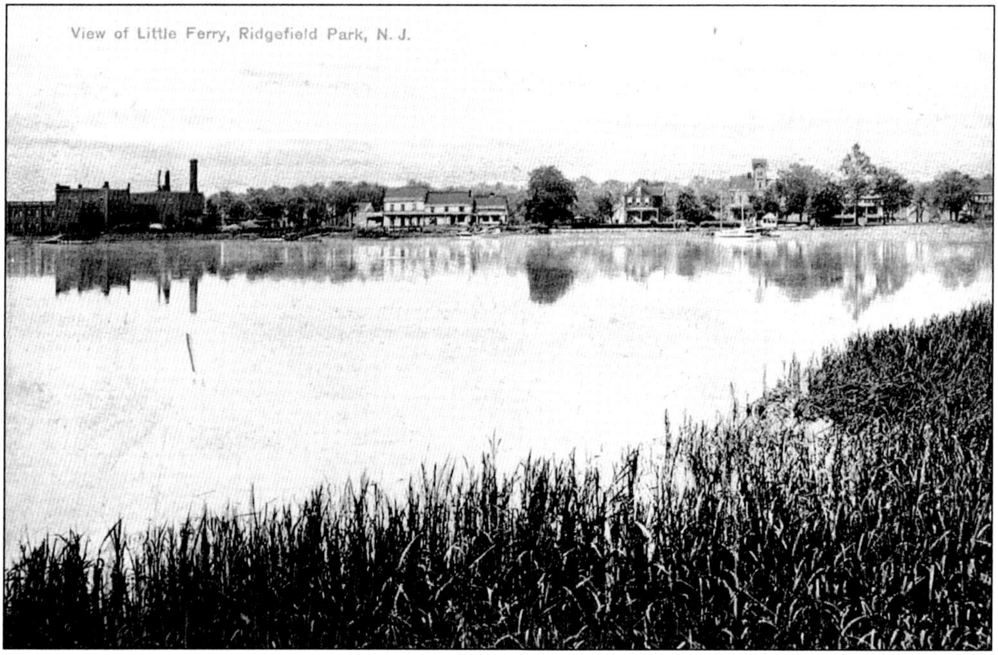

A VIEW OF LITTLE FERRY. Just west of the banks of the Hackensack River is Ridgefield Park's closest neighbor, Little Ferry.

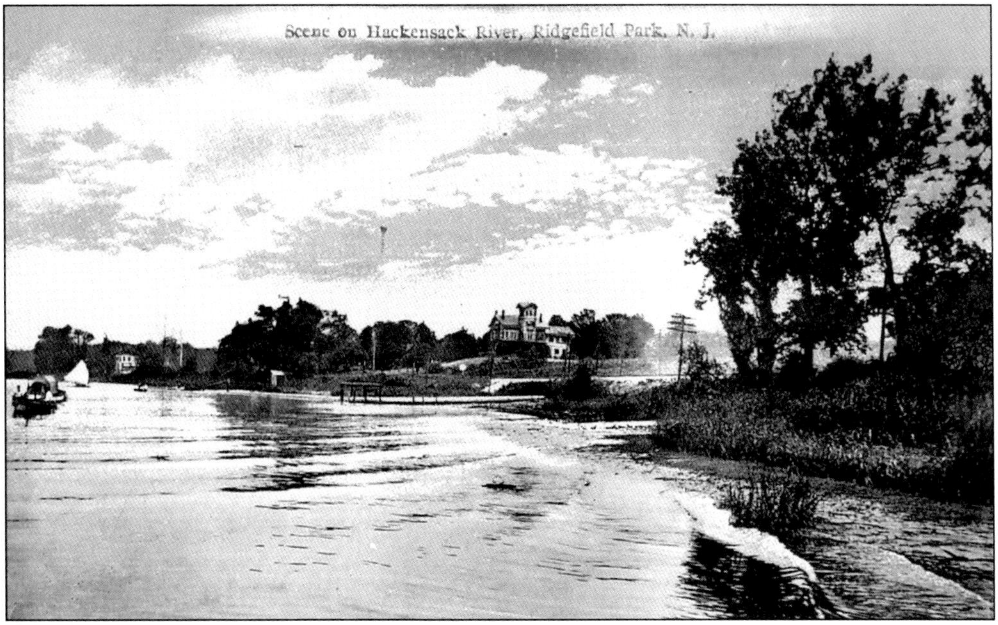

ON THE HACKENSACK RIVER. This breathtaking view of the Hackensack River looks north. The Merhoff Mansion is evident in the center of the photograph.

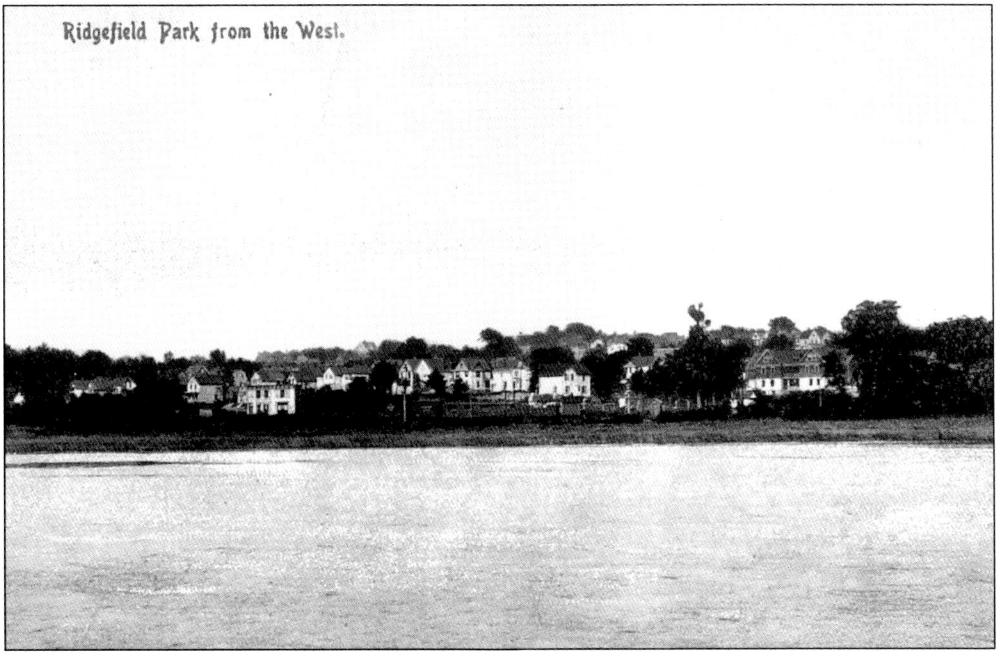

A VIEW FROM LITTLE FERRY. This was the view across the Hackensack River as seen from neighboring Little Ferry.

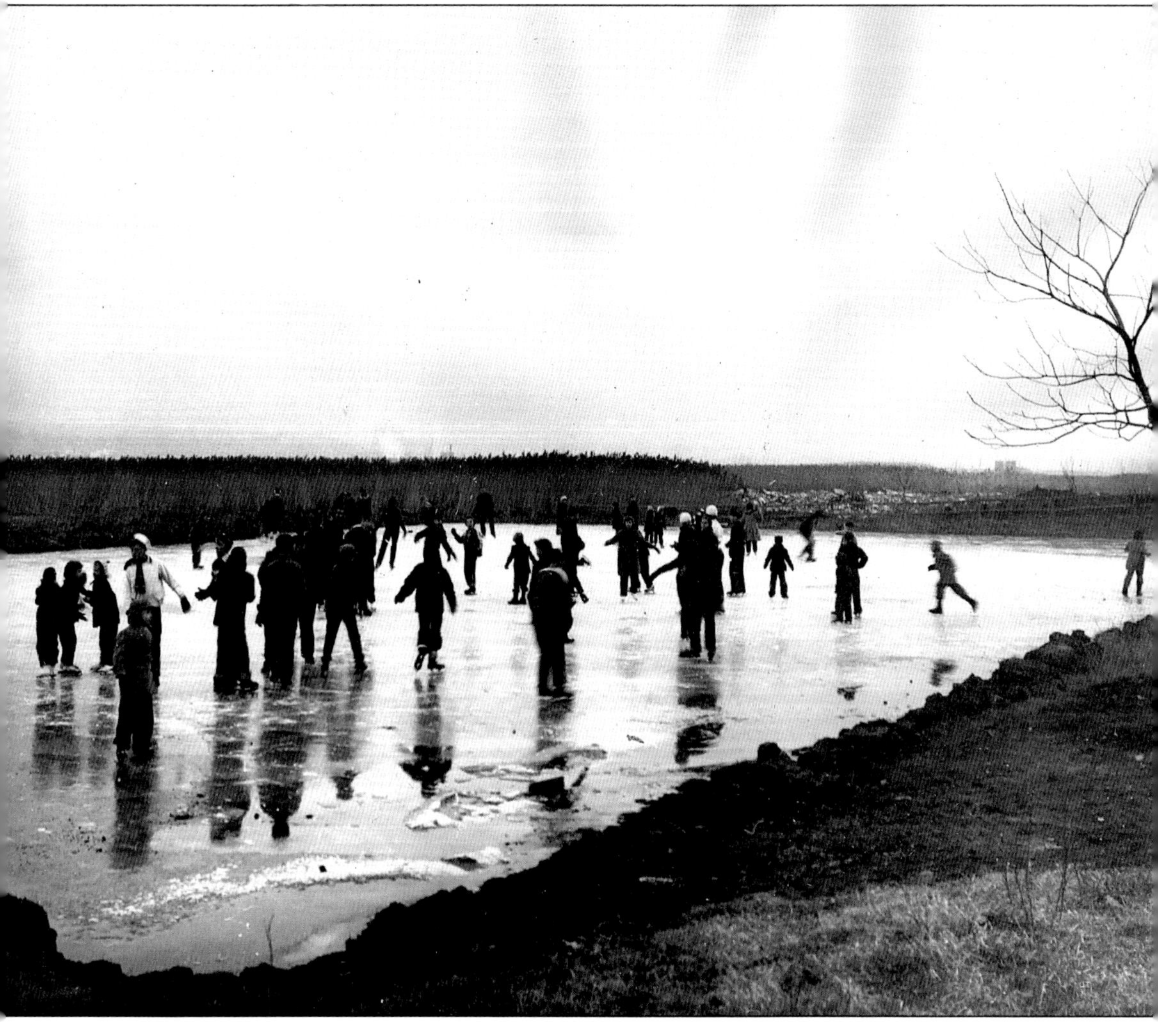

SKATING ON A COLD WINTER DAY. Children and adults enjoyed ice-skating on the pond at Dexheimer Park, which is where the current high school is.

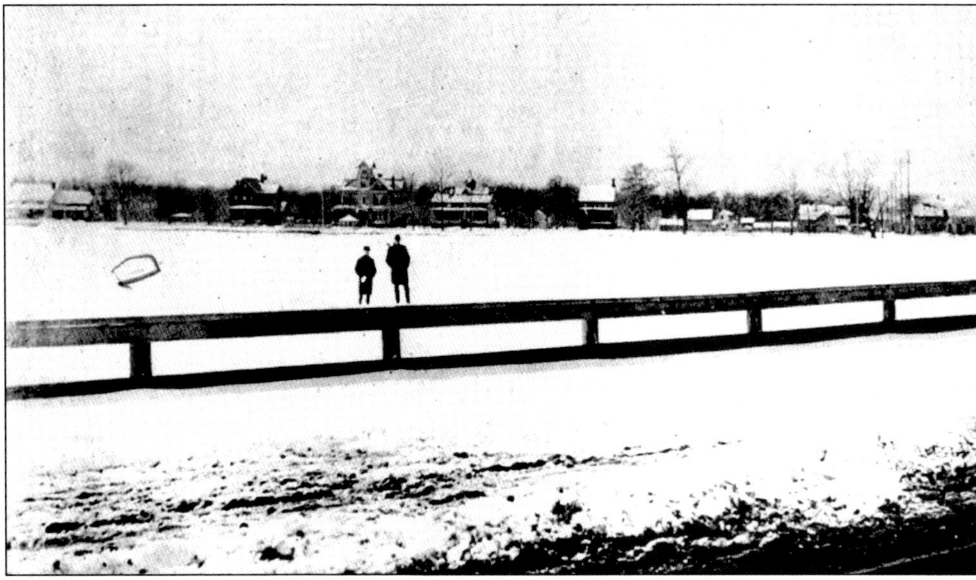

ANOTHER COLD DAY. This view of Ridgefield Park was taken from the Little Ferry side of the Hackensack River. Notice the people standing on the frozen river in the center of the photograph.

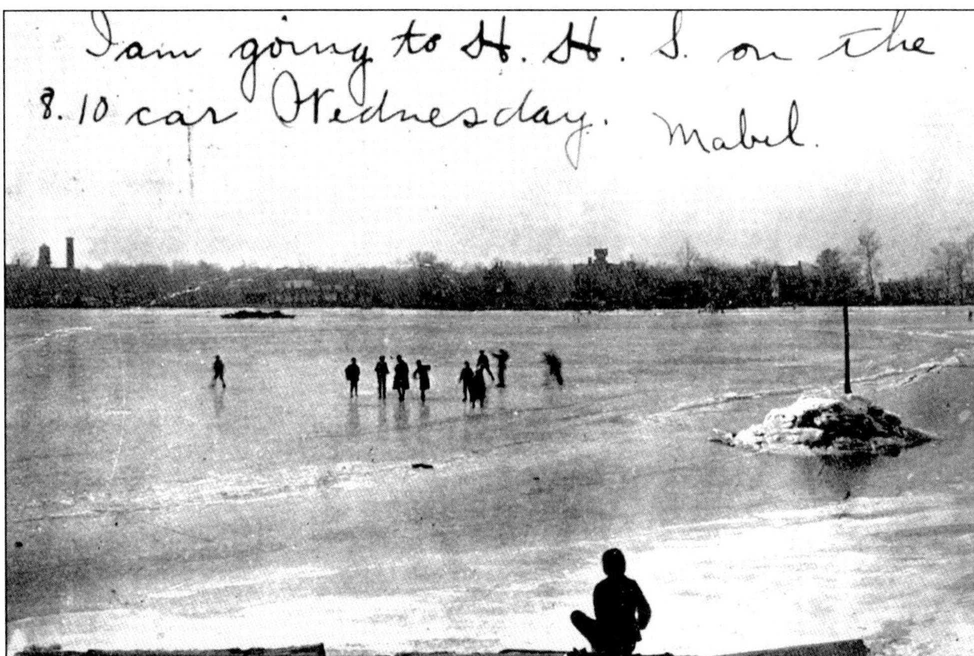

ANOTHER WINTER DAY. When the Hackensack River froze over, everyone grabbed their ice skates and headed out for a day of fun.

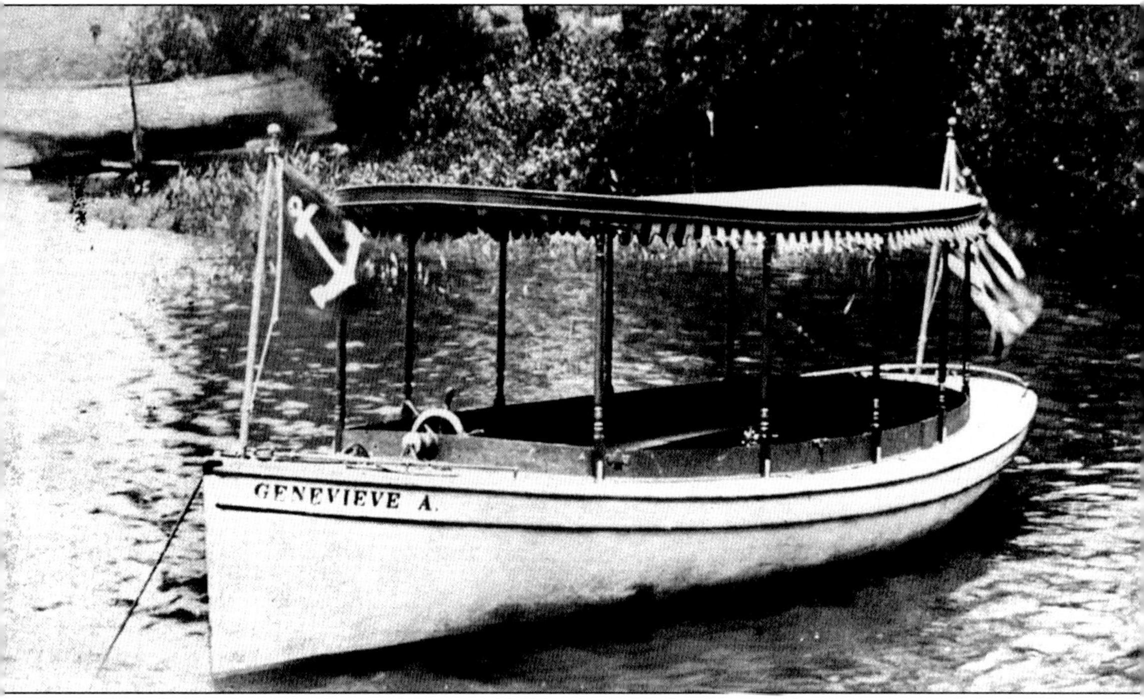

THE *GENEVIEVE A.* This 1905 postcard shows an excellent example of the wooden boats that took people on leisurely rides along the Overpeck Creek. Covered by a canopy, this boat allowed passengers to enjoy the scenery while staying cool.

Six

Athletics and Activities

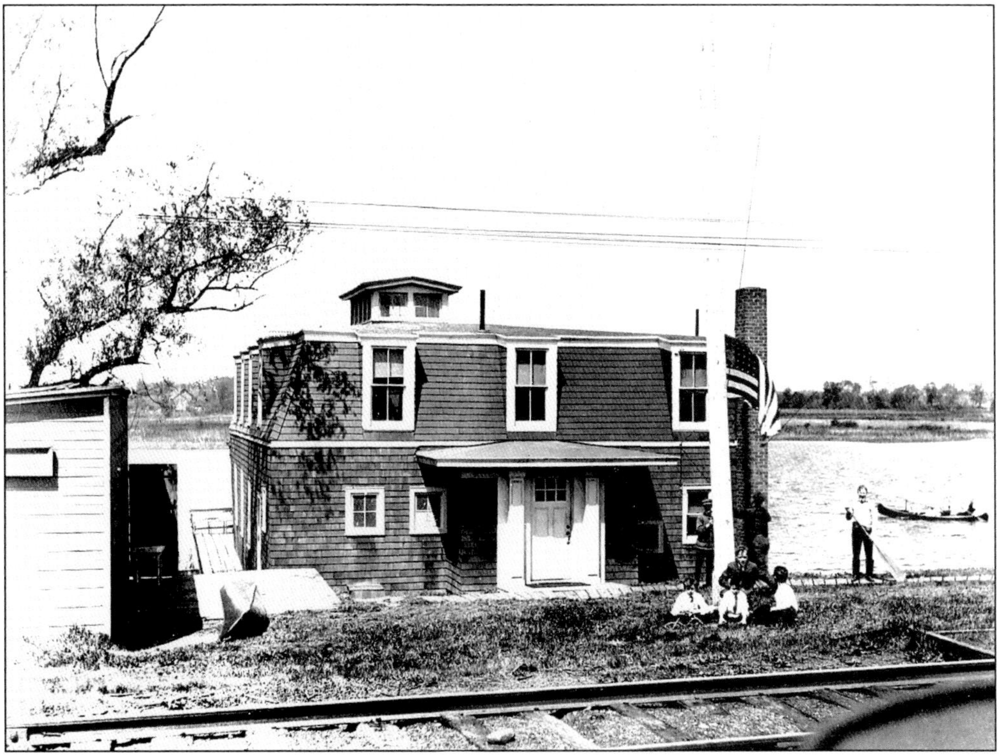

Raising the Flag. This is another view of the Ridgefield Park Boat Club, as seen from the railroad tracks.

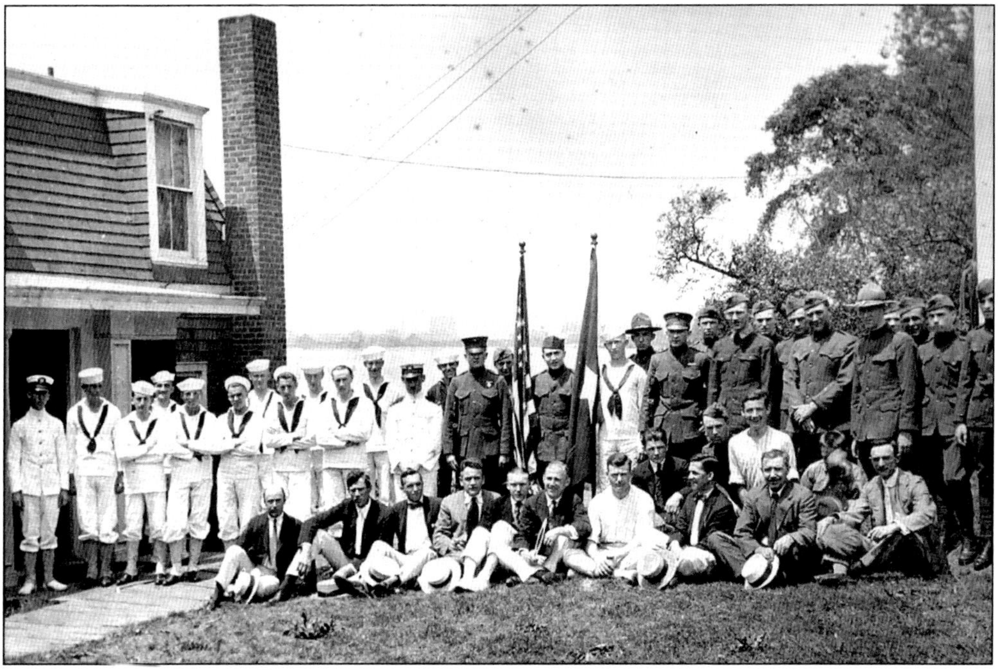

THE RIDGEFIELD PARK BOAT CLUB. Members of the boat club pose proudly in uniform. The club was formed for the promotion of social interaction and aquatic sports. Club history shows that 75 percent of the members served in World War I.

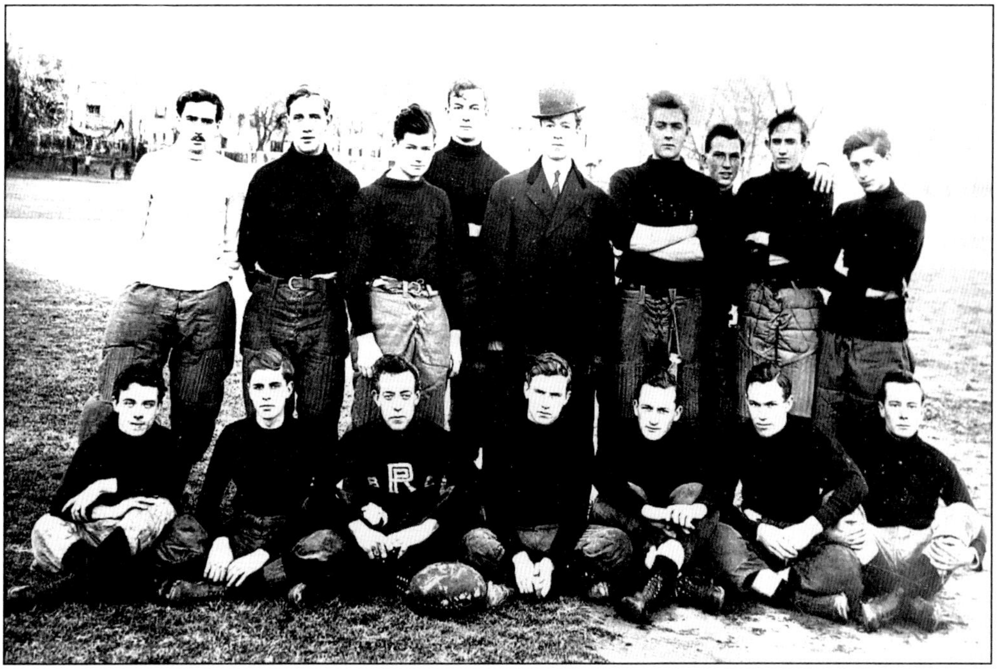

THE 1910 FOOTBALL TEAM. The Ridgefield Park Boat Club sponsored this team. Seen here are, from left to right, (front row) Frank Cunningham, Jim Green, Bob Hamilton, Frank Morrison, Basil Grey, Ed Weiss, and Paul Diaz; (back row) Russell Diaz, Gordon Lees, Frank Murphy, Fred Friend, Fred Biller, Elwood Gregory, Leo Welsh, Tim Sullivan, and Sam Squires.

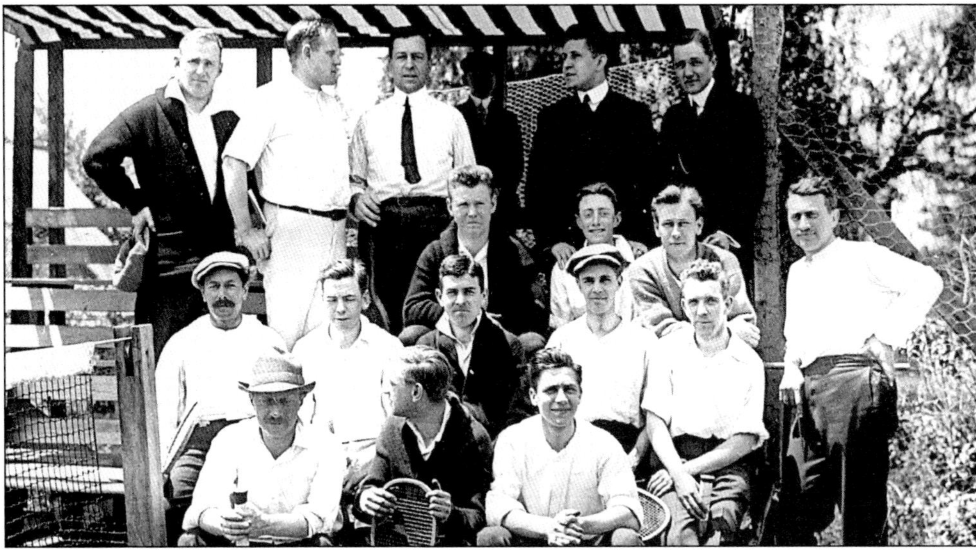

THE PINE TENNIS CLUB. For many years, the village had an active tennis club. Tennis courts were located on the west side of Bergen Avenue between Poplar and Preston Streets. This photograph from 1960 shows some of the members. They are, from left to right, (first row) ? Ehrman, Bill Ehrman, and Willoughby Chapman; (second row) ? Harvey, Bill Ingles, Mark Biddion, Joe Green, and Joe Miles; (third row) Alex Milhoman, Alin Ehrman, Ernest Harvey, and H.L. Berman; (fourth row) Claude Meredith, Charles LeRue, George Leigh, Paul Overhage, and unidentified.

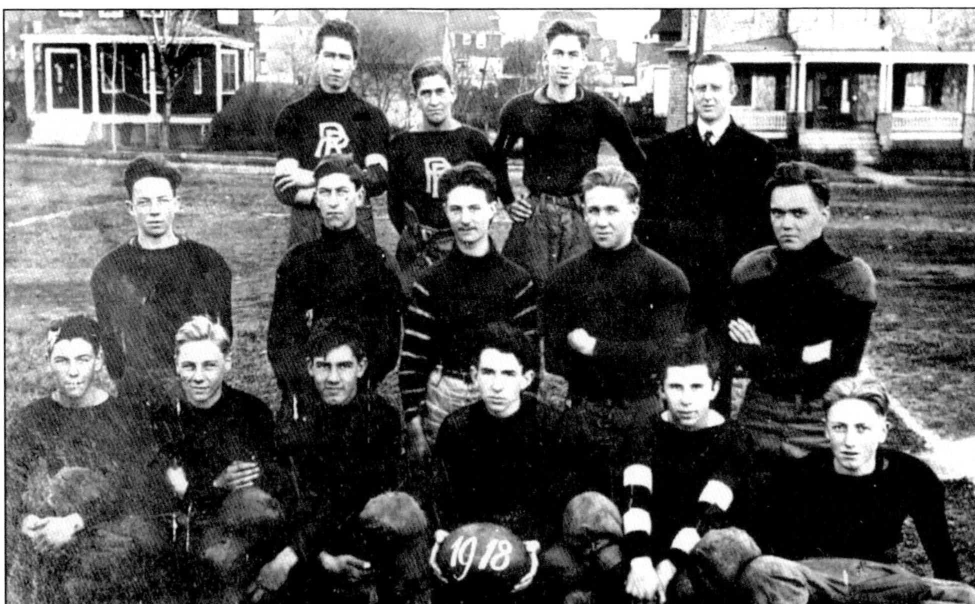

A LONGSTANDING TRADITION. The high school football team gathered at the Union Church athletic field in 1918 for a team photograph. This was the last year the team played without a full-time coach. Pictured here are Sherman Mallory, Herb Gneiding, Oscar Higbee, ? Randall, Ralph Lowe, ? Bell, Ray Lindley, Everett Beech, Ralph Terhune, Jim Maher, Al Nelson, Hadley Case, ? Hershfield (captain), Tom Bell, and Ernie Beamish.

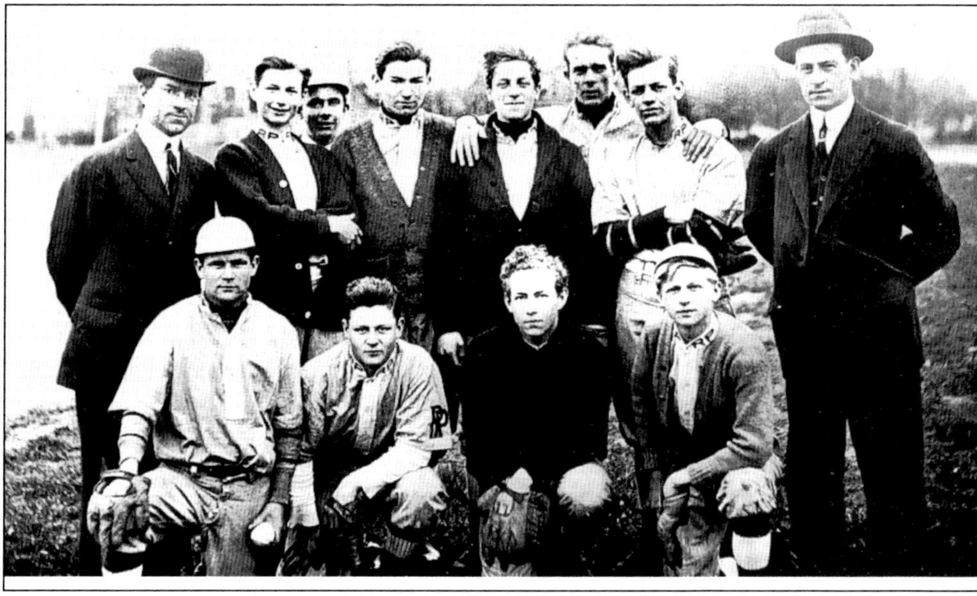

TEAMMATES GATHER FOR A PHOTOGRAPH. The Ridgefield Park High School baseball team poses on the field in 1913. Seen here are, from left to right, (front row) Frank Smith (captain), Ed Hallberg, Bill Drodge, and Bernie Diekman; (back row) Bill Heyliger, Arthur Frank, unidentified, Art Campbell, Willoughby Chapman, Lionel Wright, Francis Lloyd, and John McCarthy (principal).

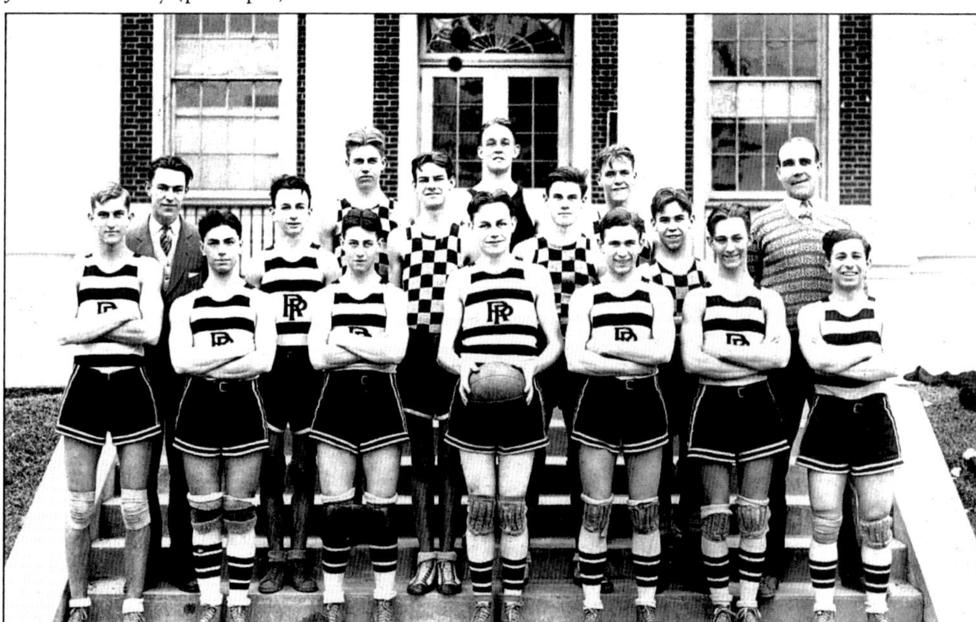

THE BASKETBALL TEAM. The 1926–1927 Ridgefield Park High School basketball team poses in their eye-catching uniforms. Only last names were available. Seen here are, from left to right, (front row) Theil, Friedman, Galliant, Oellermann, Bell, Preston, and Isolde; (middle row) Sumner (manager), unidentified , Redding, Darte, unidentified, and Coach Biggs; (back row) Robinson, Moffett, and unidentified.

Seven

Homes and Street Scenes

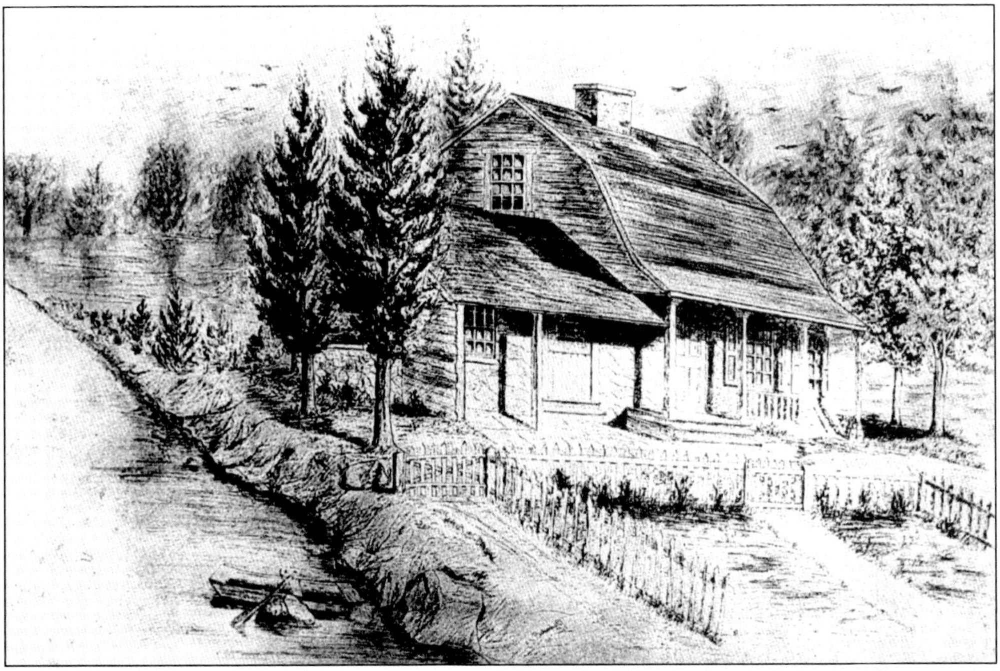

The Brinkerhoff Home. Located on the east bank of the Hackensack River, this was the home of one of Ridgefield Park's first families. It was later known as the Old Christie Homestead. Hendrick Brinkerhoff is considered to be the first white settler in the village, arriving in 1685.

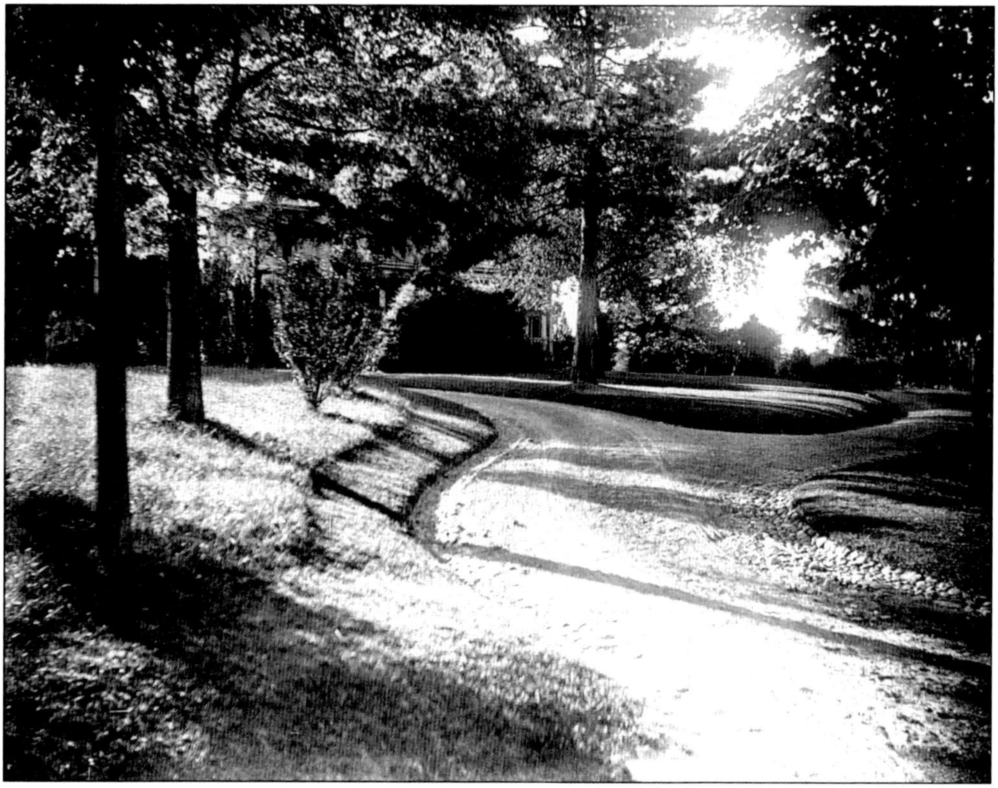

THE SMITH RESIDENCE. This is the driveway to the home of Mortimer Smith. The home was located on Teaneck Road and what is now Barnes Drive. Smith was one of the first commuters when the railroad was built through Ridgefield Park. He had a coachman drive him to the station.

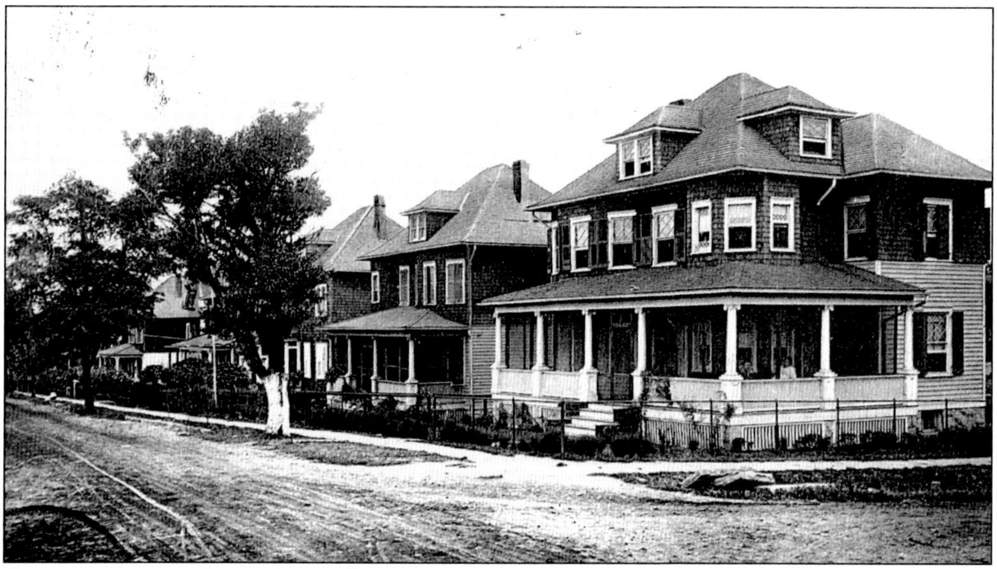

TEANECK ROAD. This is the southwest corner of Teaneck Road at Mount Vernon Street.

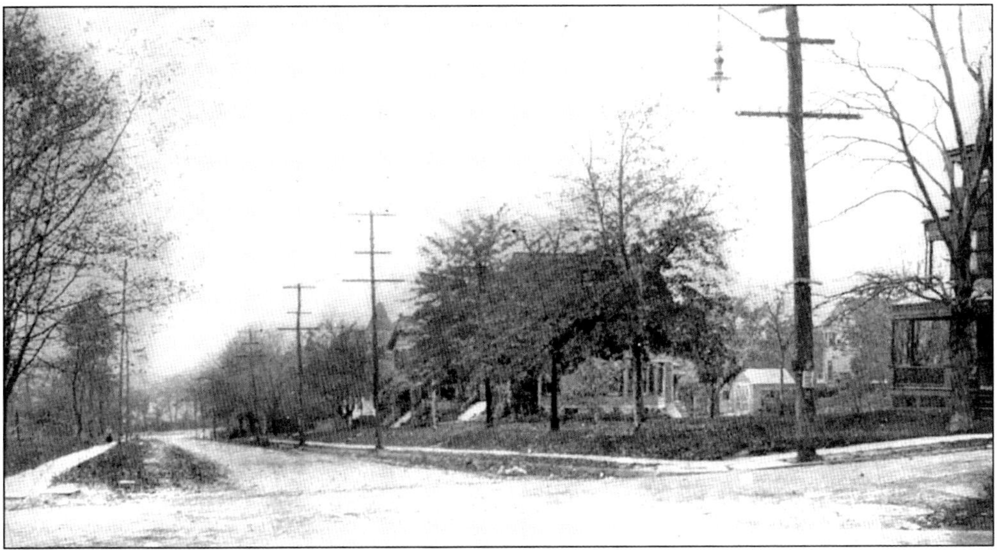

MOUNT VERNON STREET. From the vicinity of Hudson Avenue, this 1905 view looks west on Mount Vernon Street.

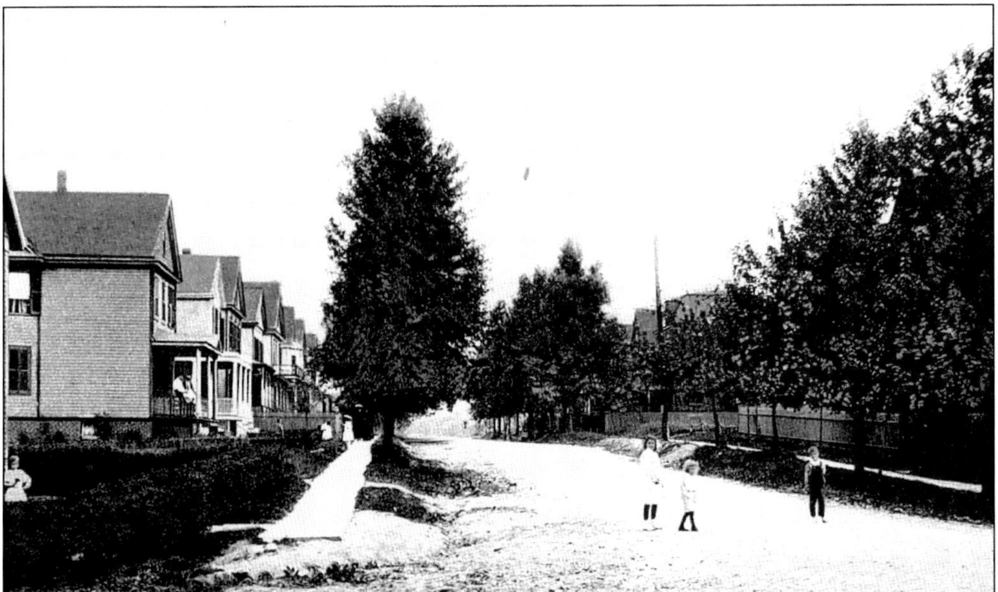

NORTH SIXTH STREET. A row of homes in the West View section of Ridgefield Park line the dirt road. Many of these homes were torn down when Route 80 was constructed in the late 1950s.

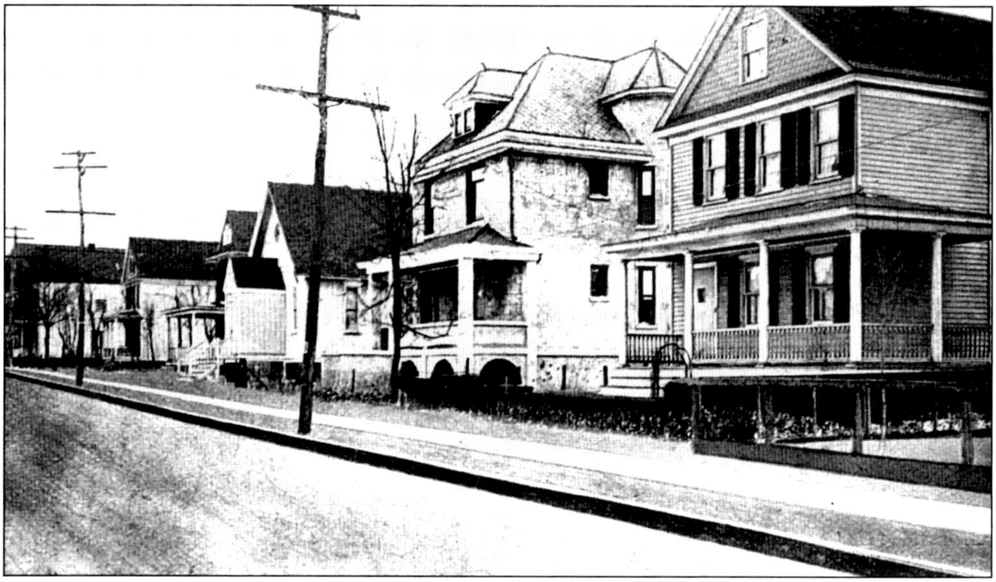

WINANT AVENUE. Now known as Route 46, Winant Avenue is a main highway leading through the village to New York City.

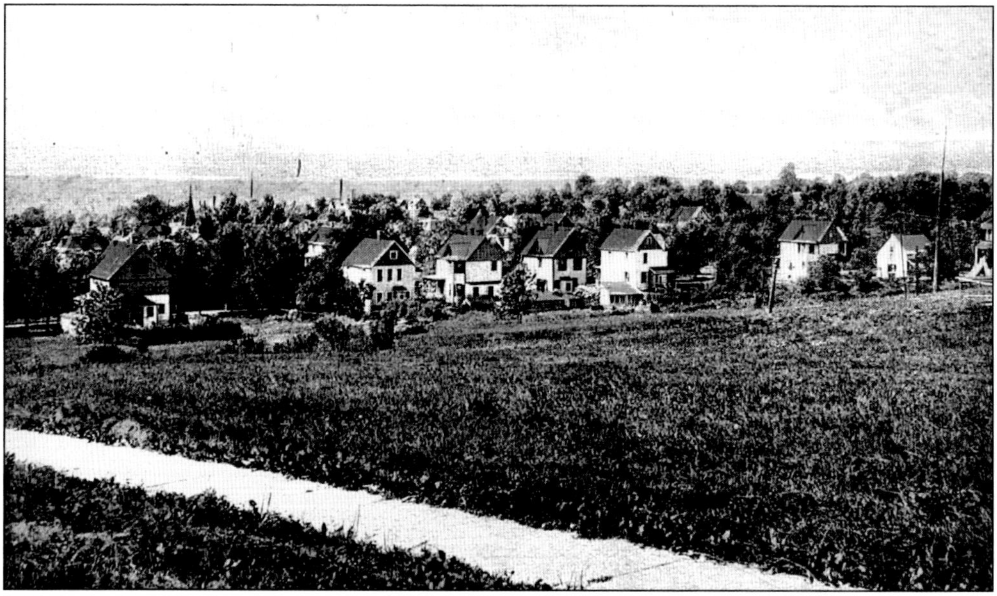

WEST VIEW. This development, still known today as the West View section, was started in 1894 by a land corporation that advertised lots for as little as $300. The development was located on the northwest side of Ridgefield Park, and its streets were numbered from First Street through Eighth Street.

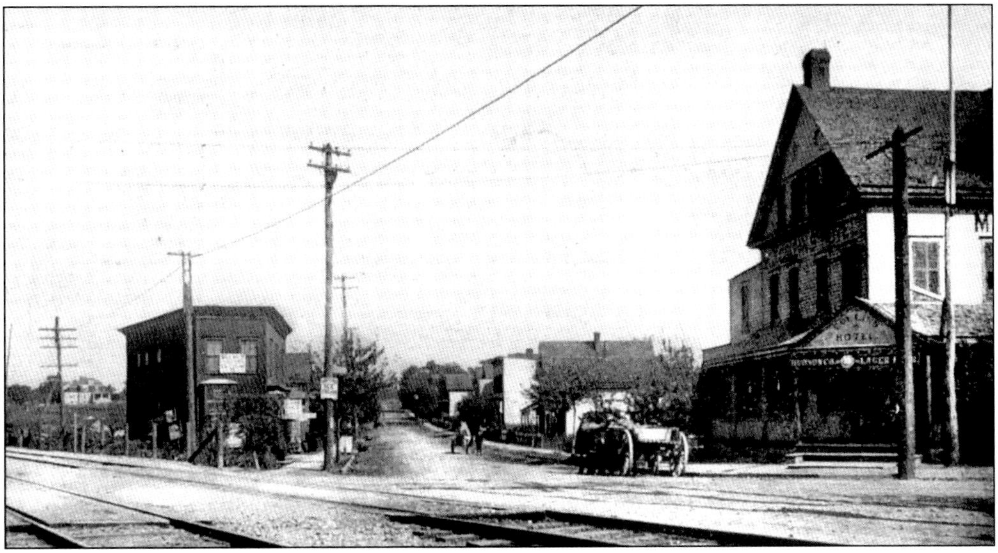

RIDGEFIELD AVENUE. This view looks north on Ridgefield Avenue from the Bergen Turnpike area. The large building on the right is the Collins Hotel.

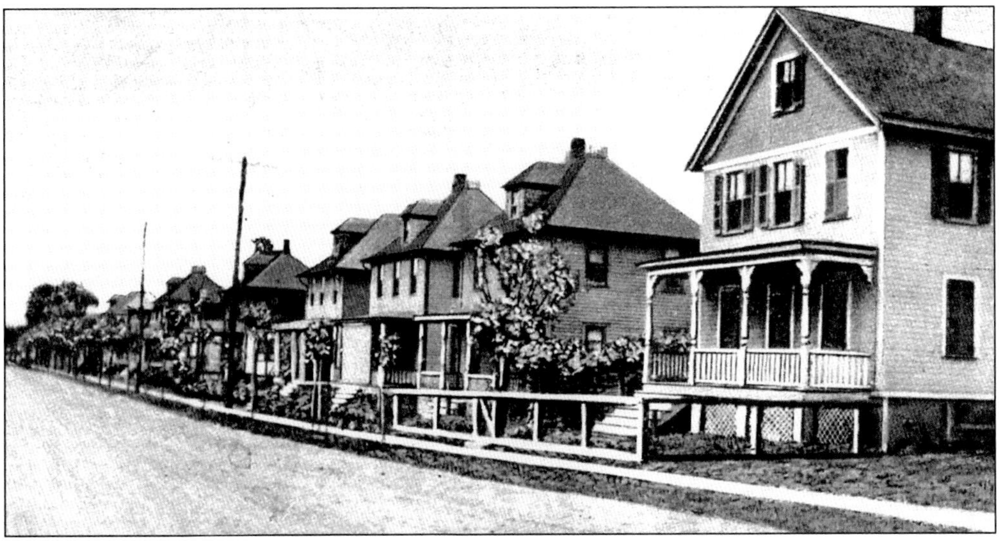

A VIEW OF ELM STREET FROM TEANECK ROAD. Located in the southern part of the village, Elm Street is now bordered by Chestnut Street Park.

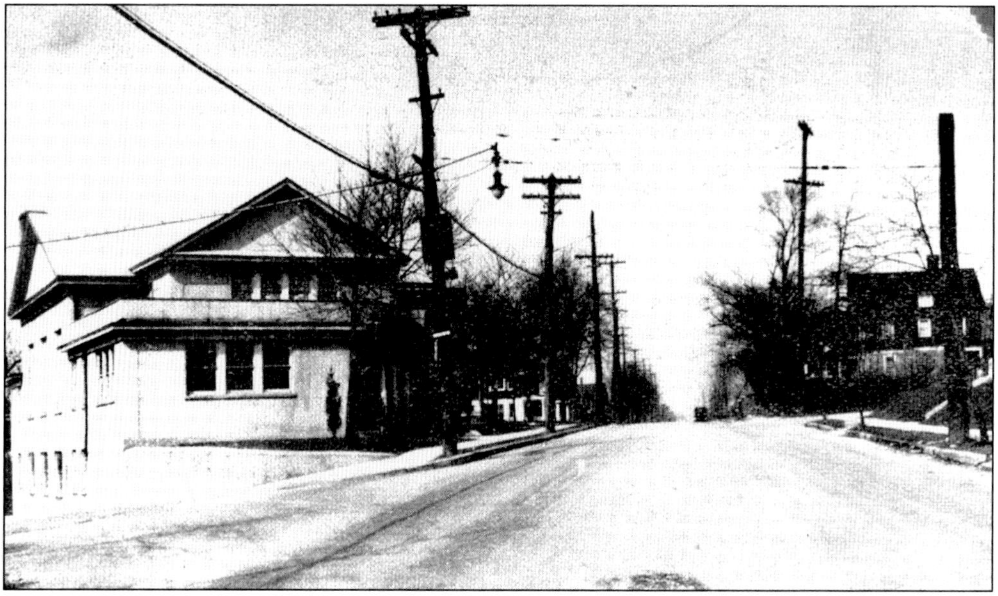

MAIN STREET. The large building on the left was once the Christian Science church, located on the corner of Hackensack Avenue and Main Street.

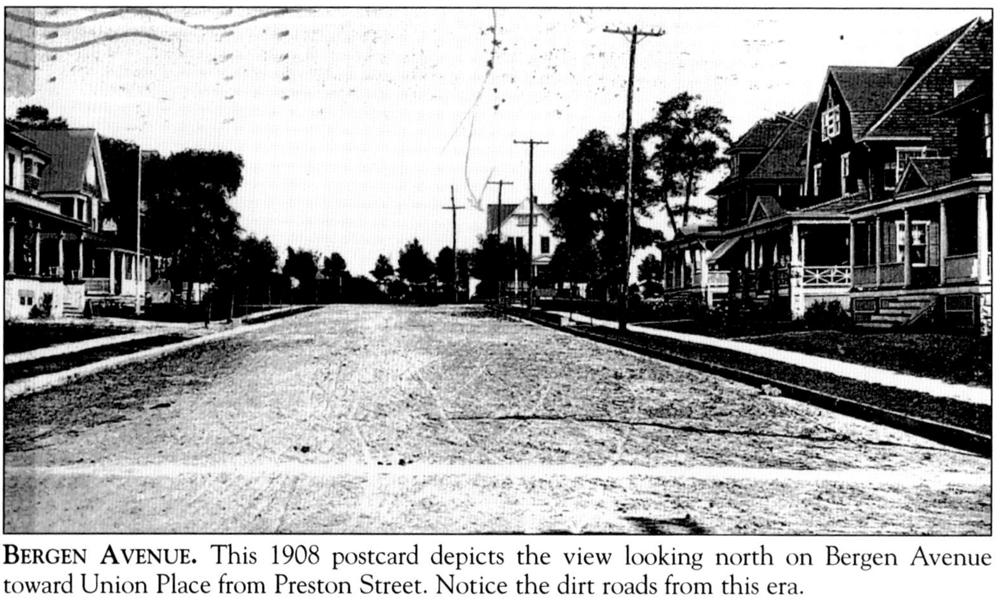

BERGEN AVENUE. This 1908 postcard depicts the view looking north on Bergen Avenue toward Union Place from Preston Street. Notice the dirt roads from this era.

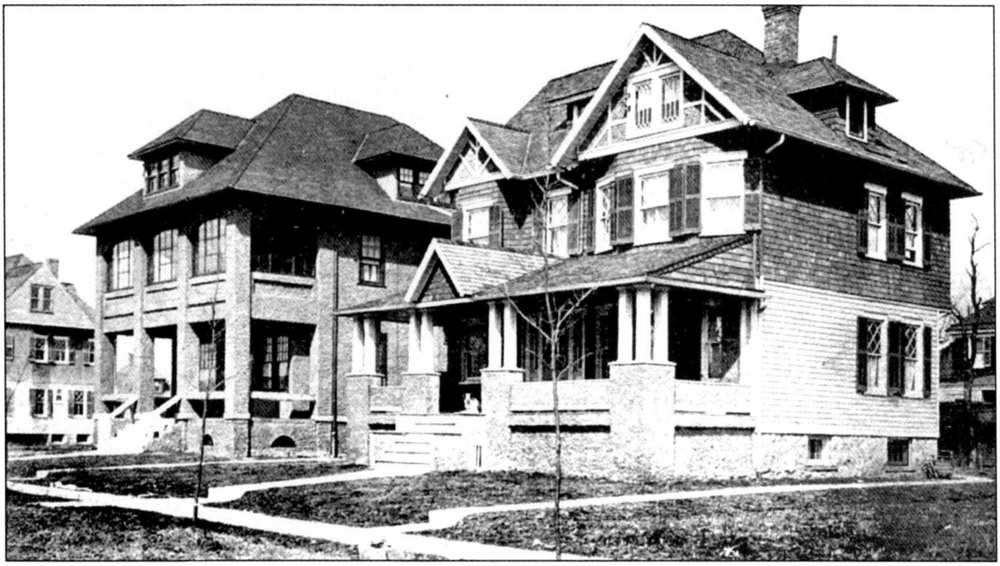

GRAND AVENUE. Large homes line this lovely avenue, which runs between Teaneck Road and Main Street.

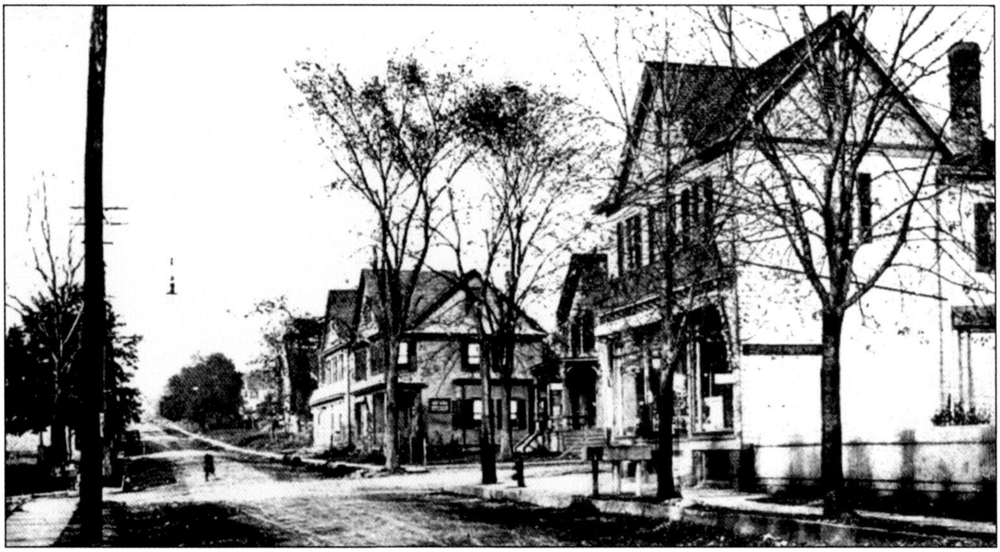

HACKENSACK AVENUE. These homes are on the border of the West View section of town.

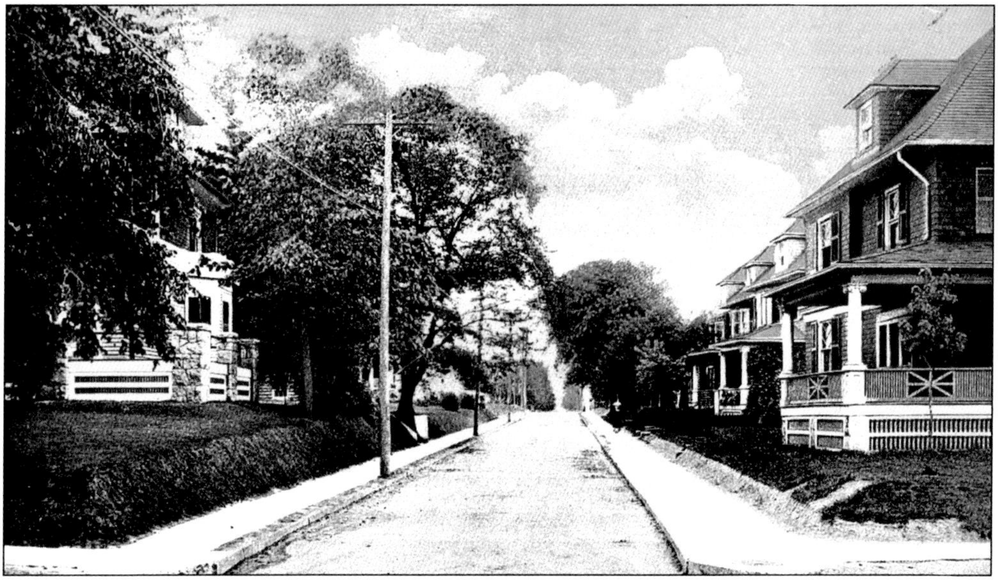

PRESTON STREET. This view of Preston Street looks east from Hackensack Road, which is now known as Main Street. Preston Street was named after the son of R.A. Robertson, an early developer in the village.

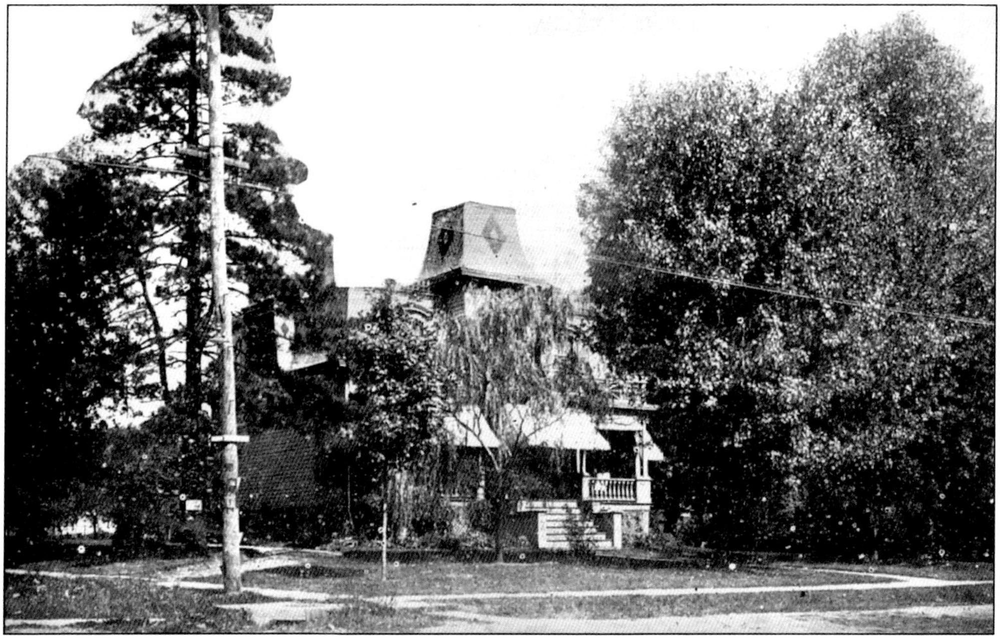

PARK STREET AND BERGEN AVENUE. This property, built in 1870, was owned by William Donald. It eventually became the Temple Emanuel and is now a Korean church.

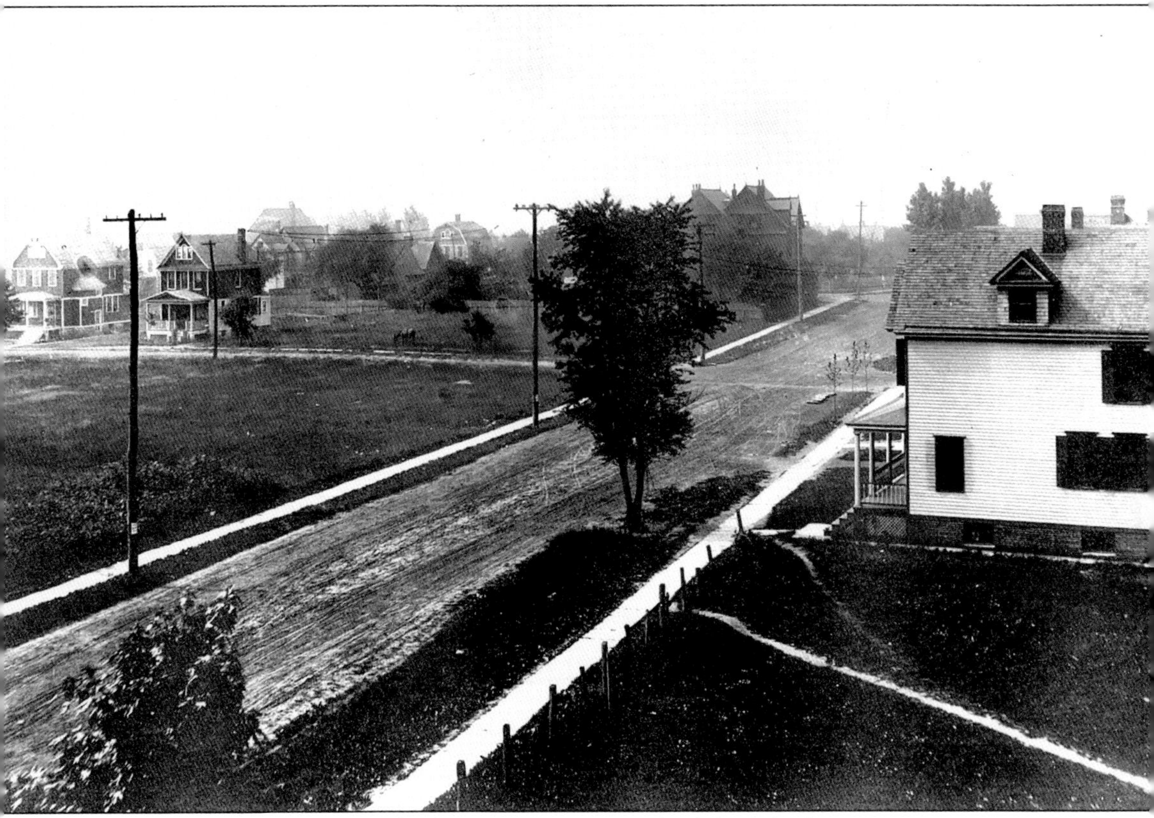

A Street Scene. Horses graze lazily in a grassy area to the left of the large tree.

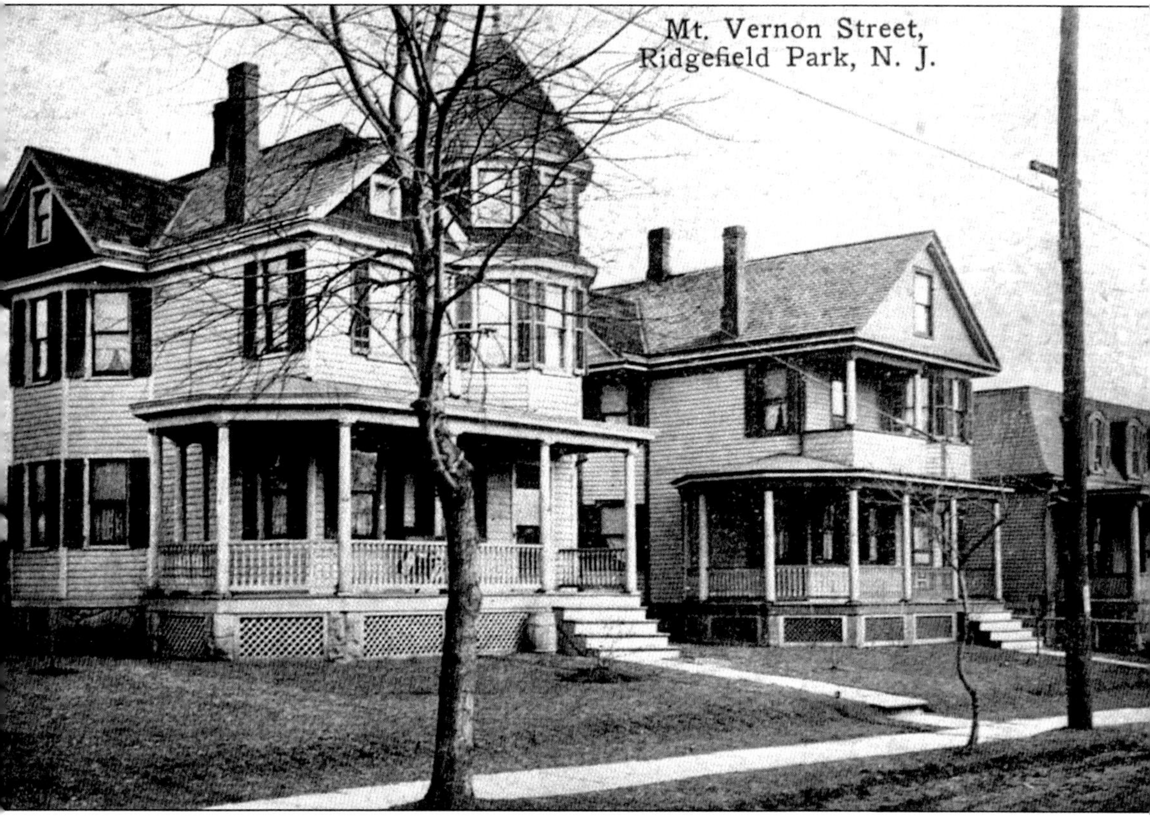

MOUNT VERNON STREET. Located between Euclid Avenue and Hudson Street, this Victorian-style home was completed in 1904. The home still looks exactly as it did when this picture was taken 1906. The home is the residence of Donna Rose-McEntee, the author. It is being lovingly restored by her and her husband, Phil.

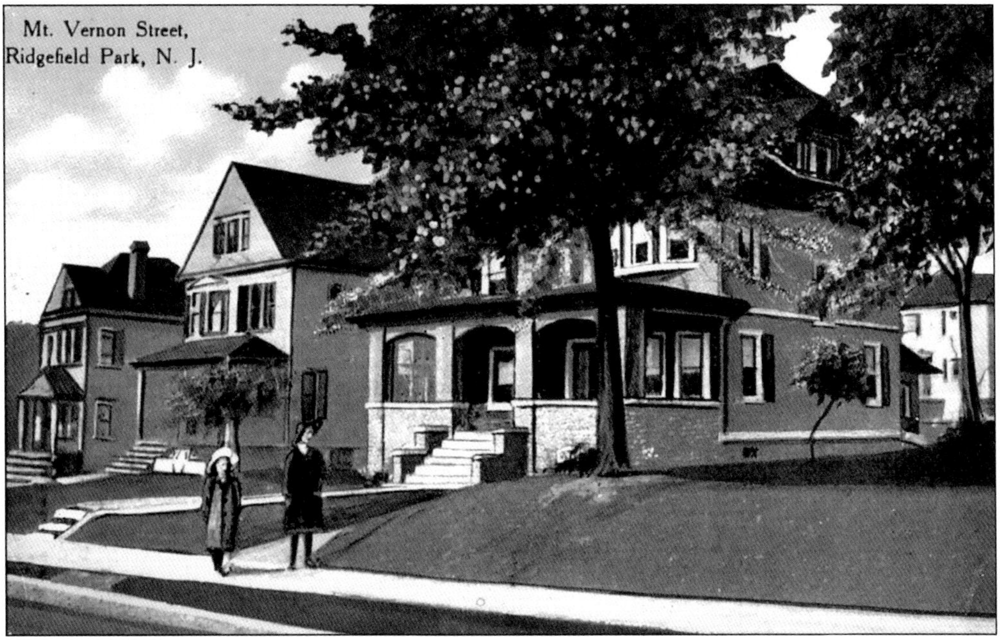

OUT FOR A STROLL. Two young ladies enjoy an afternoon stroll along Mount Vernon Street.

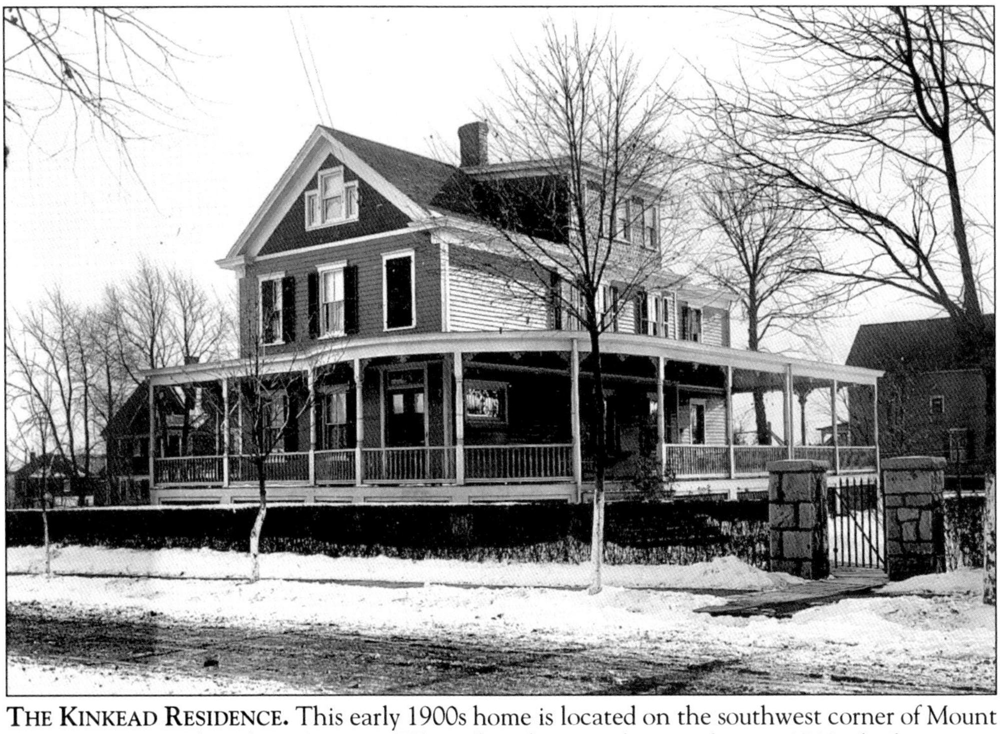

THE KINKEAD RESIDENCE. This early 1900s home is located on the southwest corner of Mount Vernon Street and Hudson Avenue. When this photograph was taken in 1910, the house was owned and occupied by Willie Hoppe, a famous billiards player.

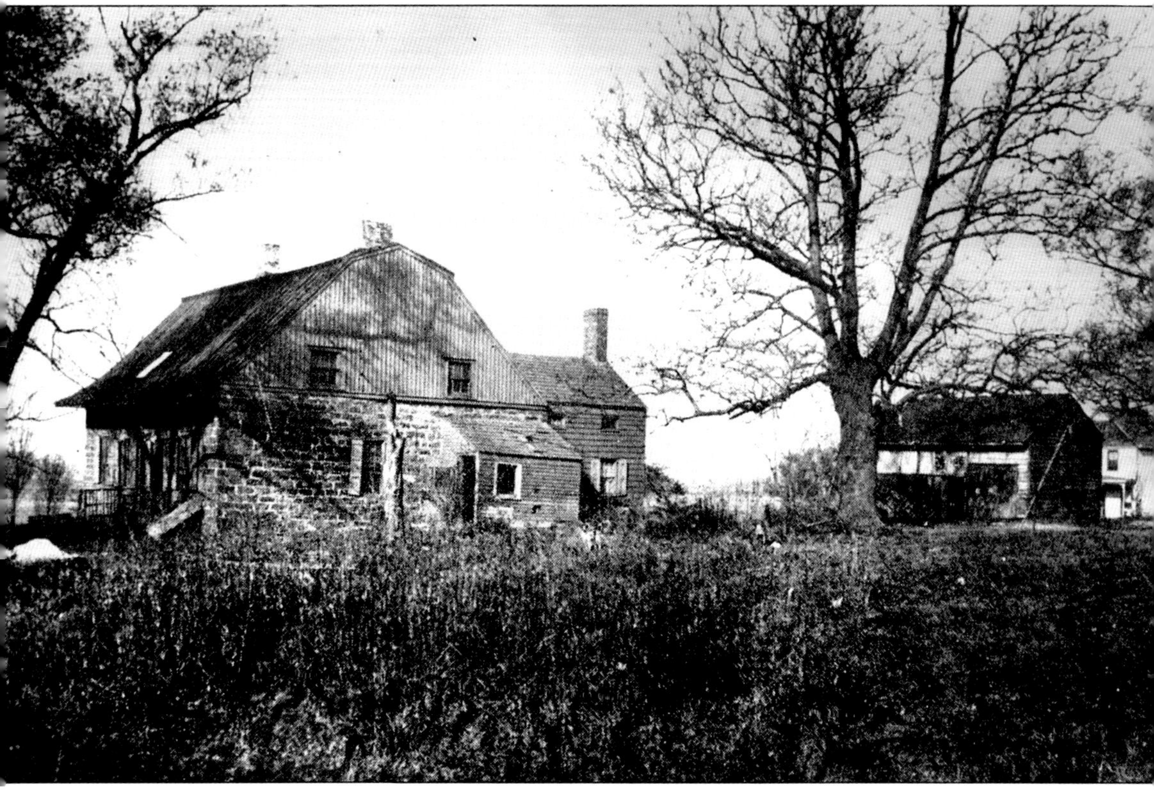

The Old Homestead of Revolutionary Fame. Known today as the Paulison-Christie House, this home overlooks the Hackensack River. Originally built by Hendrick Brinkerhoff and later occupied by Paul Paulison, this property was purchased by David Christie in 1844.

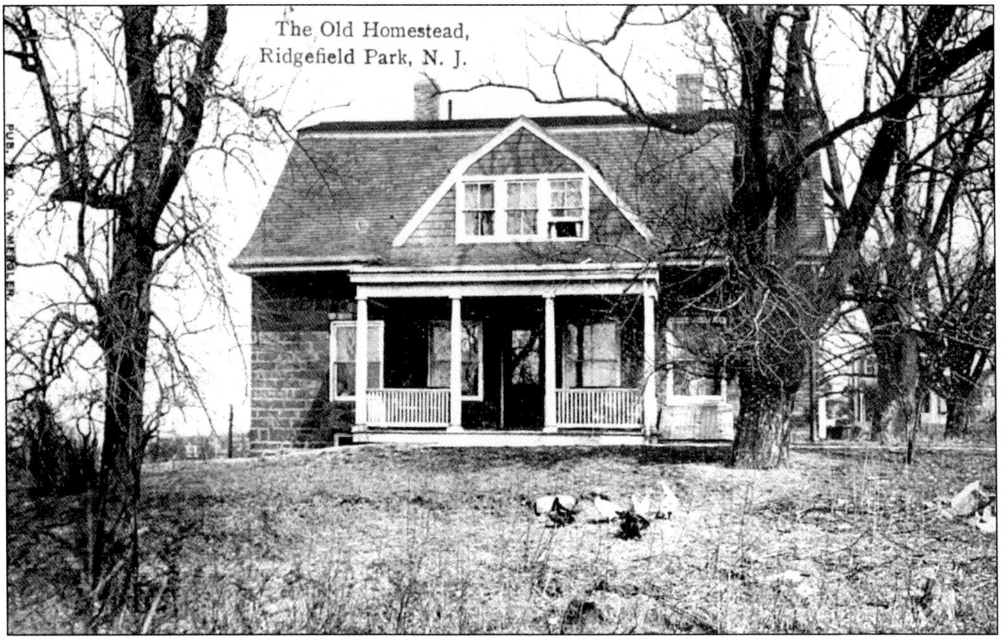

ANOTHER VIEW. The Paulison-Christie House is the oldest building in Ridgefield Park.

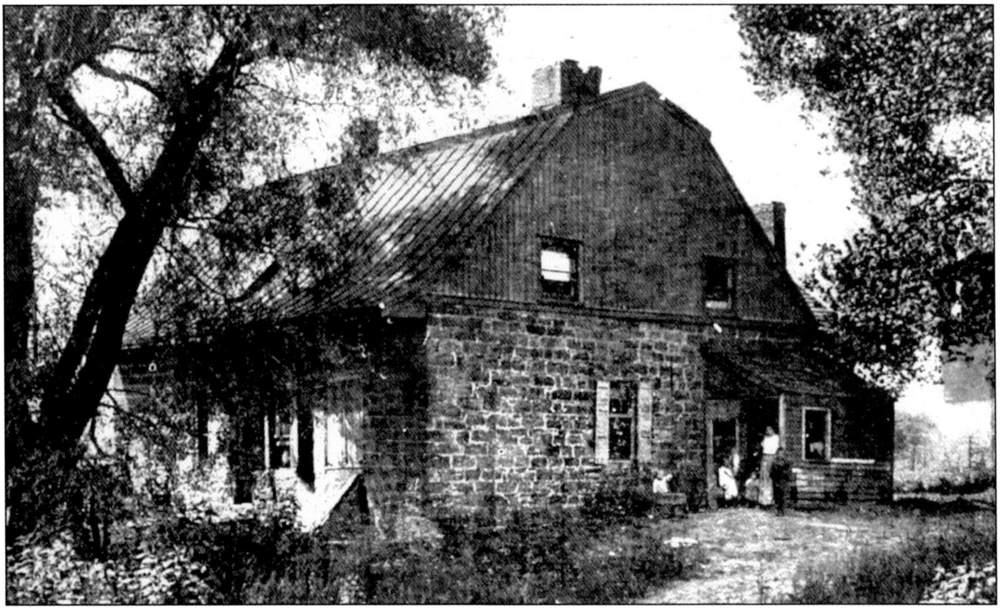

THE OLD HOMESTEAD. The Paulison-Christie House is on the National Register of Historic Places. It is located near the Hackensack River on Homestead Place. Built by Hendrick Brinkerhoff, it is estimated to be 295 years old. David Christie purchased this property for his son in 1844.

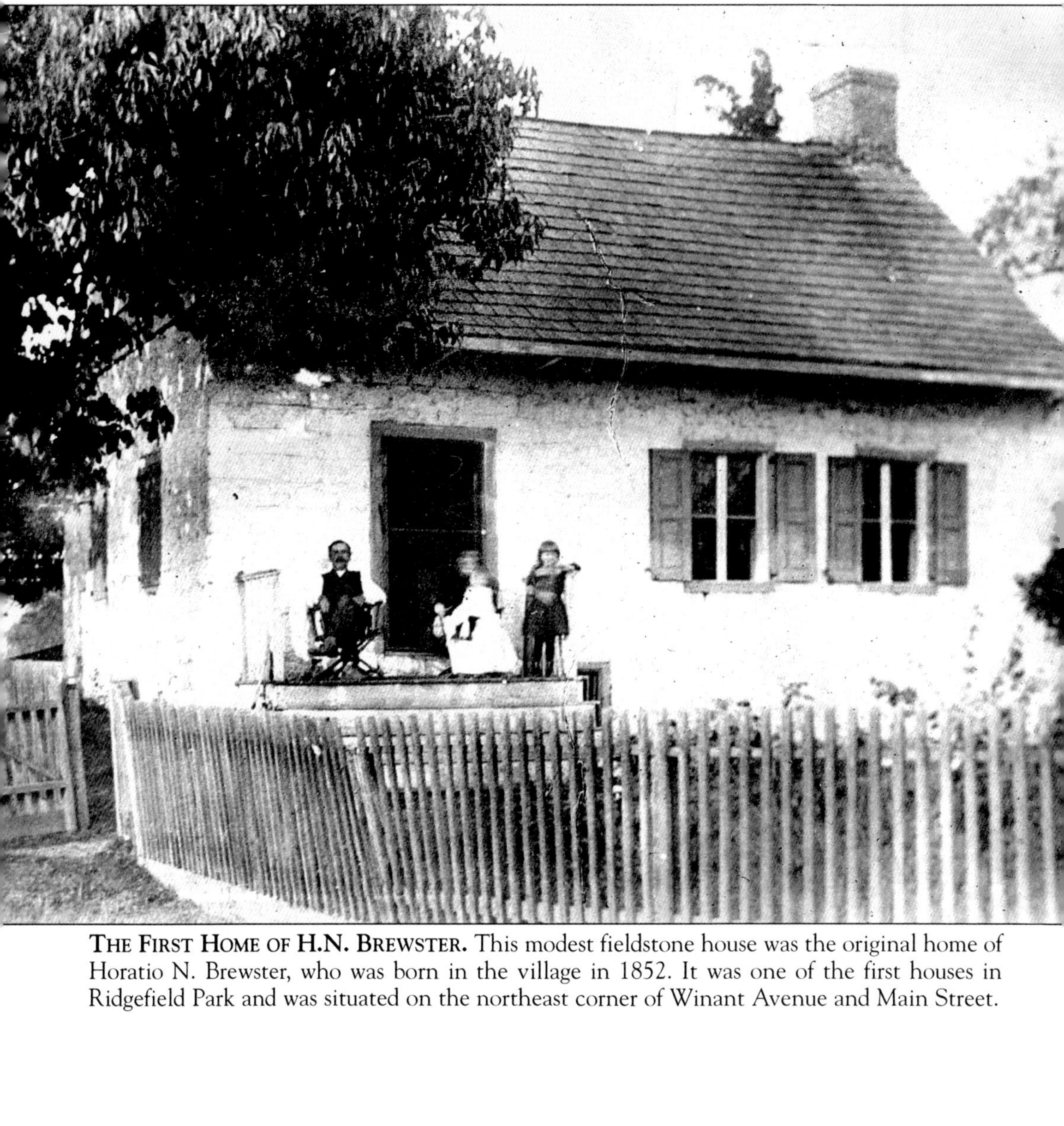

THE FIRST HOME OF H.N. BREWSTER. This modest fieldstone house was the original home of Horatio N. Brewster, who was born in the village in 1852. It was one of the first houses in Ridgefield Park and was situated on the northeast corner of Winant Avenue and Main Street.

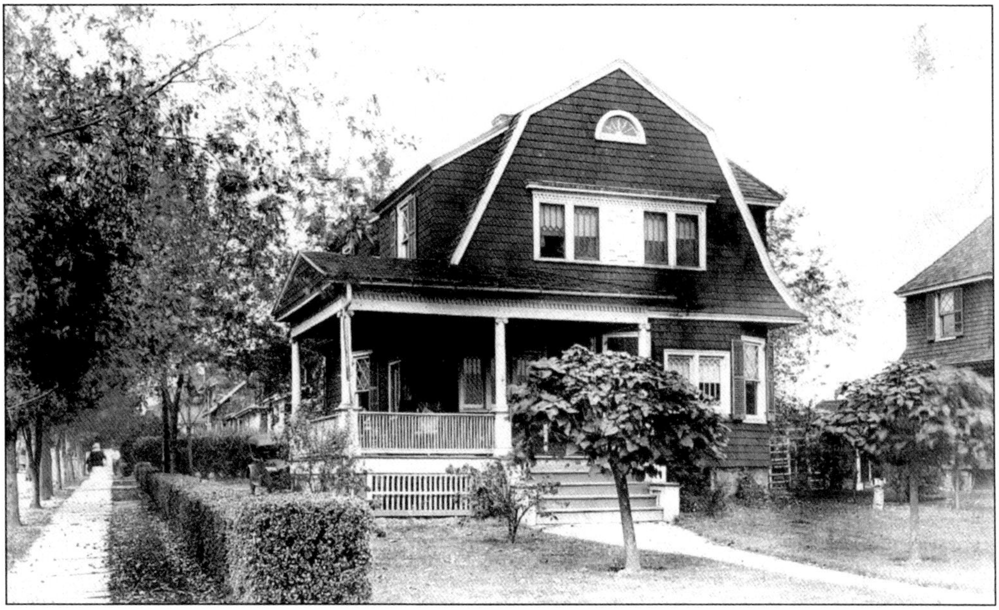

A Dutch Colonial. This lovely home is located at the corner of Teaneck Road and Union Place. Large porches were very common in the early 1900s.

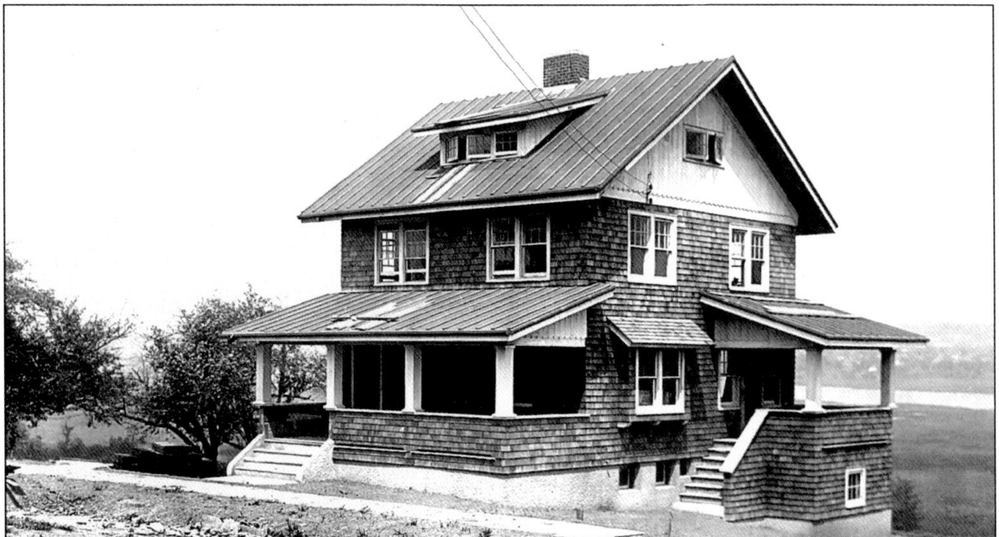

The Poole Residence. Ralph Poole made his home along Overpeck Avenue. Notice the expanse of land in the background. The Overpeck Creek is visible.

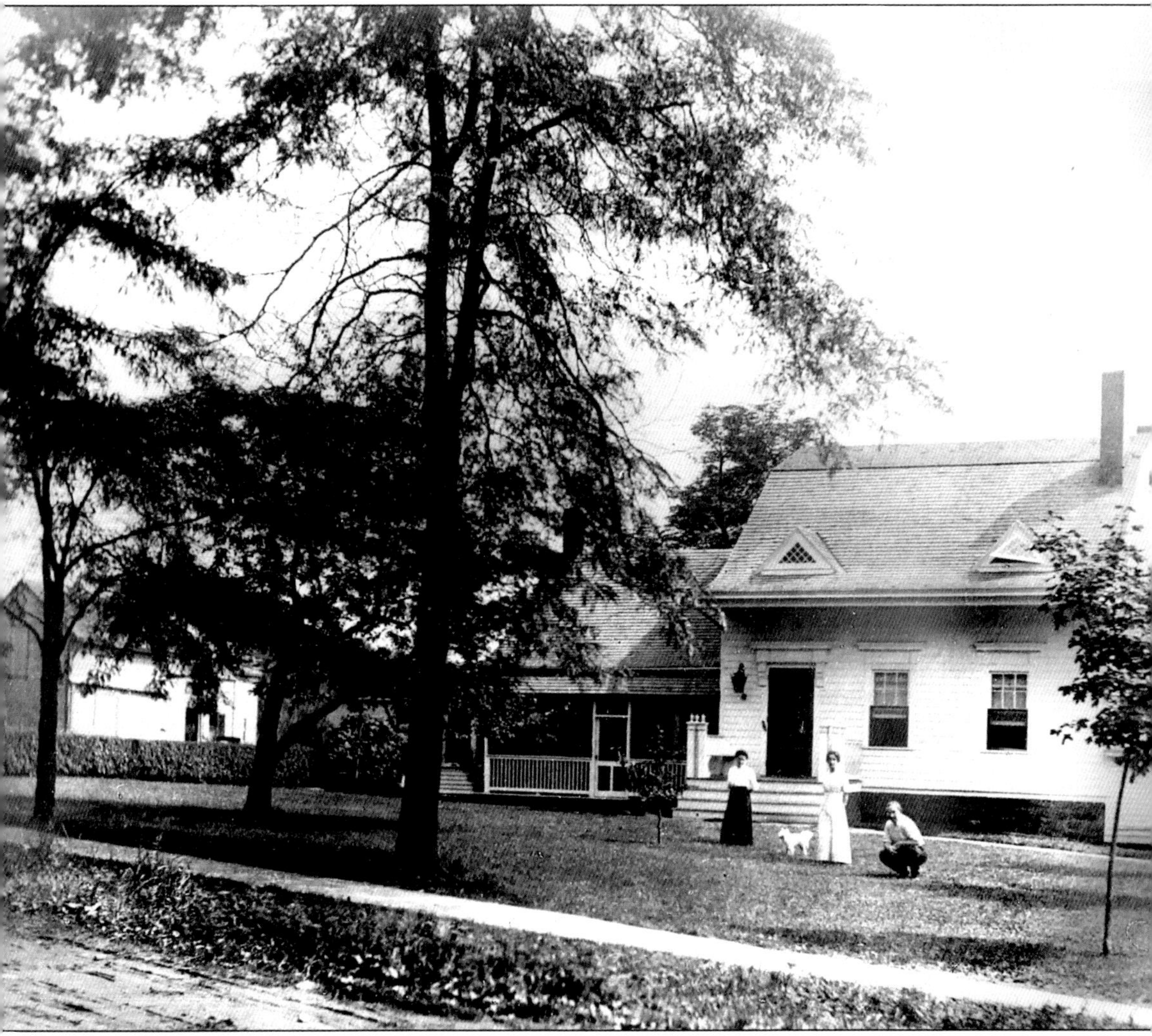

THE HOMESTEAD OF PAUL R. PAULISON. Located on the southeast corner of Main and Park Streets, this house later became the residence of Archibald D. Lees.

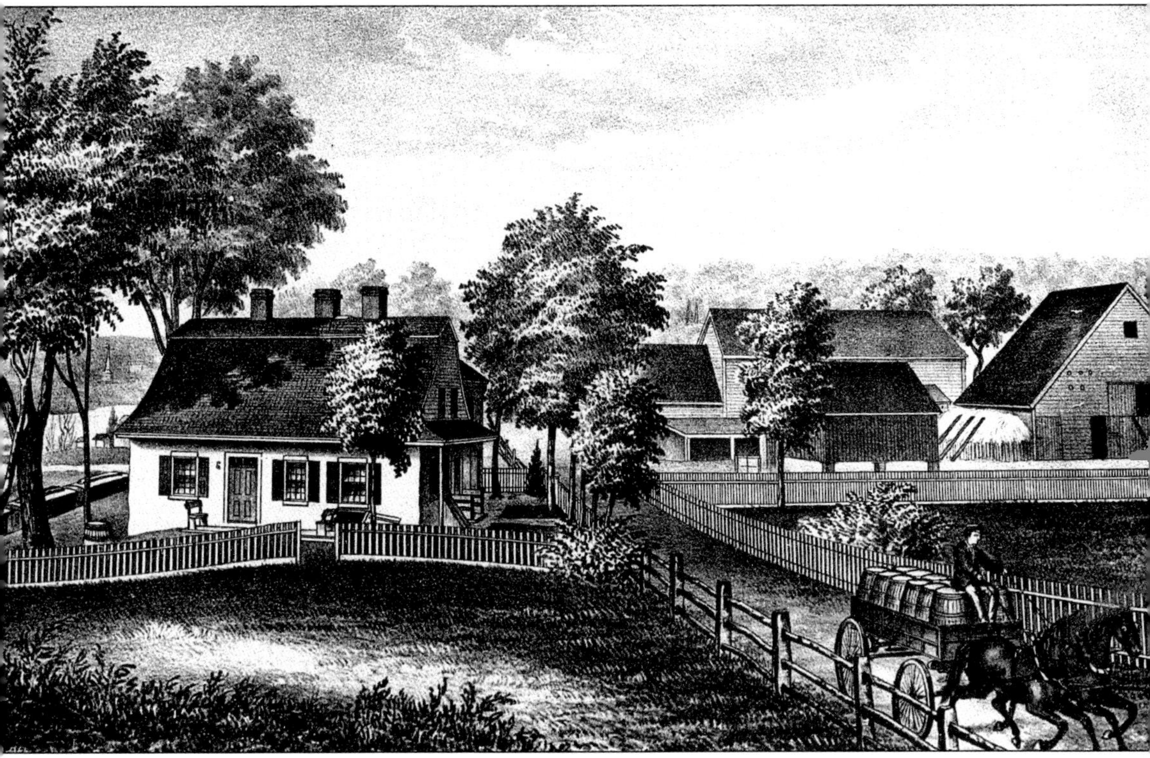

THE PAULISON RESIDENCE. This is the home of John R. Paulison as seen in 1876. It was located in the area of Hackensack and Railroad Avenues.

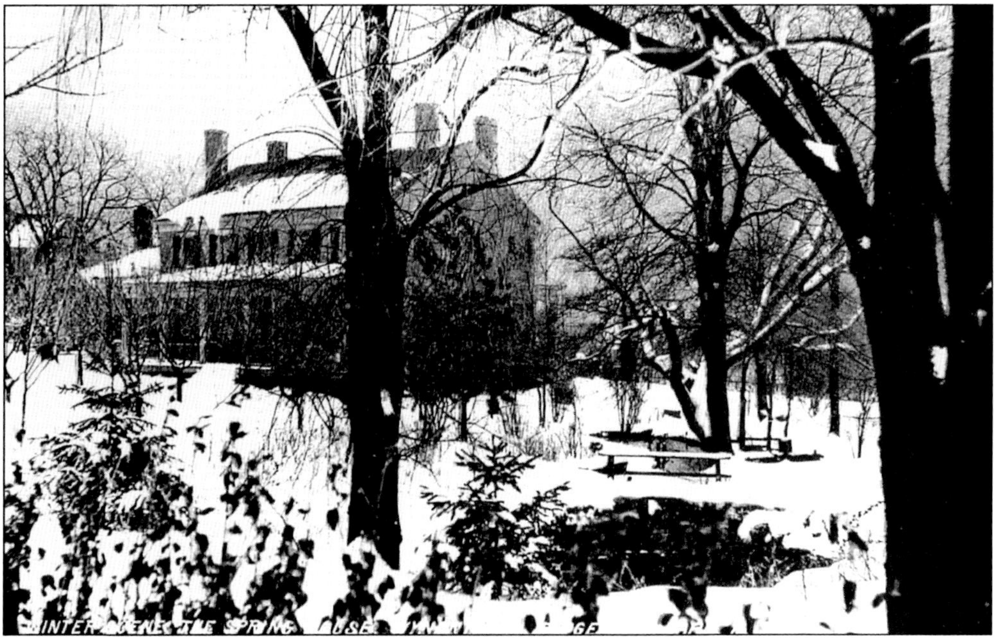

A Spring Scene. A spring snow covers the parklike property surrounding the Spring house. The house was located on Winant Avenue, which is now Route 46.

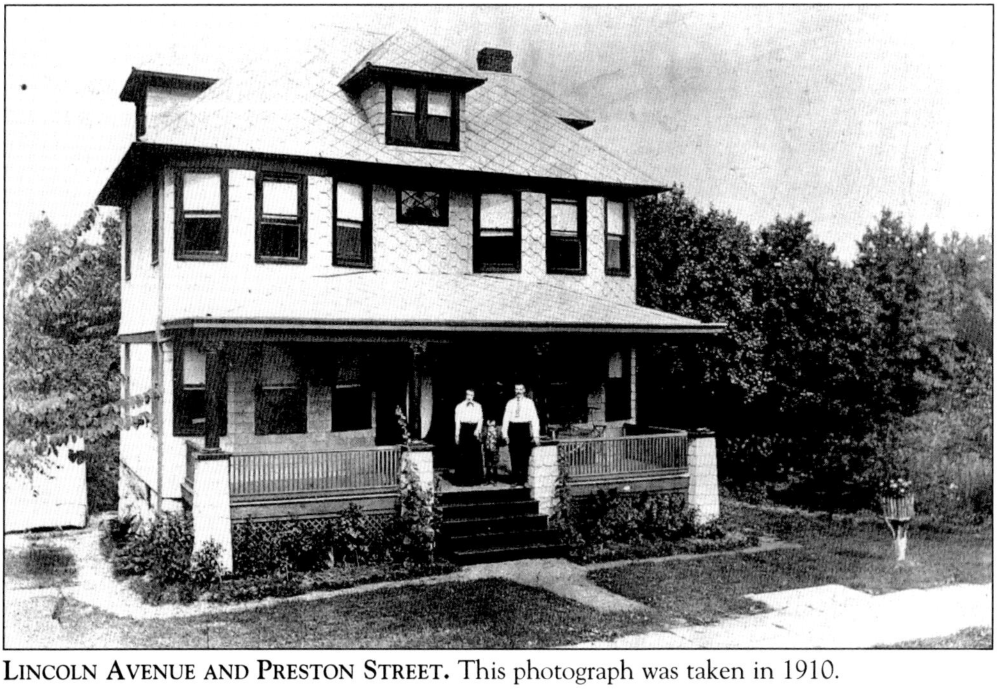

Lincoln Avenue and Preston Street. This photograph was taken in 1910.

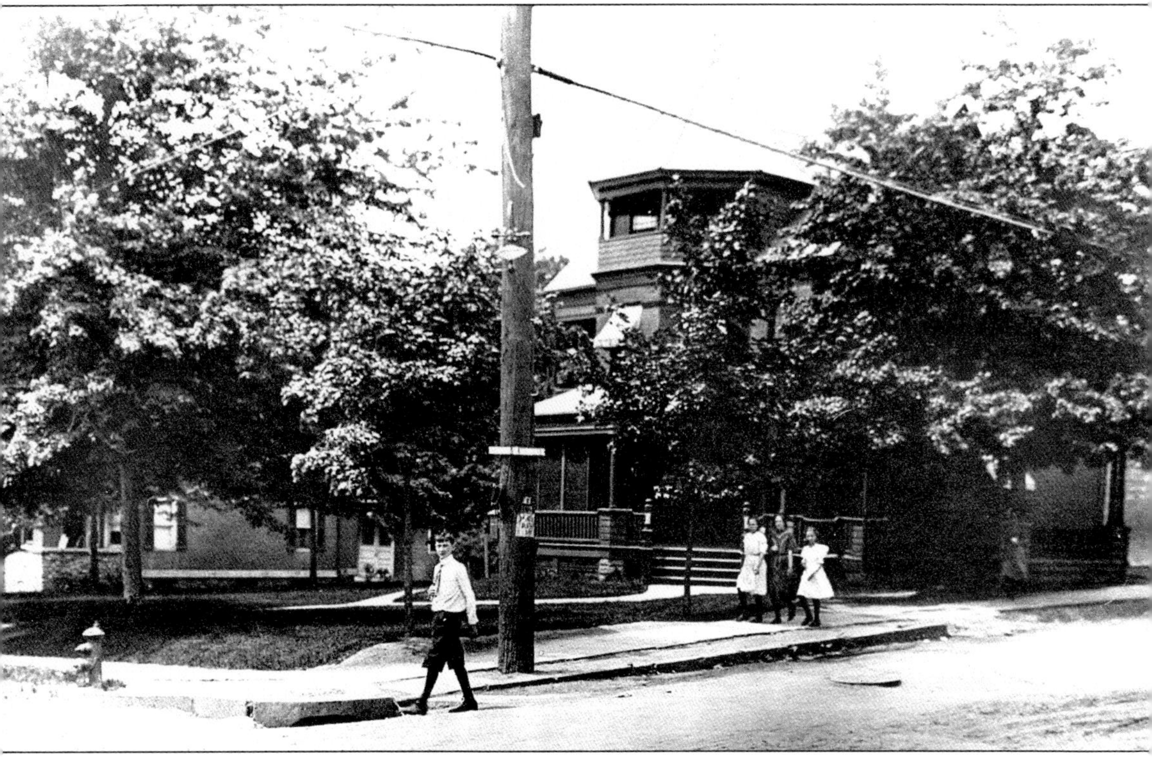

THE A.V. SMITH RESIDENCE. This home was located on the corner of Hackensack Avenue (now known as Main Street) and Mount Vernon Street. Smith was an American Civil War veteran and a prominent businessman. He manufactured window glass with his partner Ezra Cornell, founder of Cornell University.

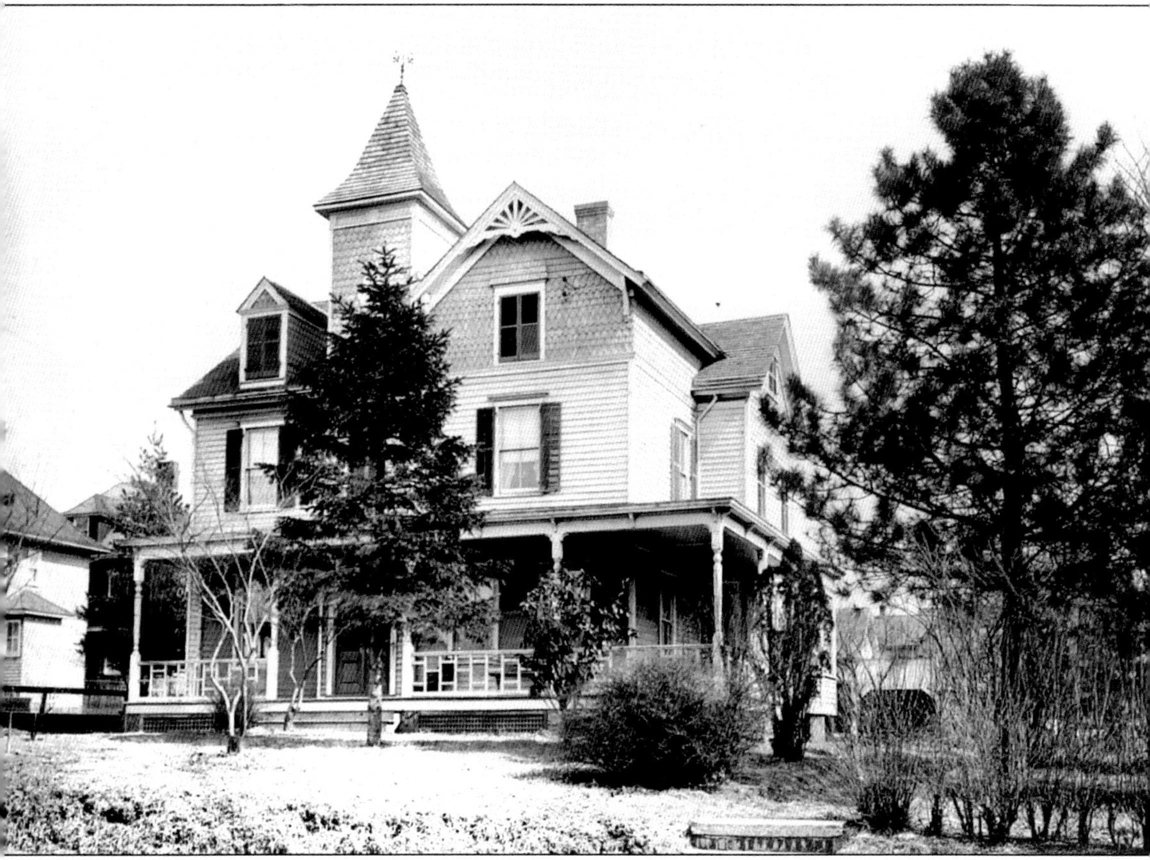

THE O'BRIEN RESIDENCE. This grand home was located on Main Street between Poplar and Preston Streets. Today, it is the site of the Marlboro House Apartments.

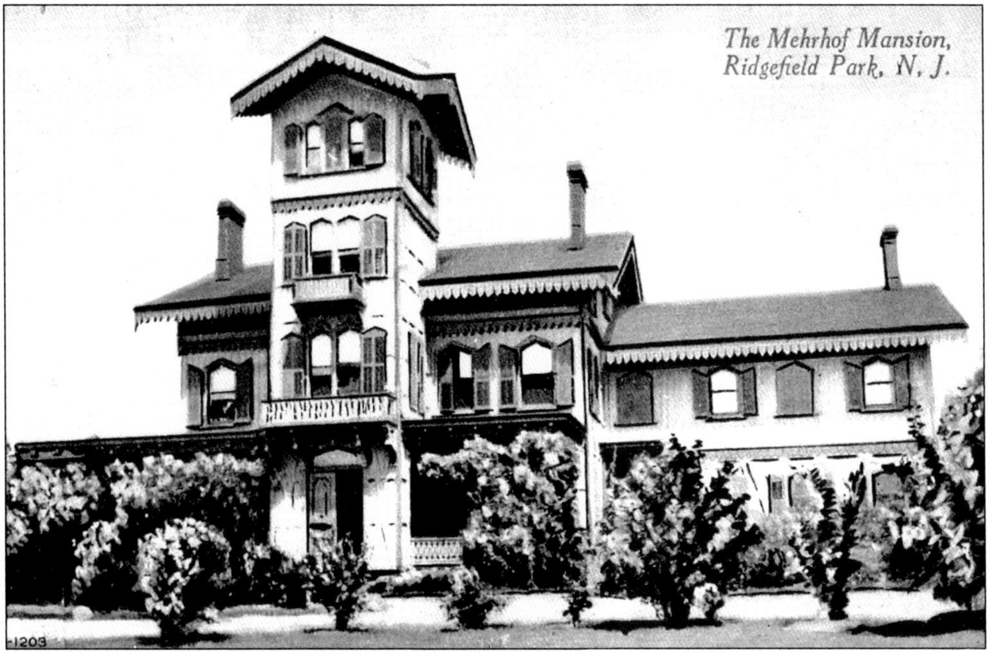

THE MERHOF MANSION. This home was once the gathering place for many villagers. The Merhofs held many social events in its grand rooms and on its parklike grounds. The mansion was originally built by R.A. Robertson, a local developer, in the 1870s.

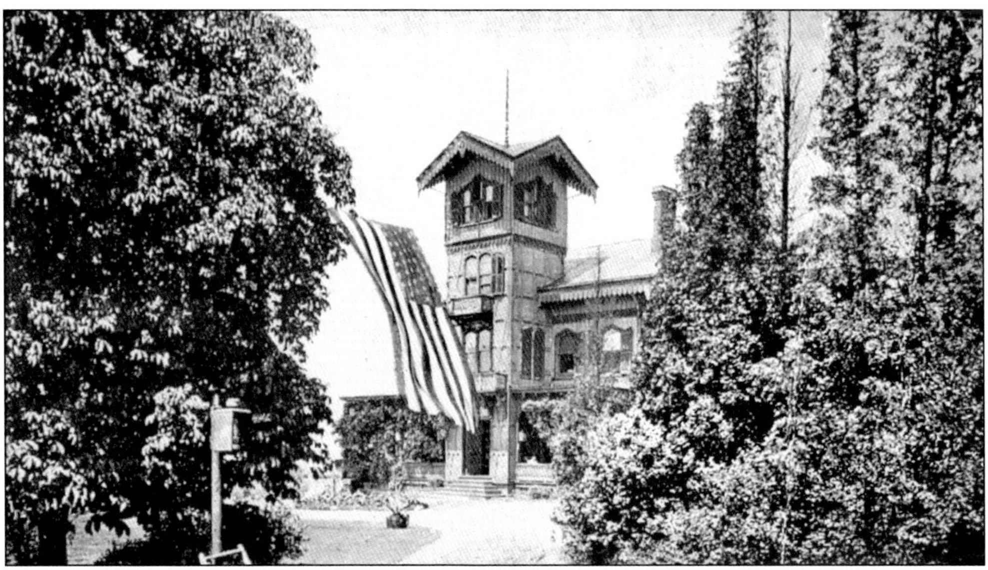

THE MERHOF MANSION. The Merhof Mansion was one of the most grand homes in Ridgefield Park. Located along the Hackensack River, the property surrounding it was known as Merhof Park. At one time, the building was a boardinghouse, and some of the first teachers in the village lived here. This property eventually was torn down and is the present site of the Elk's club.

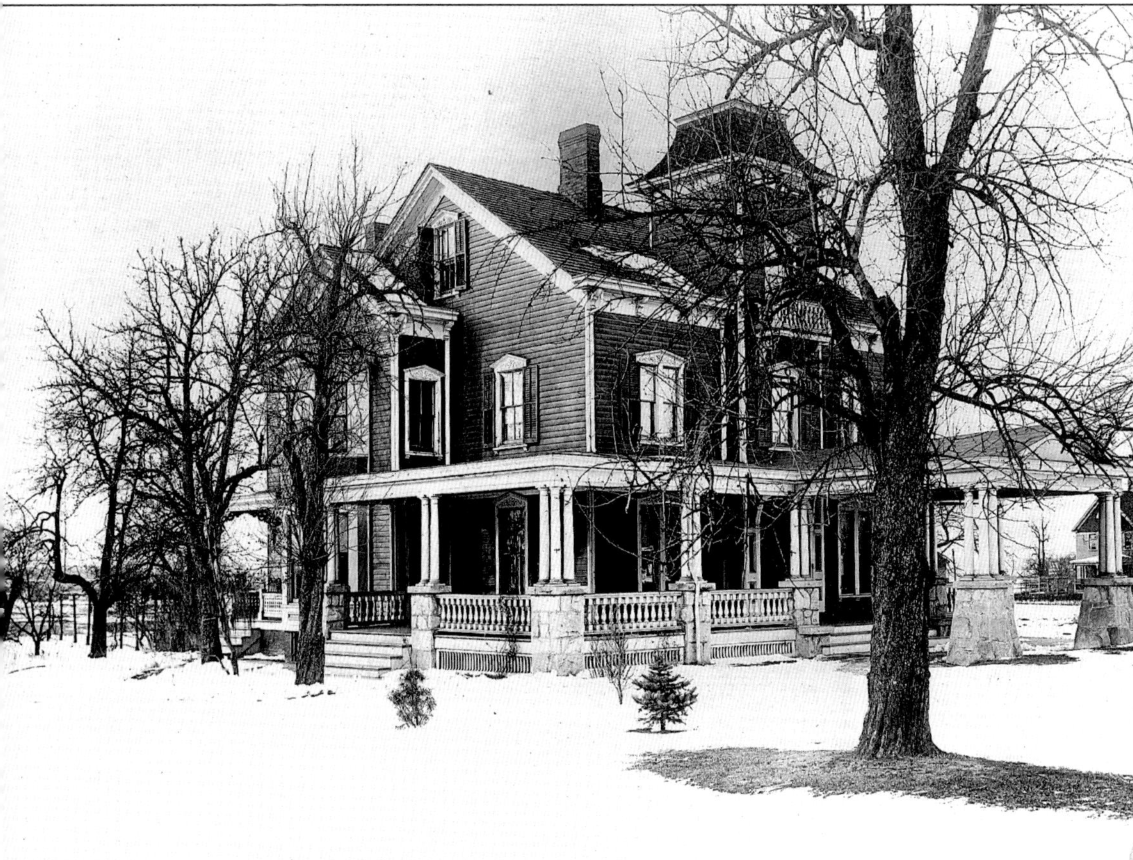

THE THOMAS MORTON BREWSTER RESIDENCE. This house later became the home of Eva Brewster Peard. It was located on Main Street and is now the site of Brewster Park. This property was part of the original Brewster farm, which was divided among the three Brewster sons: Thomas, Charles, and Horatio.

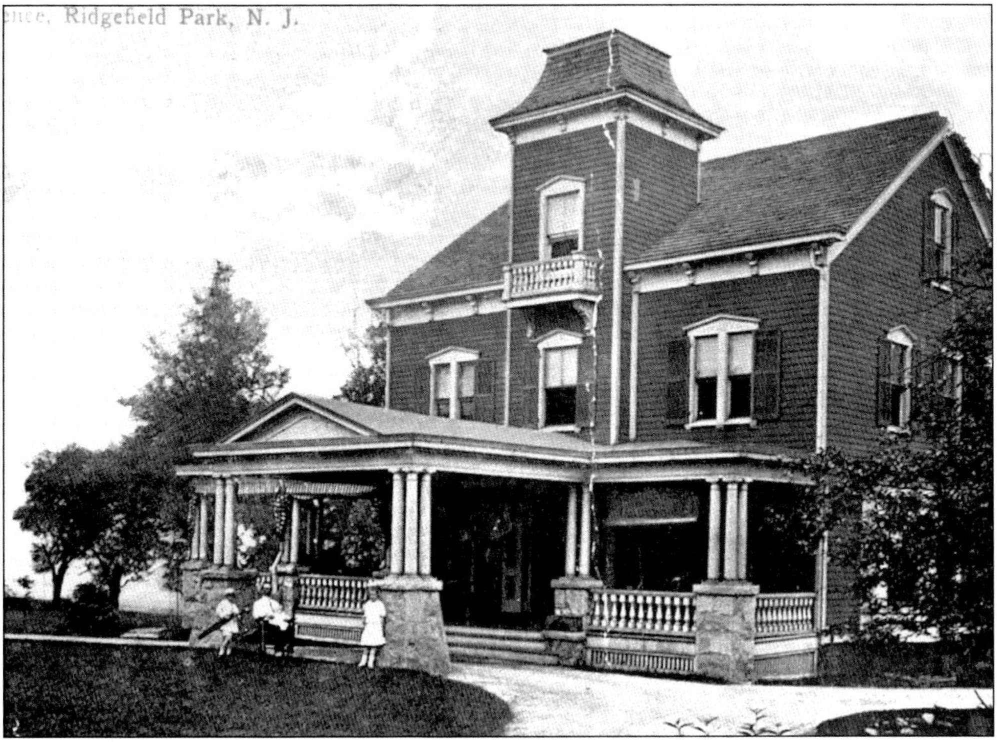

The T.M. Brewster Residence. The Brewster family was one of the village's earliest families. Their grand home was located on Main Street. T.M., or "Tom," as he was known to friends, owned and operated the Brewster and Son Coal and Lumber Company. Brewster was elected to the first board of trustees of the village in 1852. The property is now Brewster Park.

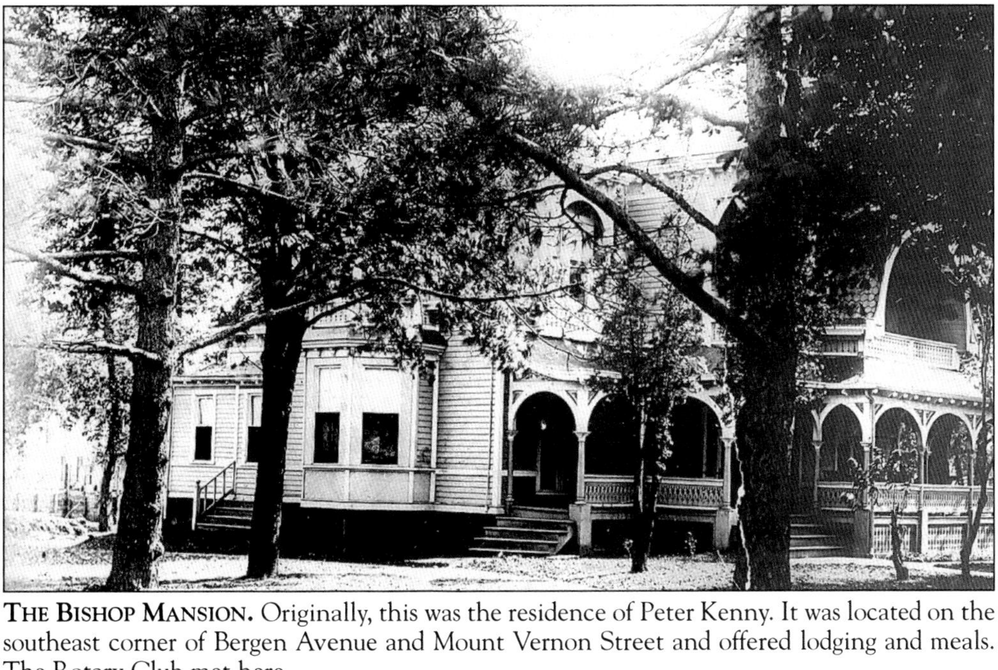

The Bishop Mansion. Originally, this was the residence of Peter Kenny. It was located on the southeast corner of Bergen Avenue and Mount Vernon Street and offered lodging and meals. The Rotary Club met here.

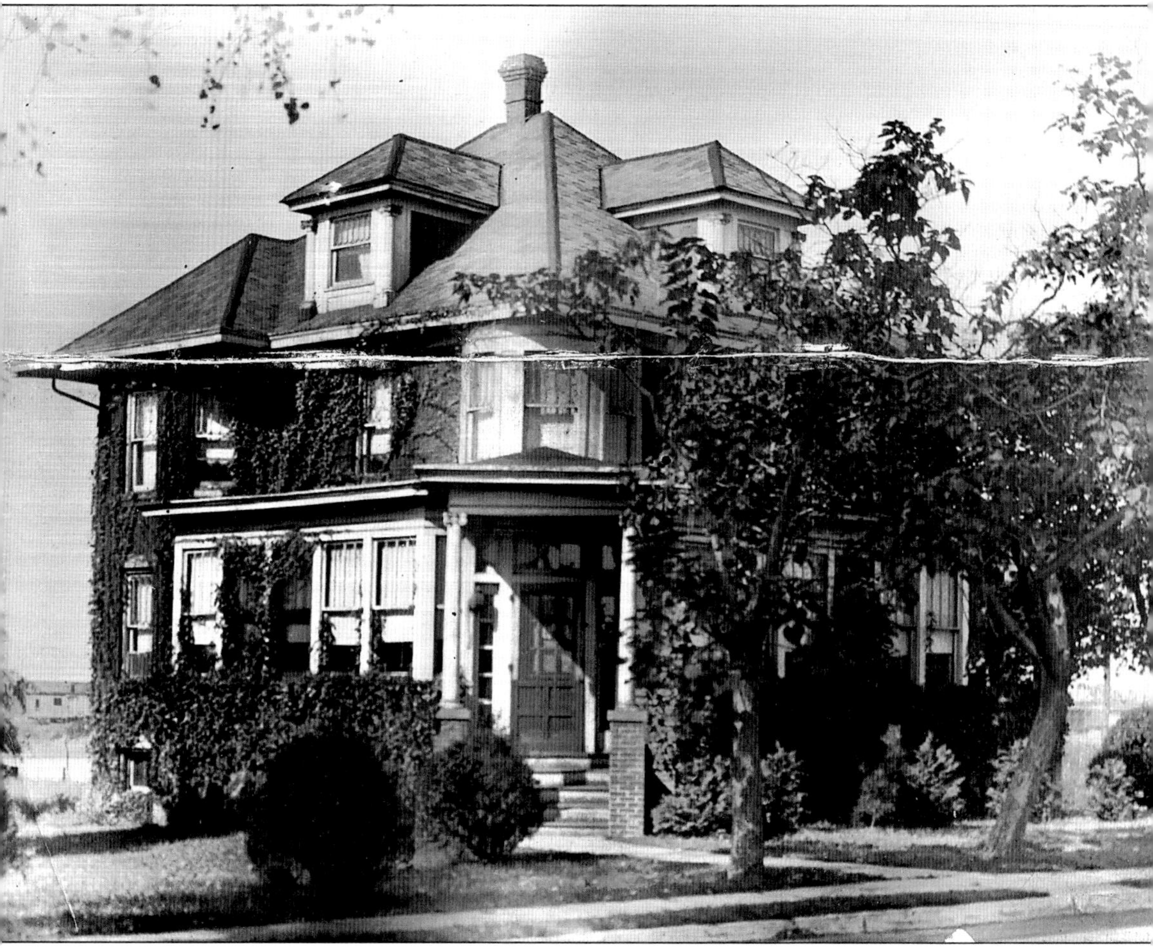

THE EUCKER RESIDENCE. Located on the corner of Eucker Street and Bergen Turnpike, this was the home of Louis A. Eucker, one of Ridgefield Park's most prominent citizens. Eucker was the first police chief in the village, as well as a fire chief and one of the first commissioners of the village.

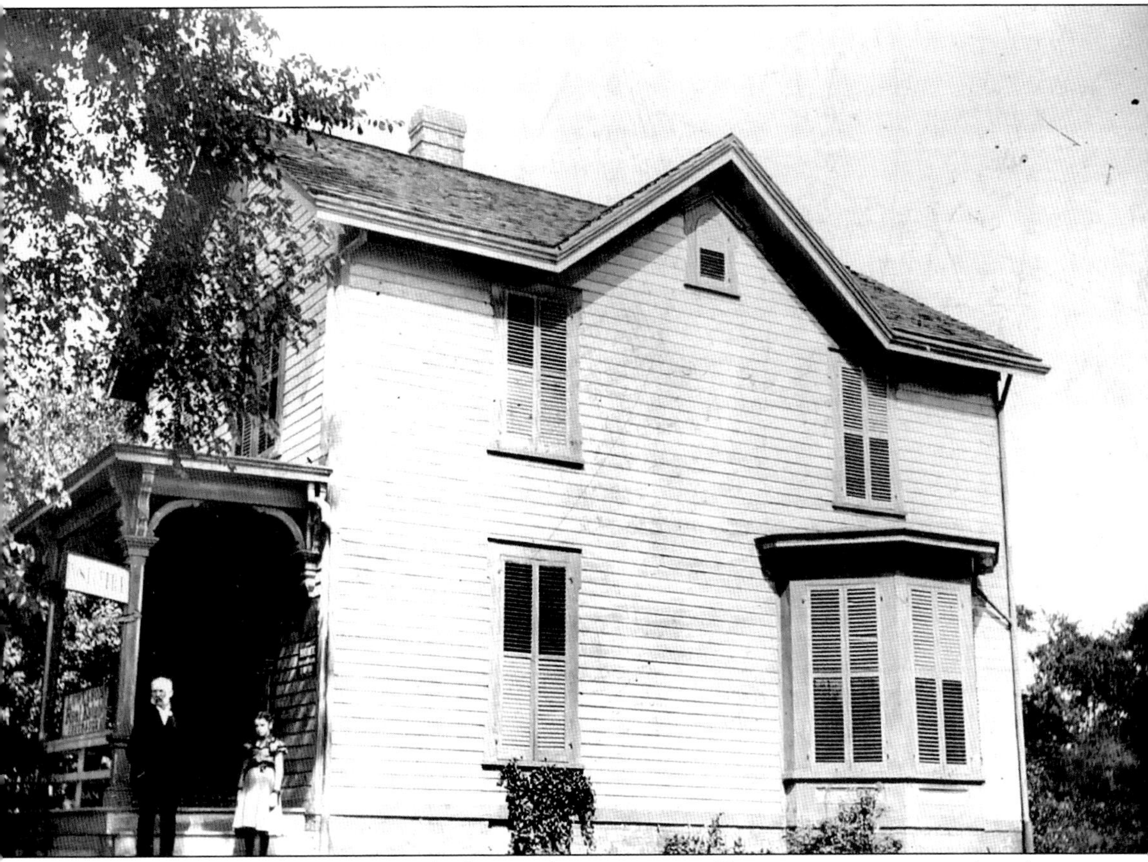

THE LOWE RESIDENCE. This was the home of George Lowe. For many years, it served as the village post office. It was located on the northeast corner of Main and Mount Vernon Streets.

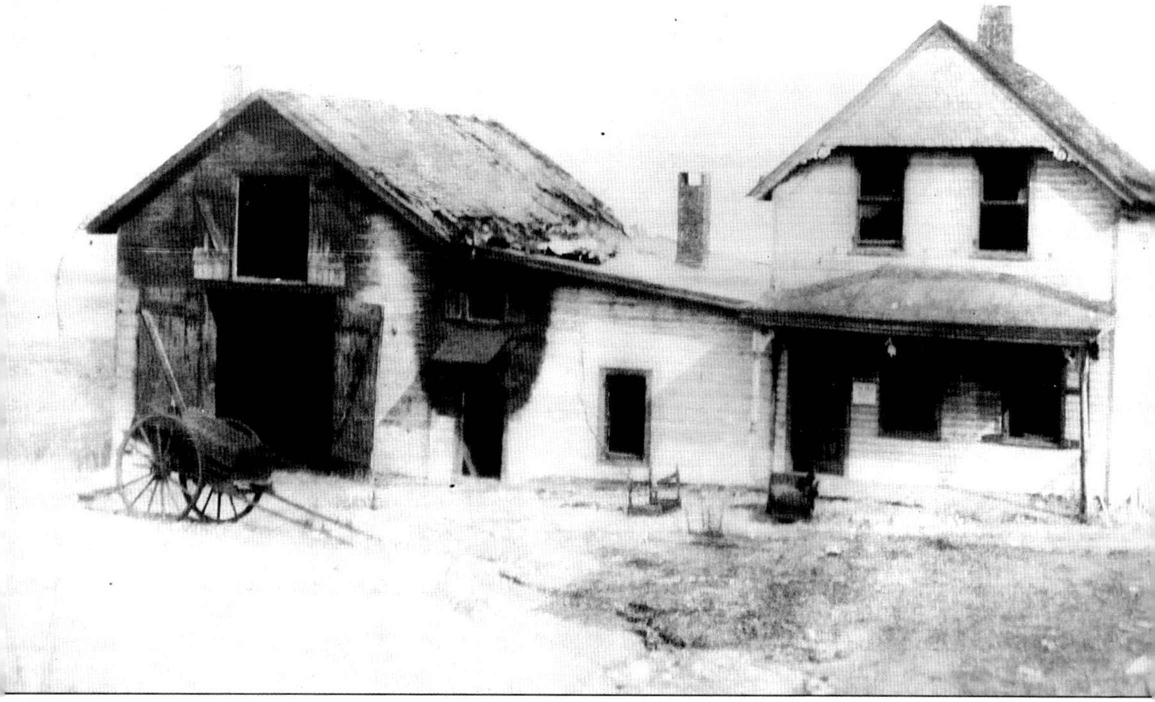

THE CLAUSEN FARM. This farm stretched from Preston Street to East Grand Avenue on the east side of Teaneck Road. The house was destroyed by fire in 1921.

Eight

Hotels and Businesses

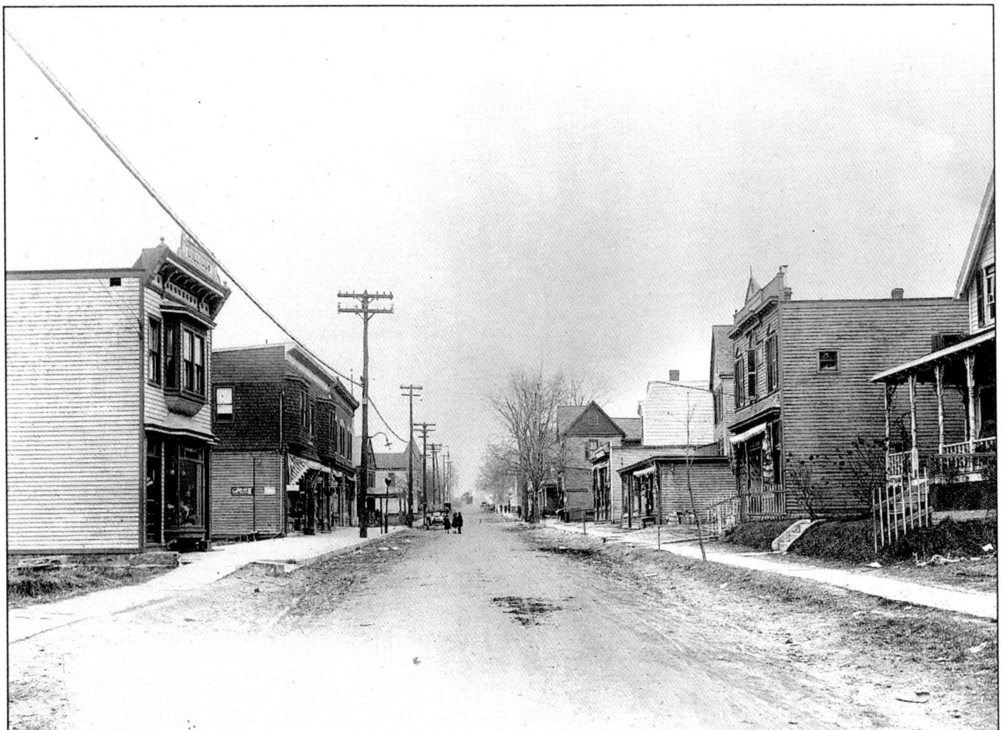

Main Street in 1910. This photograph was taken at the intersection of Main and Cedar Streets looking north. Notice the dirt road and wooden sidewalks.

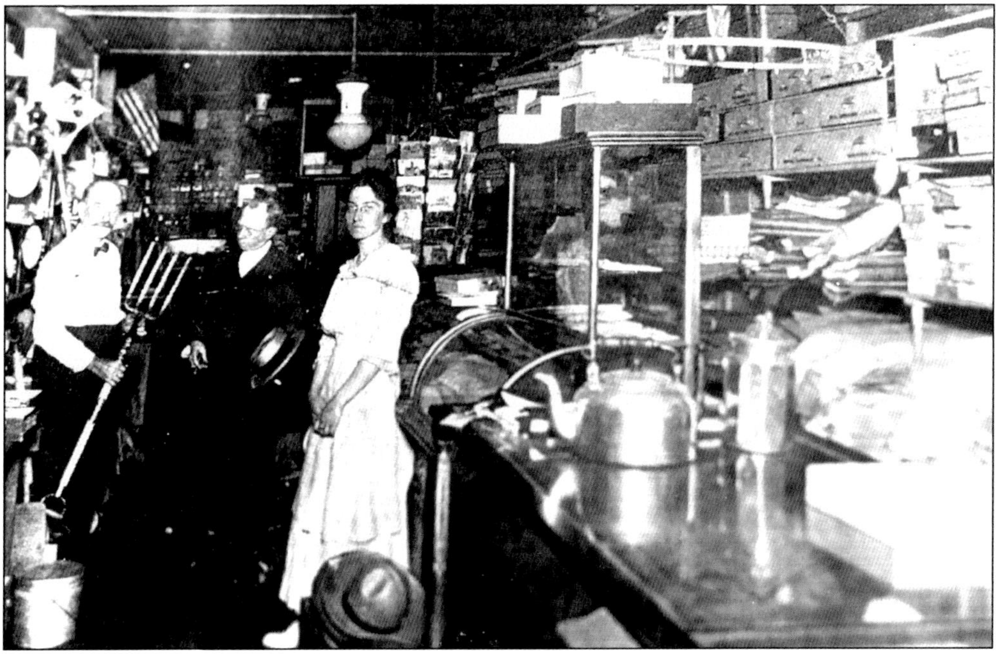

INSIDE MERGLER'S. Conrad Mergler came to the village in 1887. He opened a general store that carried everything from lamp wicks to a baby carriage. He was called the Wanamaker of Ridgefield Park.

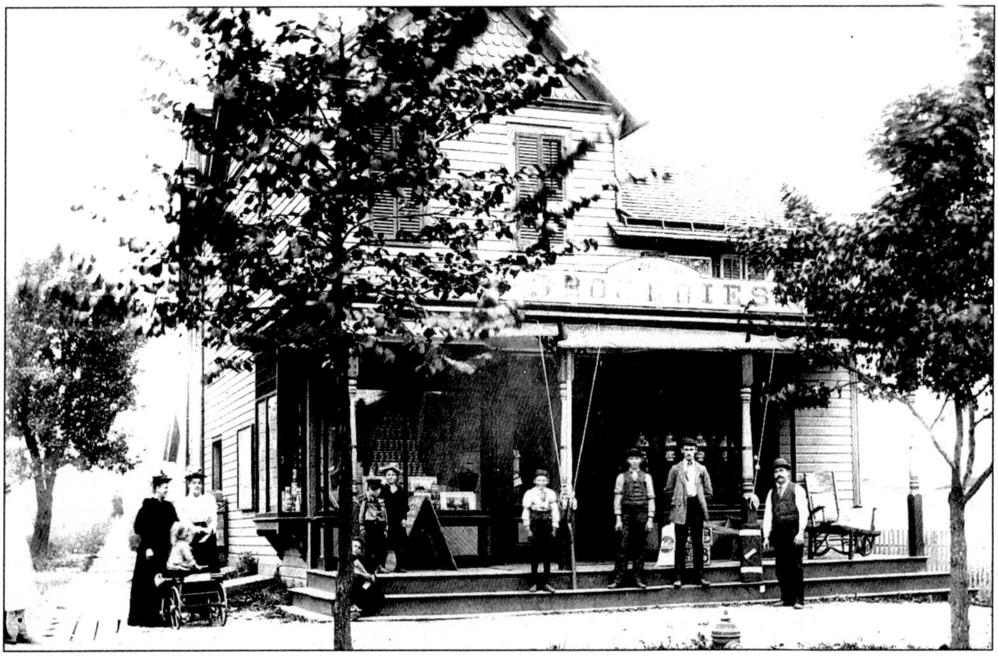

MERGLER'S CORNER STORE. This photograph was taken in the summer of 1895. Mergler's store was in business from 1889 to 1919. Mergler made his first deliveries with a wheelbarrow. Mrs. Stroltmeyer and her sister (with a child in the carriage) are on the left. In the center are, from left to right, Abe Hascup, Daniel Mergler, and George Tukey. C.W. Mergler is standing on the far right.

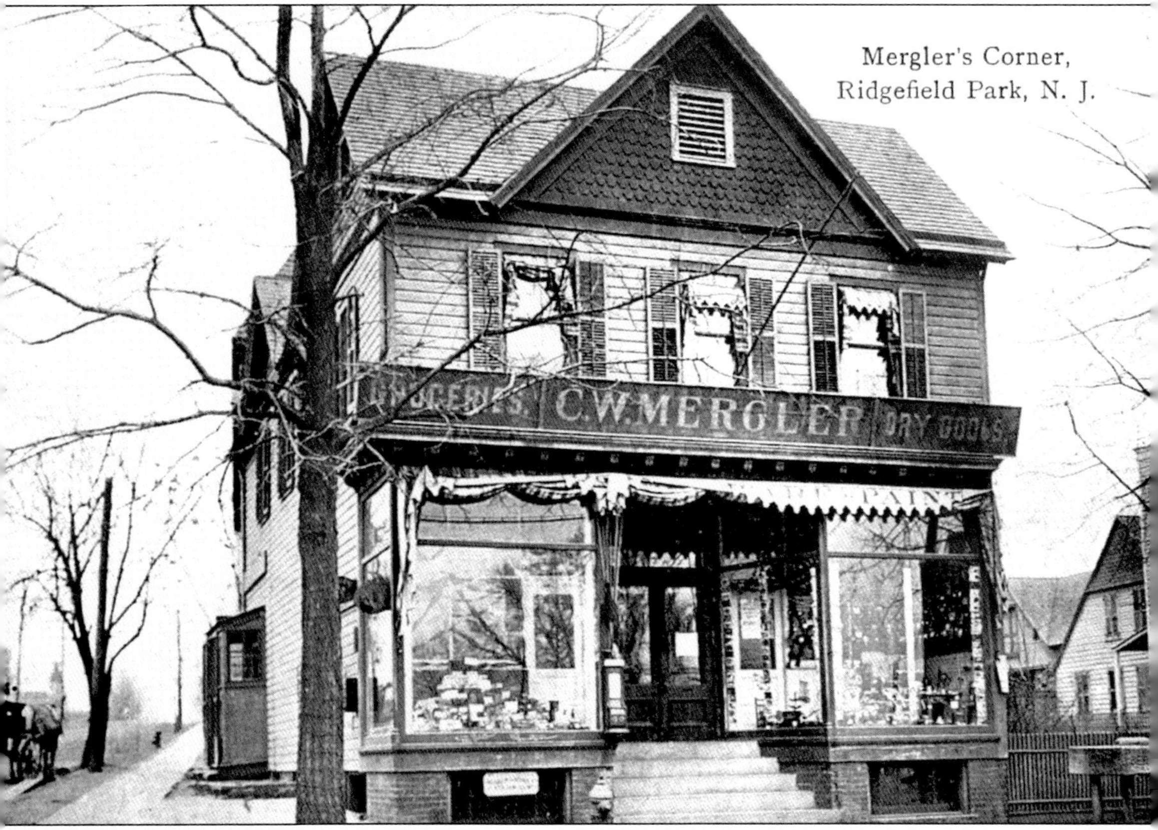

MERGLER'S CORNER. C.W. Mergler owned this store on the corner of Main and Mount Vernon Streets. At various times, it served not only as the market for villagers, but as the post office, town hall, school, and a gathering place. Conrad Mergler helped found the volunteer fire department and First National Bank. He was also the postmaster.

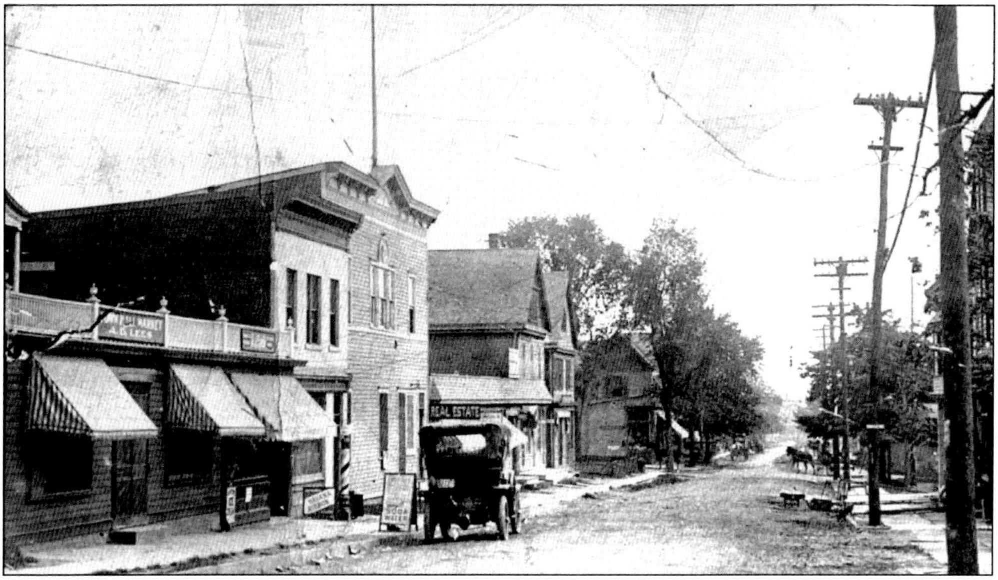

HACKENSACK ROAD IN 1903. This view of Hackensack Road (now Main Street) shows the Town Hall Market, run by A.D. Lees. The market sold stationery and was also a barbershop. Several signs advertised Havana cigars, soda water, and ice. On the right is the old town hall. Horse-drawn carriages can be seen in the background. This was in the vicinity of what locals still call Lloyd's.

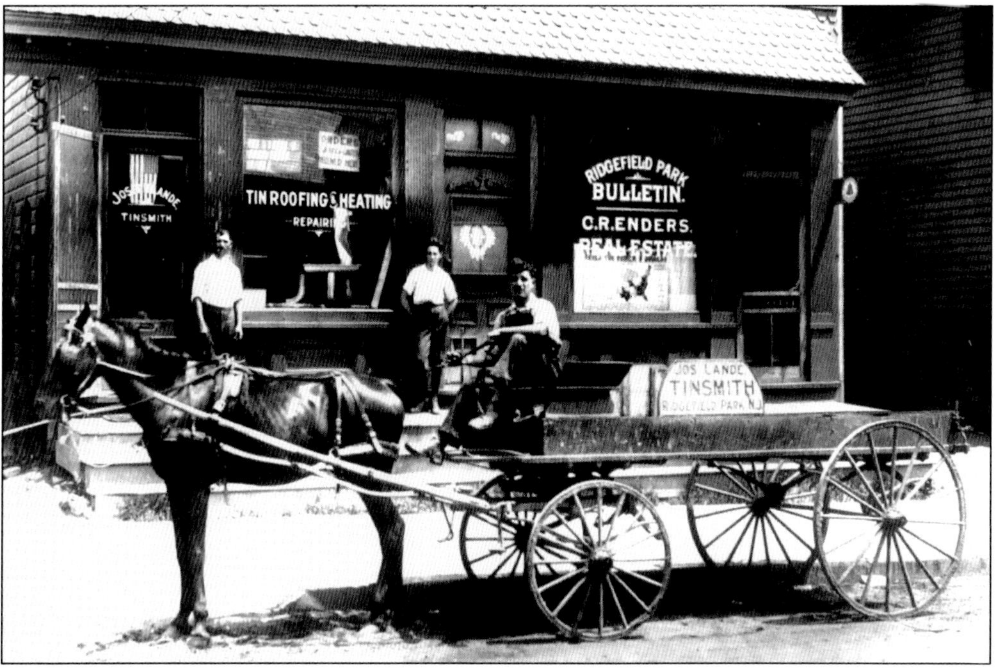

MAIN STREET IN 1916. Joseph Lande is seated in his horse-drawn cart, which was used for his tinsmith business. In the storefront next to Lande's was the office of the Ridgefield Park Bulletin, run by of C.R. Enders. The *Ridgefield Park Bulletin* was a weekly paper that helped to keep residents informed. The first telephone in the village was installed in the paper's office. This is the present site of the Village I.G.A.

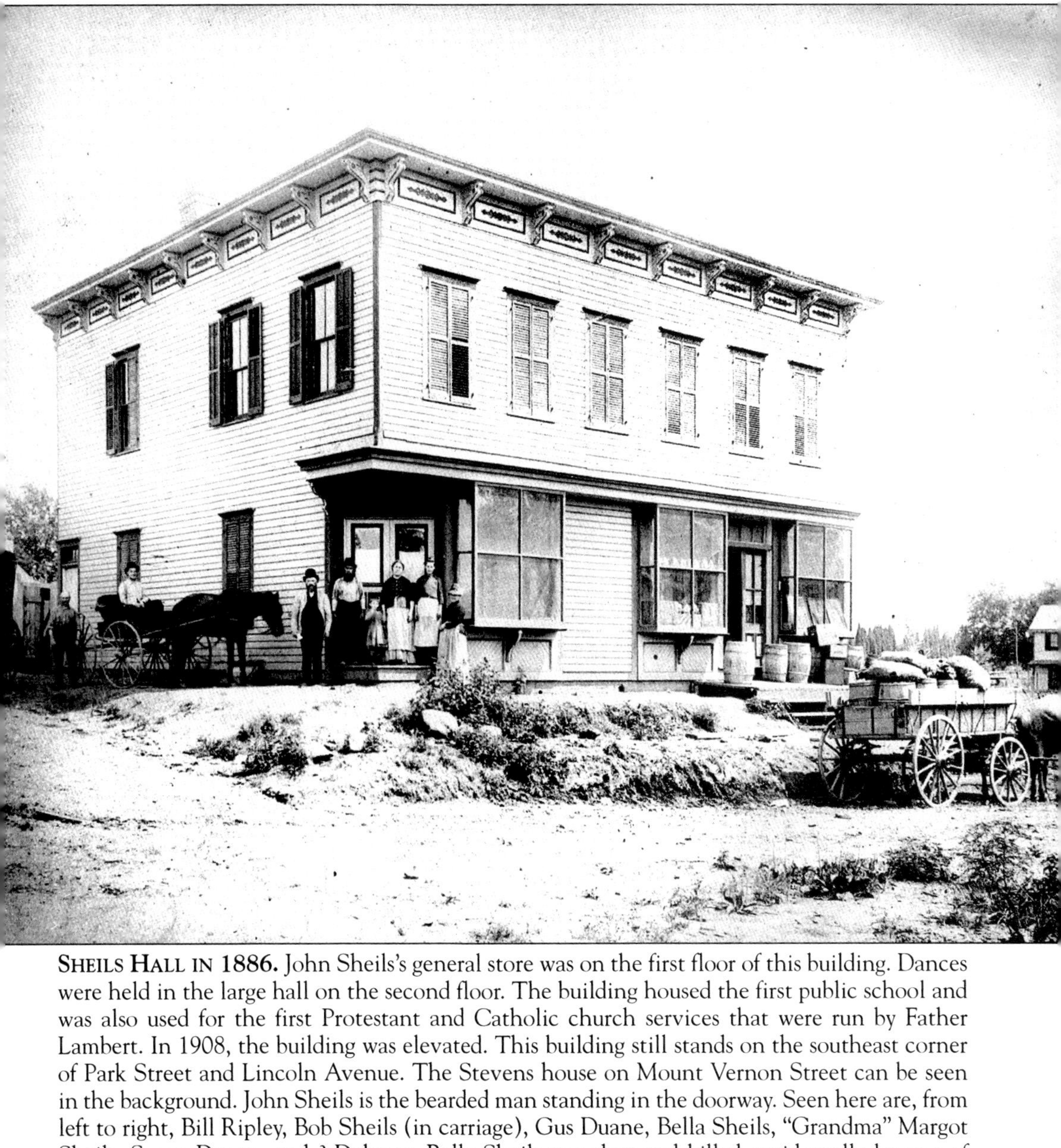

SHEILS HALL IN 1886. John Sheils's general store was on the first floor of this building. Dances were held in the large hall on the second floor. The building housed the first public school and was also used for the first Protestant and Catholic church services that were run by Father Lambert. In 1908, the building was elevated. This building still stands on the southeast corner of Park Street and Lincoln Avenue. The Stevens house on Mount Vernon Street can be seen in the background. John Sheils is the bearded man standing in the doorway. Seen here are, from left to right, Bill Ripley, Bob Sheils (in carriage), Gus Duane, Bella Sheils, "Grandma" Margot Sheils, Susan Duane, and ? Delaney. Bella Sheils was shot and killed accidentally by one of the Duane boys.

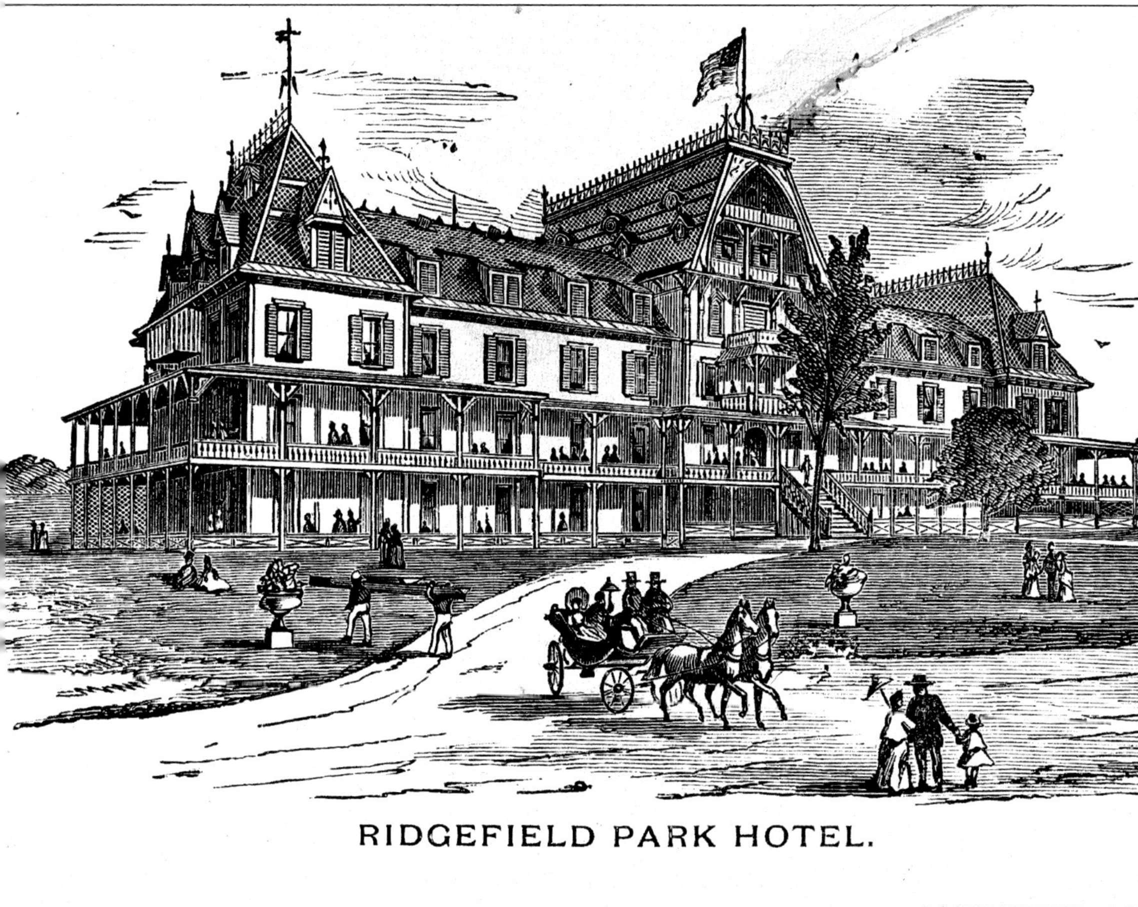

THE RIDGEFIELD PARK HOTEL. Built in 1870, this hotel was destroyed by fire in 1883. It was situated on Main Street between Mount Vernon and Grove Streets.

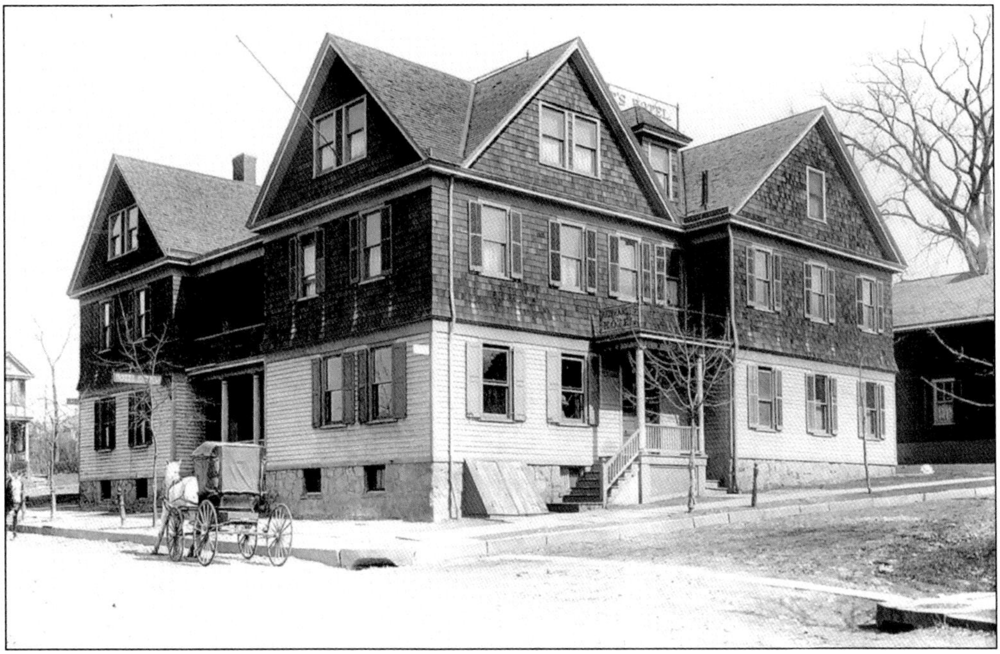

REINHARDT'S HOTEL. The hotel seen in this 1910 photograph was built in 1904.

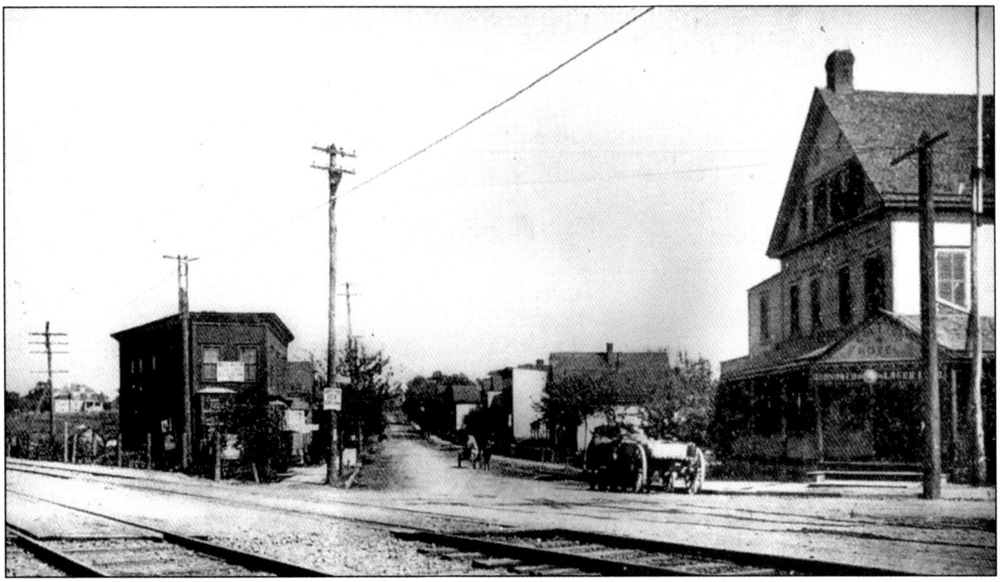

M.J. COLLINS'S HOTEL. Located at Bergen Turnpike and Ridgefield Avenue near the railroad tracks, the Collins Hotel (right) served travelers and tourists. It was later known as Bausbacks. The building on the left, known as the "Tin Triangle," was the Stephens Store. It was built in 1892. E.R. Stephens ran a newspaper delivery service from this location, as well as serving ice cream to travelers. The building was destroyed in 1913 by a terrible fire in which Stephens died.

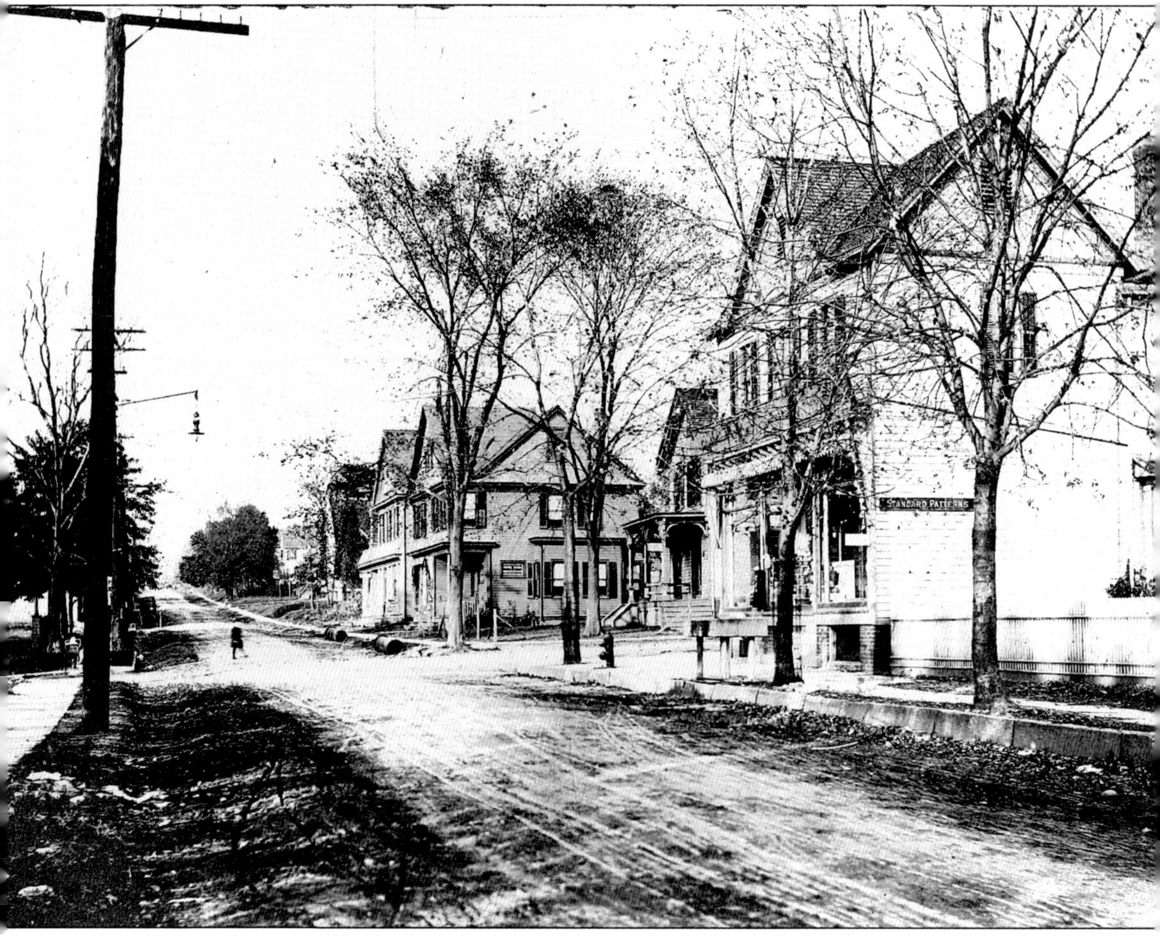

MERGLER'S CORNER. The building on the right is Conrad Mergler's store and residence.

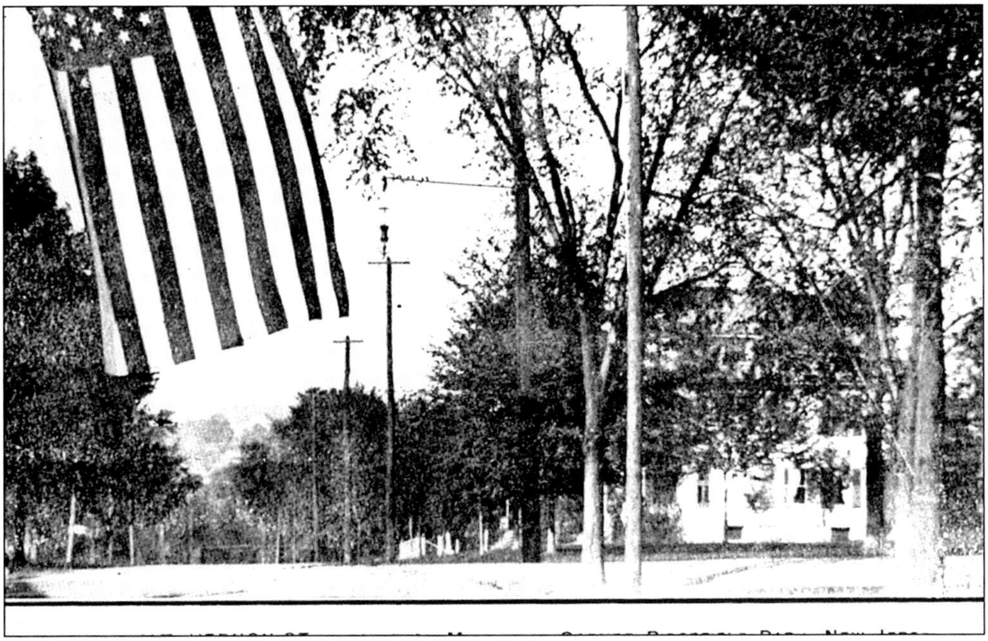

MOUNT VERNON STREET. Looking west from Mergler's Corner, this view looks down the hill of Mount Vernon Street.

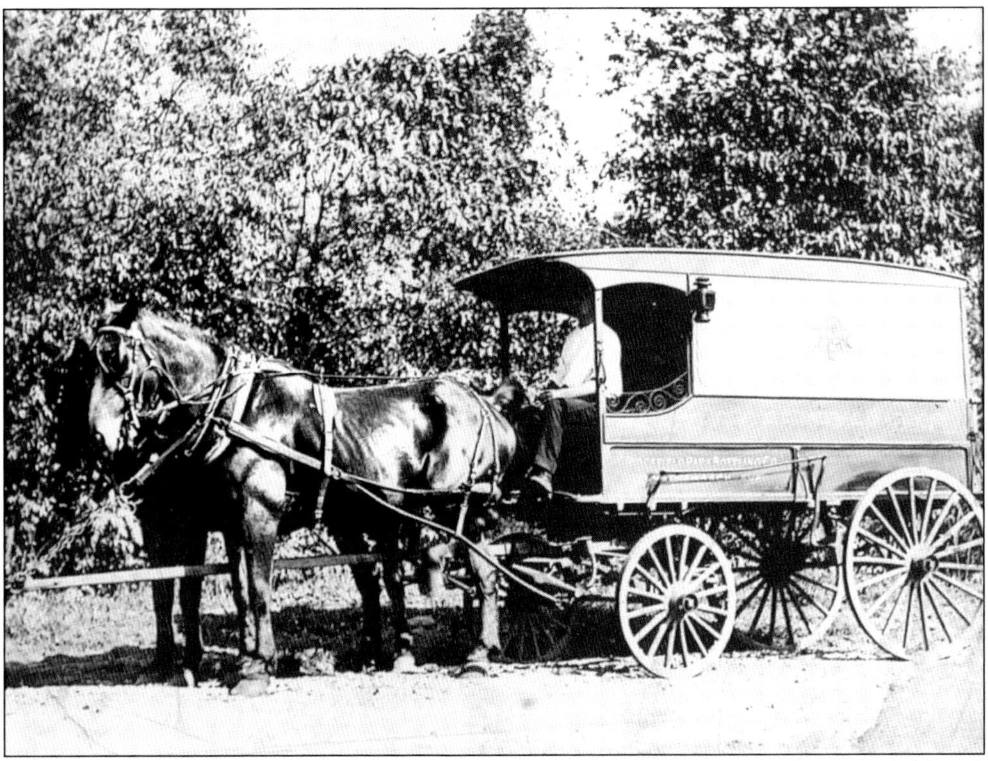

A HORSE AND BUGGY. In 1911, this horse-drawn buggy made deliveries for the Ridgefield Park Bottling Company, which was located on Hackensack Avenue. The bottling company made soda and mineral waters.

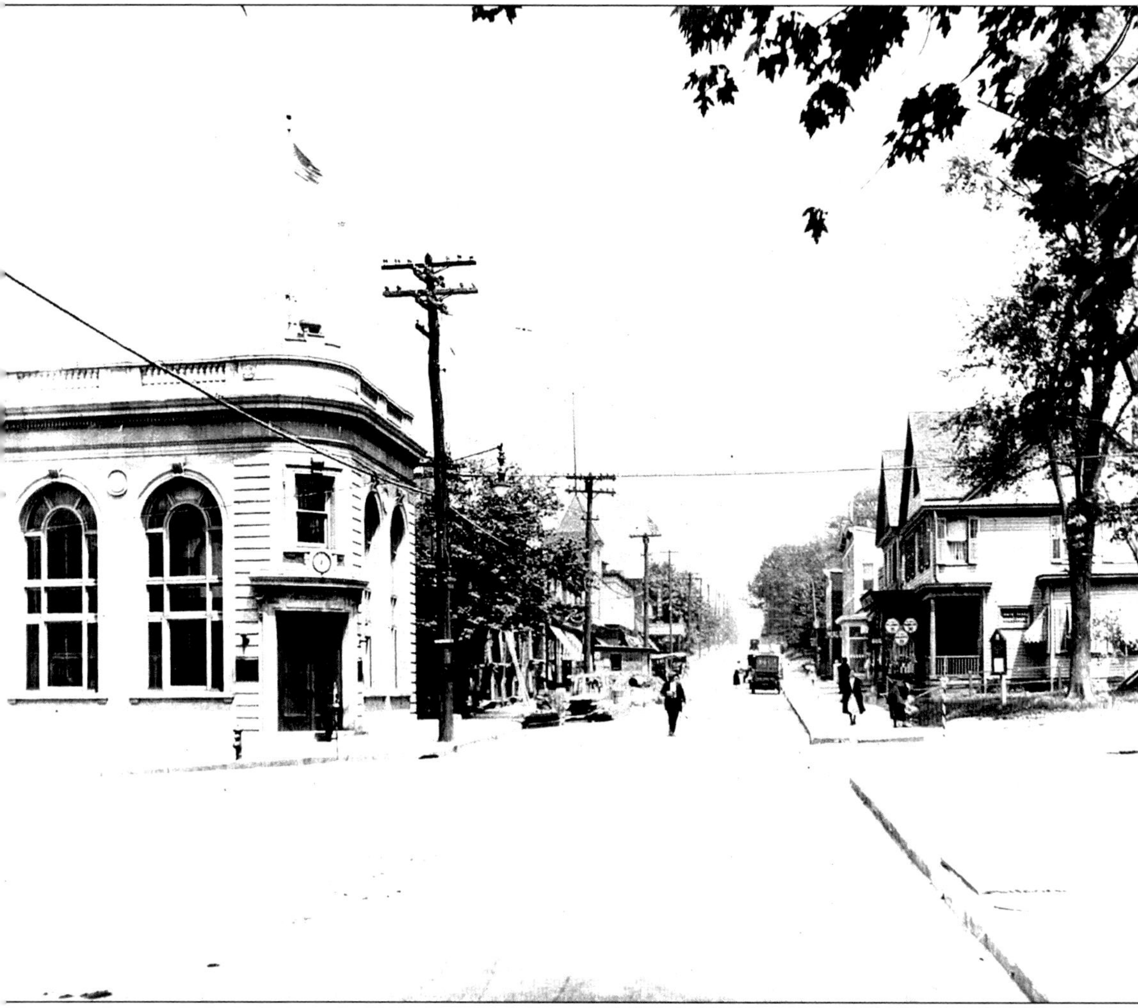

MAIN STREET IN 1919. Here, Main Street is bustling with activity. In this view, which looks north from the corner of Main and Mount Vernon Streets, the new bank building, Mergler's store, and the old post office are visible.

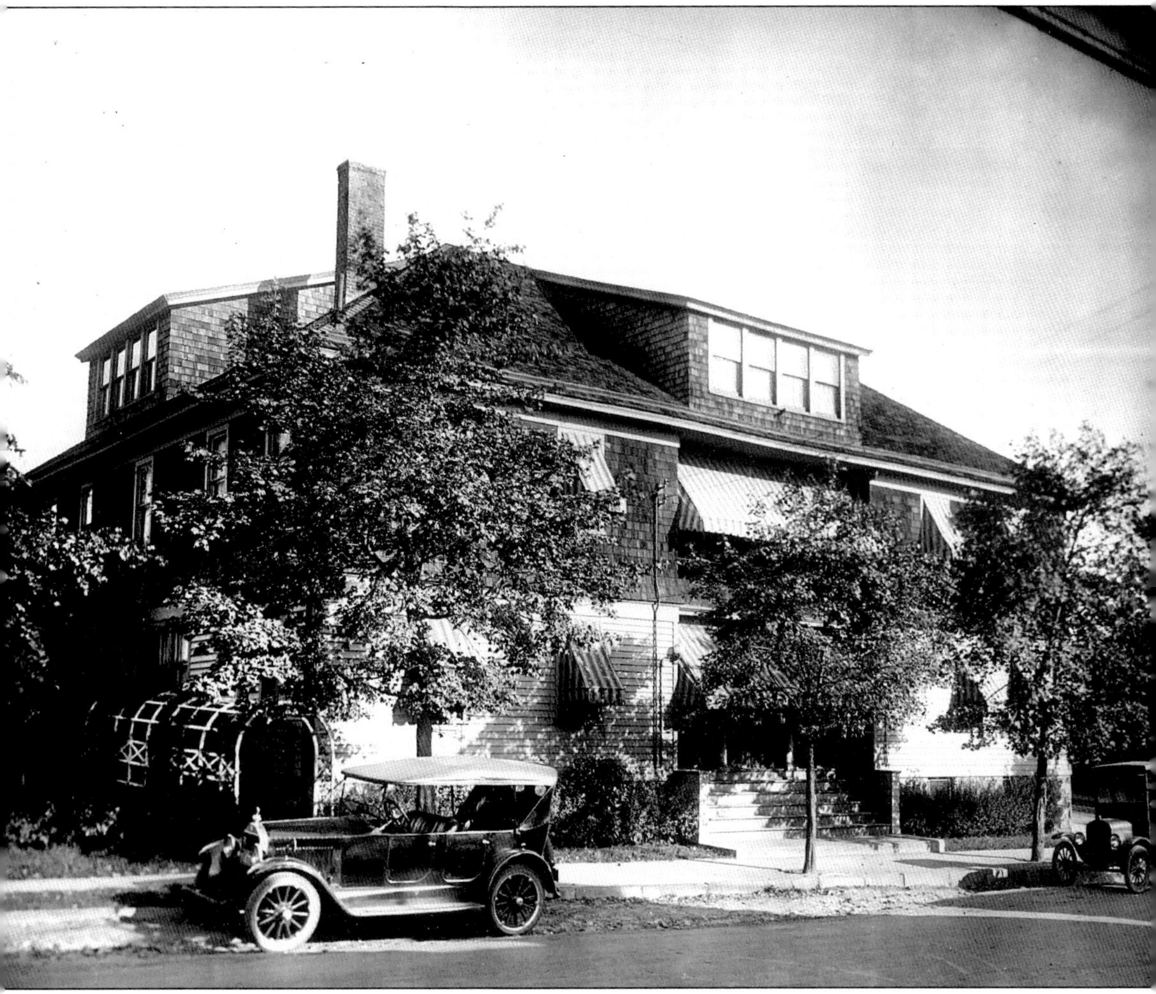

REINHARDT'S HOTEL. Located on Paulison Avenue between Park and Grove Streets, this building had a bowling alley, an auditorium, and a separate bar room. In May 1913, quick work by volunteer firemen saved the building. However, it is rumored that Mr. Reinhardt was very distressed at the loss of his liquid stock. Reinhardt rebuilt, but another fire in 1929 destroyed the hotel.

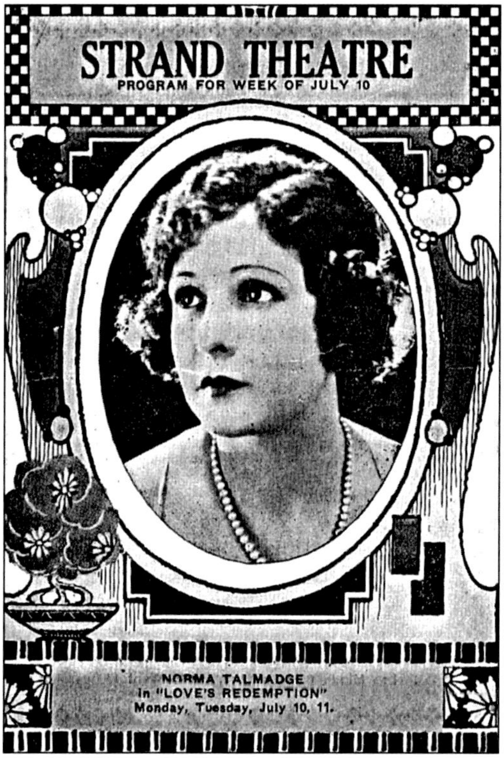

THE STRAND. Once the Opera House, the Strand Theatre continued to offer entertaining films for village residents. Located at Park and Main Streets, the Strand had three daily showings and cost between 10¢ and 25¢. *Love's Redemption* was the headline movie for the week of July 10, 1922. It starred Norma Talmadge.

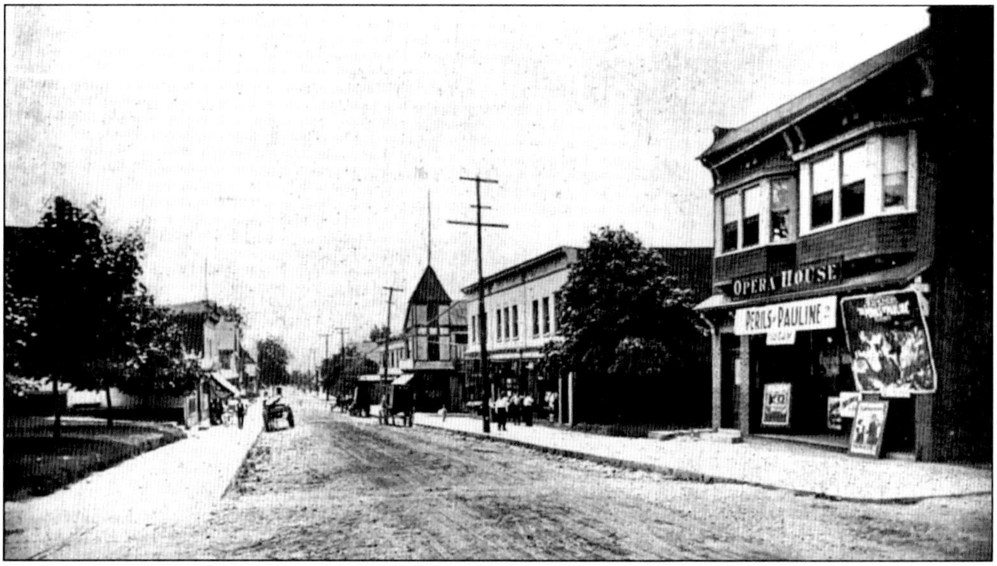

THE OPERA HOUSE. Located on Hackensack Road (now Main Street), the Opera House was a cultural icon in Ridgefield Park. As evident by the banners advertising the *Perils of Pauline*, the Opera House brought the latest entertainment to the village.

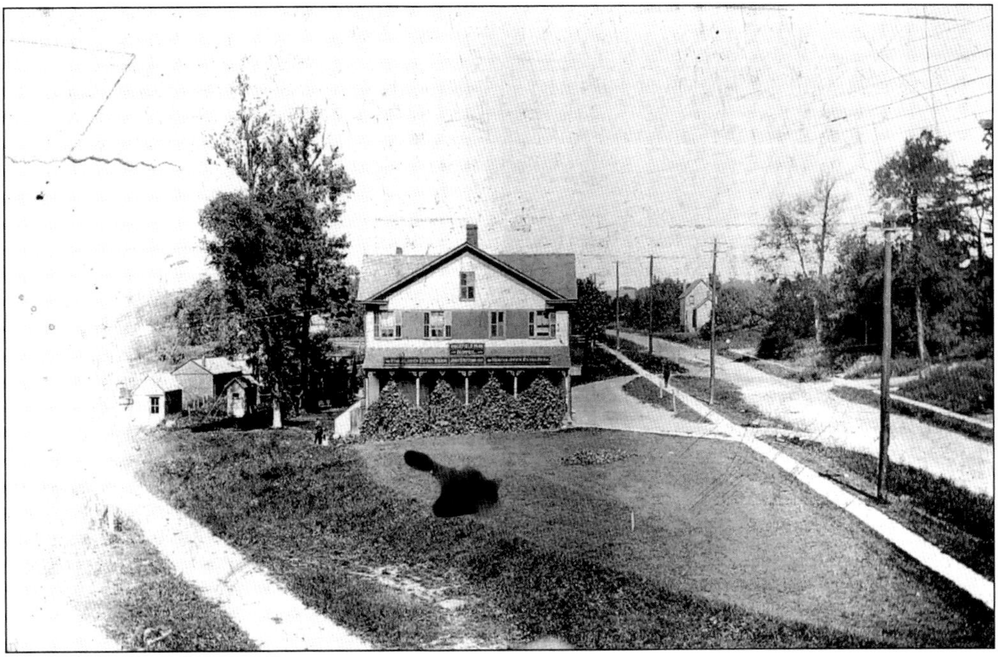

THE OLD HOTEL. Located on the triangular corner of Paulison and Railroad Avenues, this building became known as the Steffens Hotel. It was destroyed by fire. The sign on the building reads Ridgefield Park Hotel, however it was not the original. Another sign on the building harkens thirsty travels by advertising Hinchliffe's beer. Just north of this property stood the old springhouse, which pumped water to the Ridgefield Park Hotel.

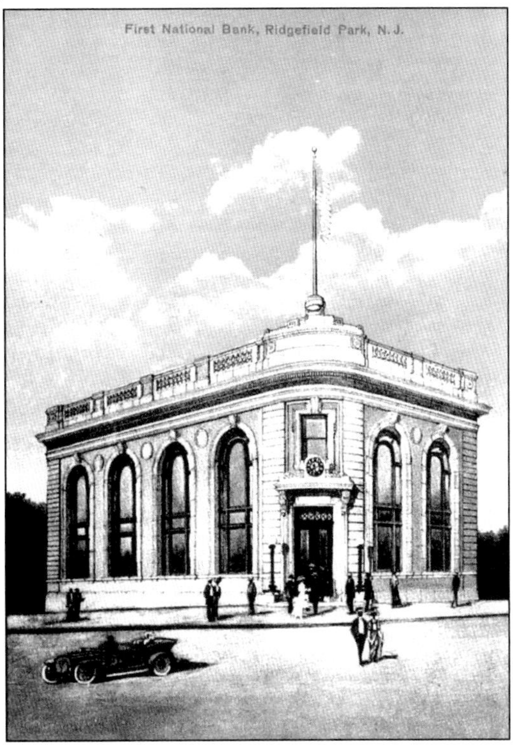

THE FIRST NATIONAL BANK. Located on the northwest corner of Main and Mount Vernon Streets, this building still stands. The bank was founded by C.W. Mergler and Cyrus Lozier.

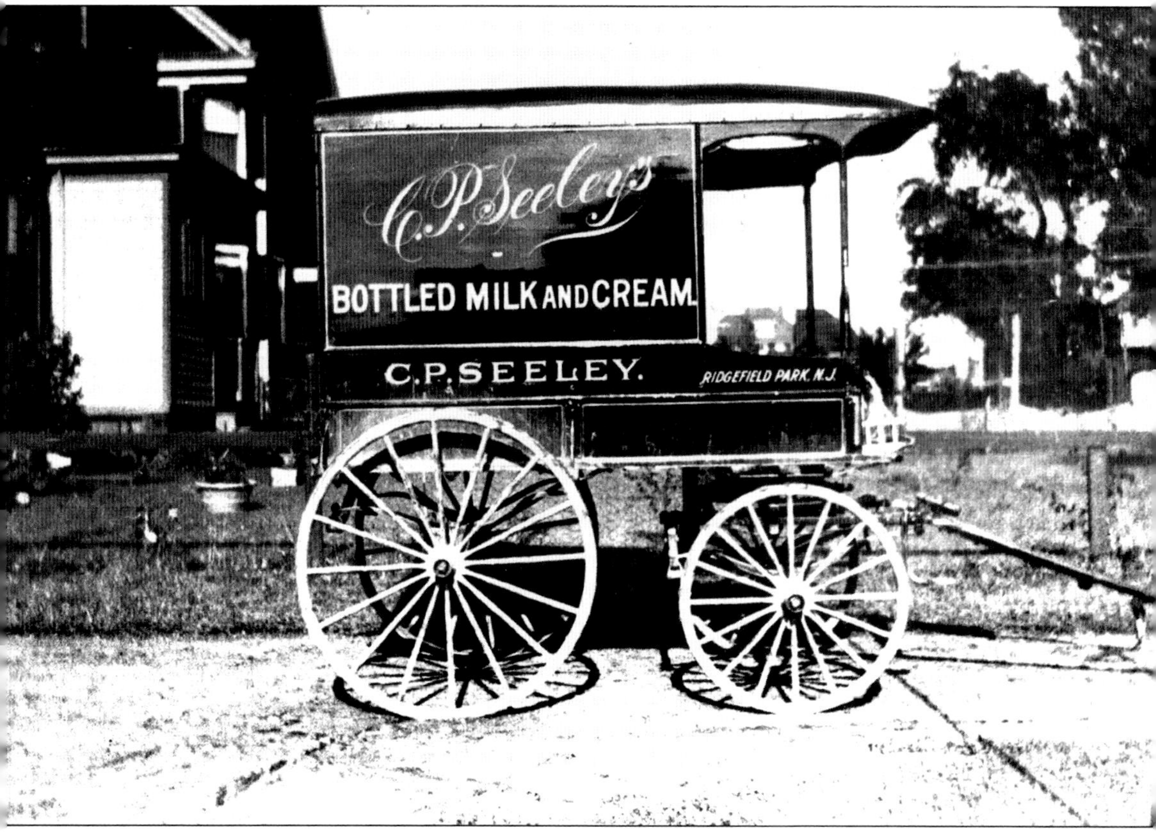

A MILK WAGON. This photograph was taken in 1912 and belonged to C.P. Seeley of Ridgefield Park. Home delivery of milk and cream was common and was made by horse-drawn carts like this one.

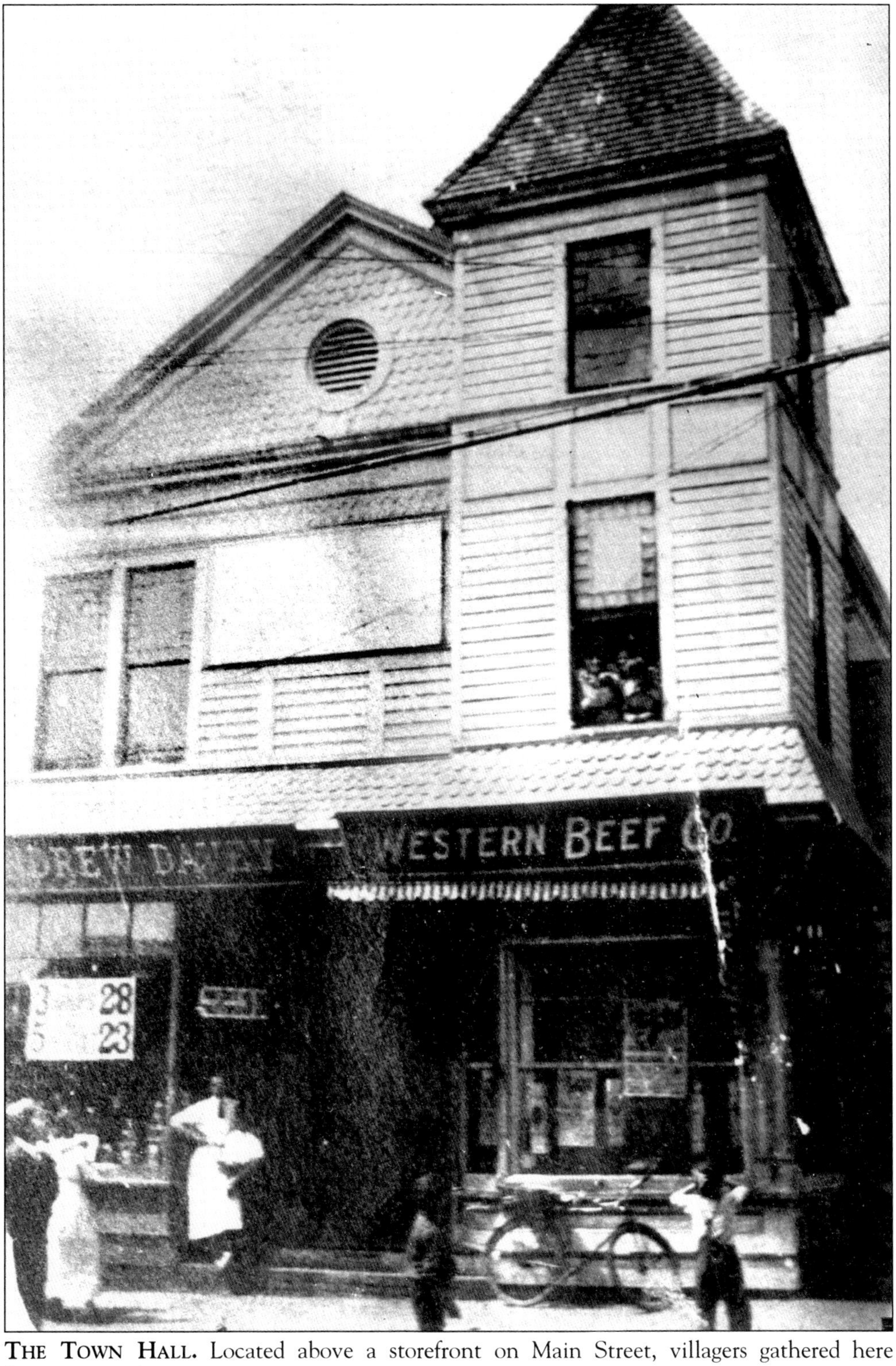

The Town Hall. Located above a storefront on Main Street, villagers gathered here for town meetings.

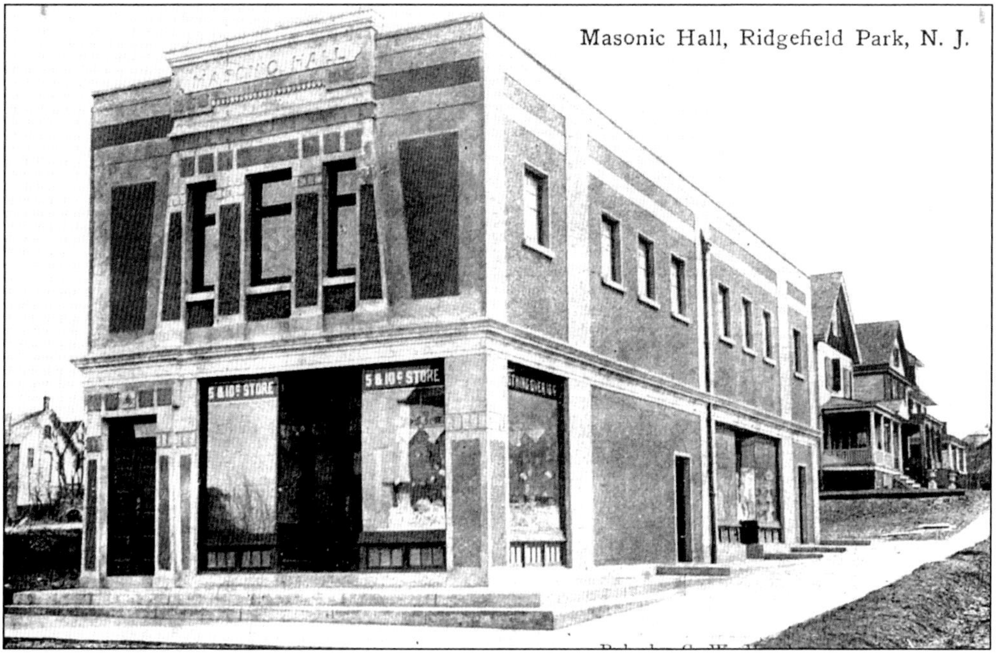

THE MASONIC HALL. This building still stands on Main Street at the corner of Hobart Street. The Masons had their meeting hall upstairs. On the street level was a five-and-ten-cent store.

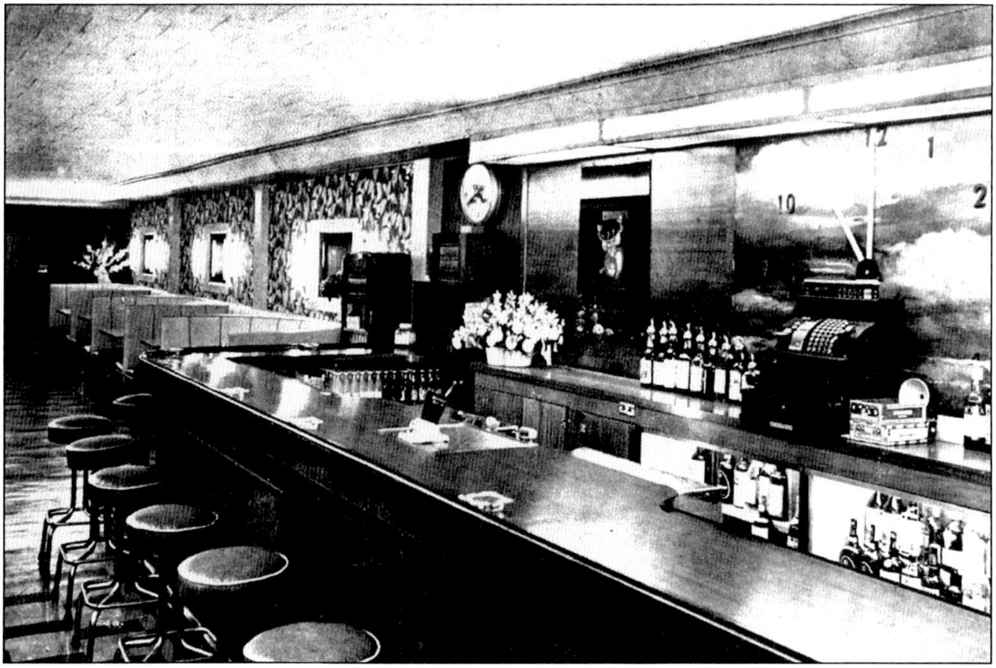

THE ELK'S GRILL. Seen here is the bar and grill at the Benevolent & Protective Order of Elks lodge. Although the bar has been remodeled, the clock mural is still there.

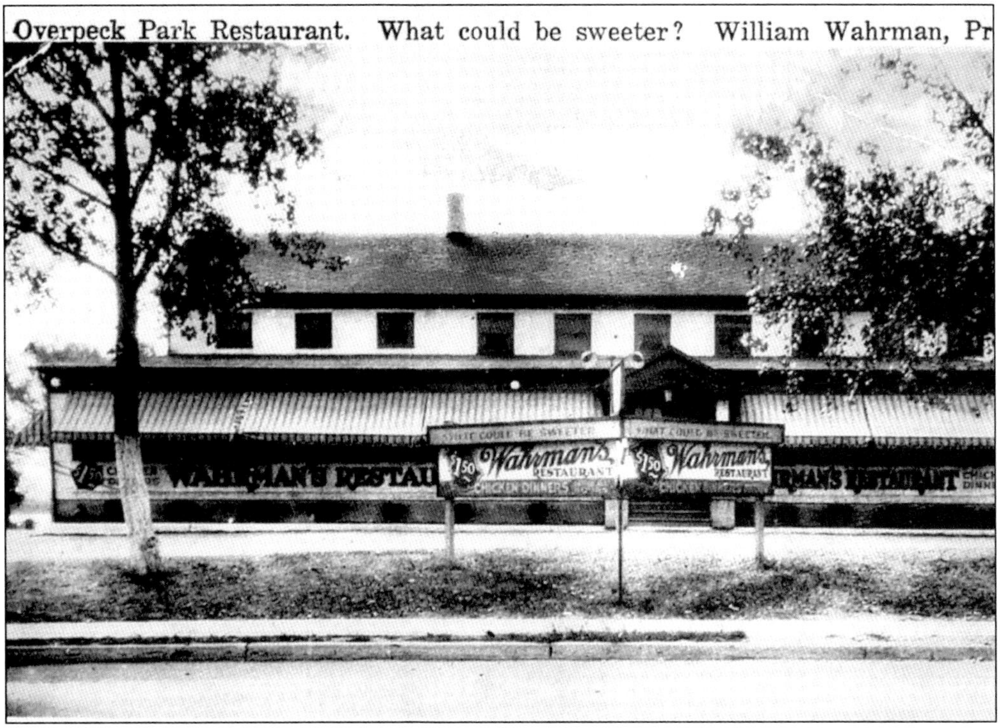

THE OVERPECK PARK RESTAURANT. Also known as Wahrman's, this large building was located on Bergen Turnpike near Teaneck Road. The restaurant served hungry patrons chicken dinners for $1.50. William Wahrman's motto was "What could be sweeter?"

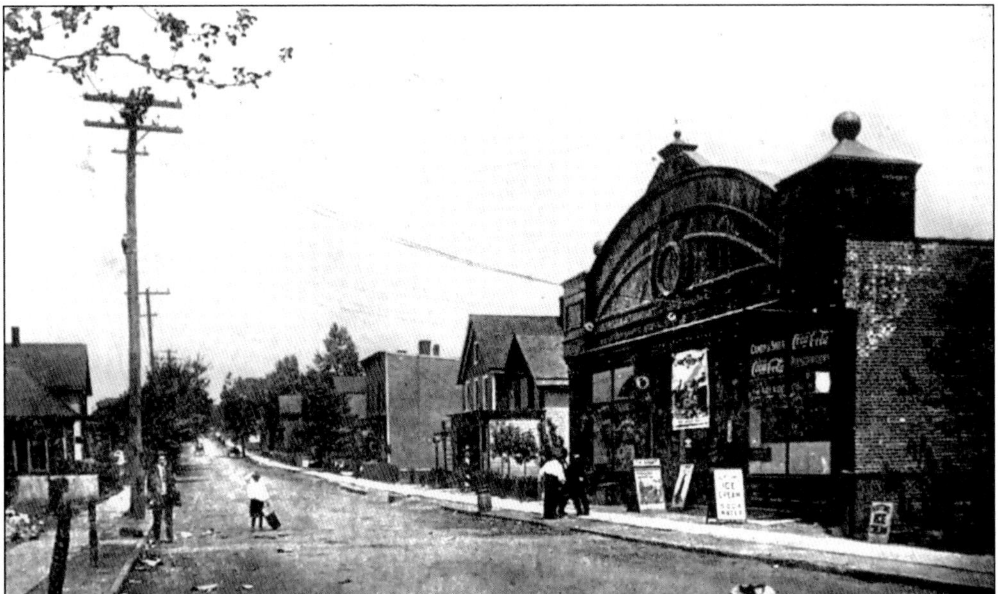

RIDGEFIELD AVENUE. This brick building on Ridgefield Avenue sold Coca Cola and ice cream and filled prescriptions.

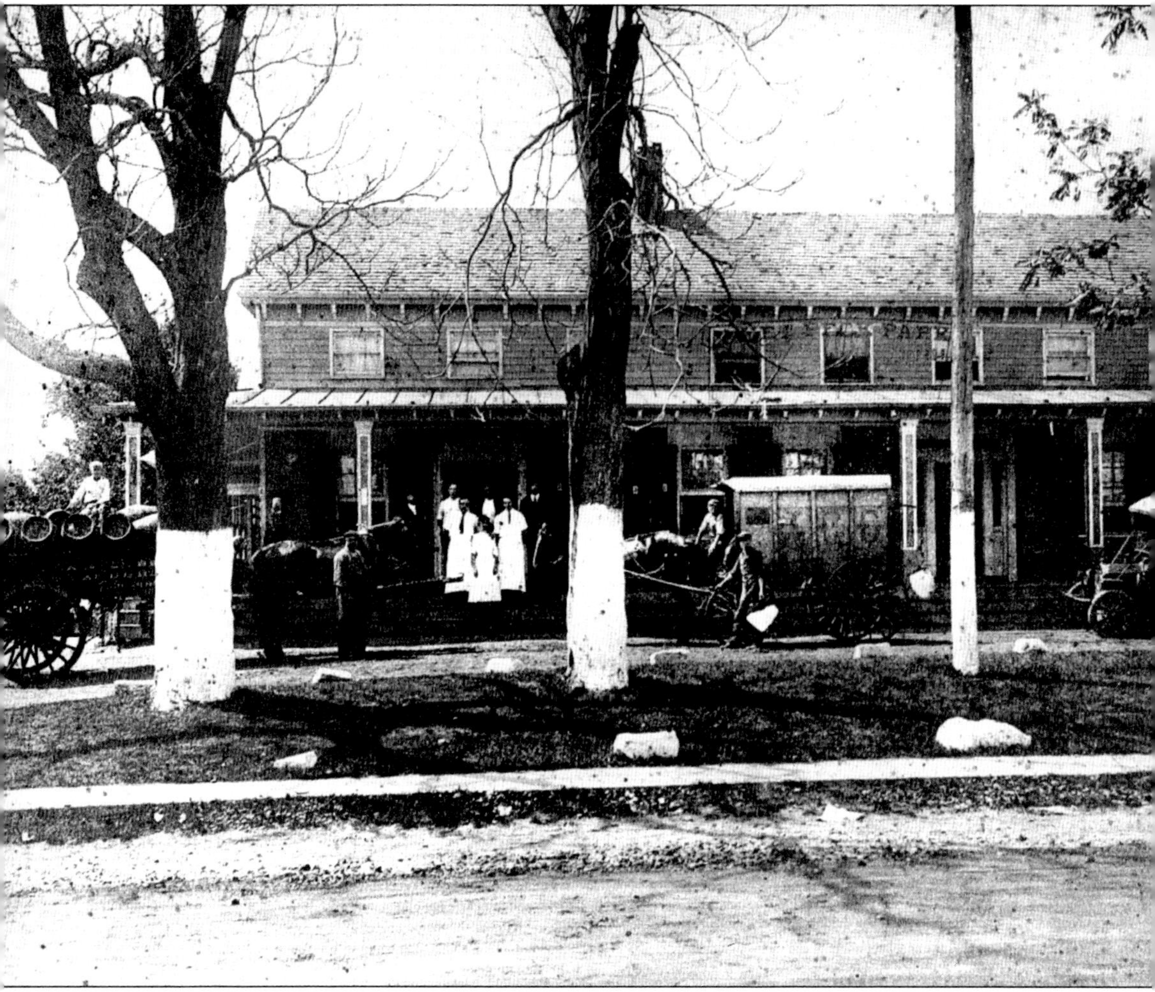

OVERPECK PARK. Located on Bergen Turnpike near Teaneck Road, this property has served the community for many years. Originally, it was a stage-coach stop. Later known as Wahrman's, it eventually became Eucker's, when Louis Eucker married Auguste Wahrman. Behind the building were a large picnic area and a bathing beach, making it a popular gathering place for locals in the early 1900s.

Nine

THE RAILROAD

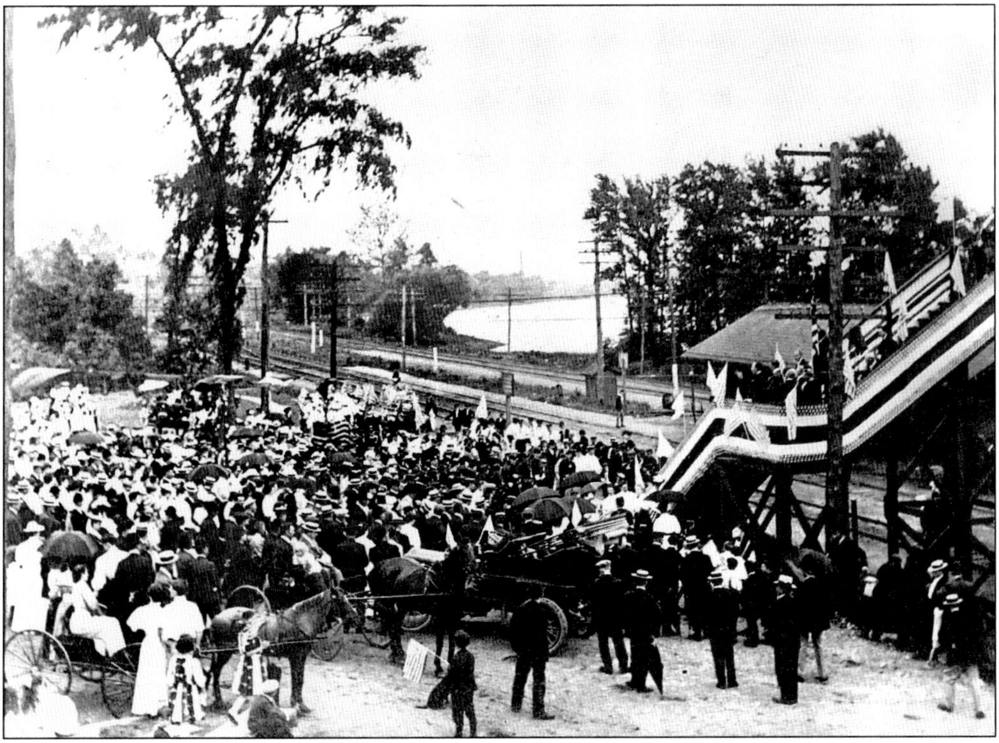

THE FOOTBRIDGE. In 1903, a footbridge was dedicated to allow passengers of the many trains that passed through the village to cross the tracks safely. The celebration drew a large crowd in spite of the rain.

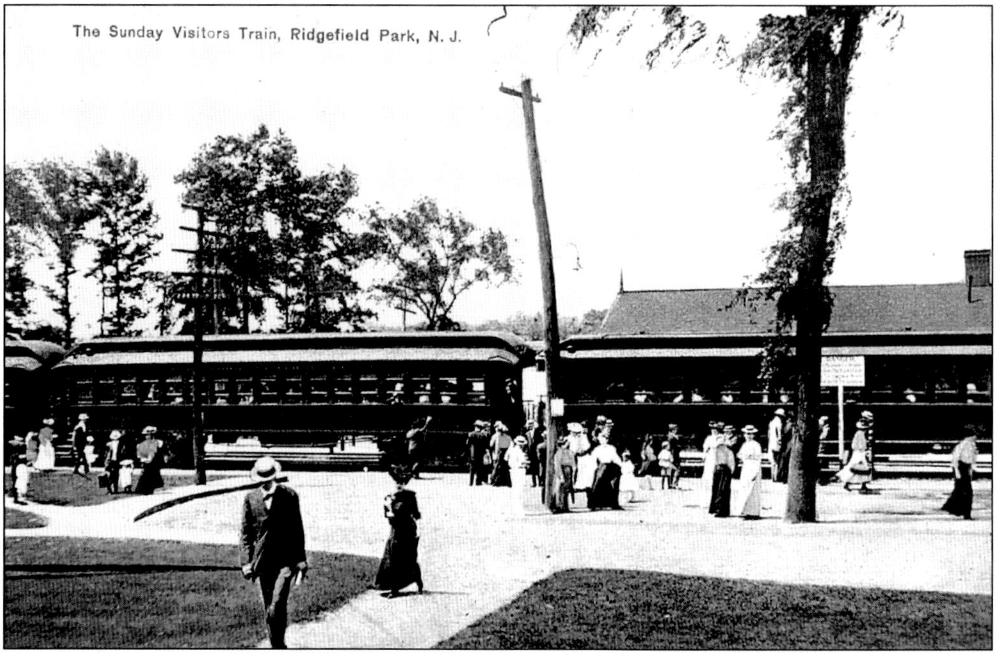

THE SUNDAY VISITORS TRAIN. Passenger trains were once the norm and brought travelers and commuters to and from the village. The small sign on the right warns passengers of the dangers of crossing the tracks and instructs them to use the footbridge.

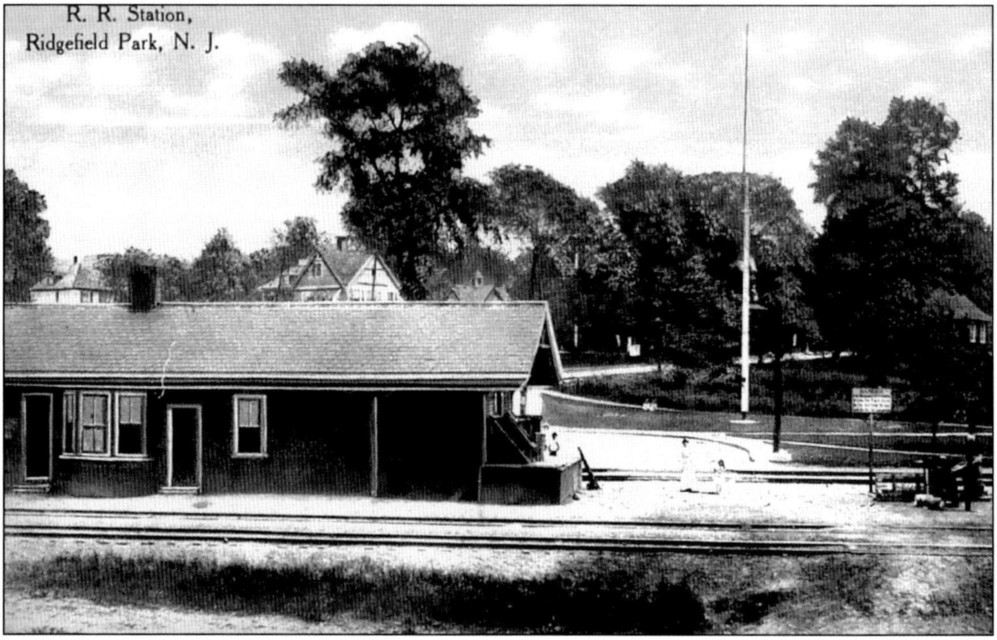

THE MOUNT VERNON STREET STATION. This is the railroad station at the bottom of Mount Vernon Street. In 1927, there were 3,269 commuters from the village.

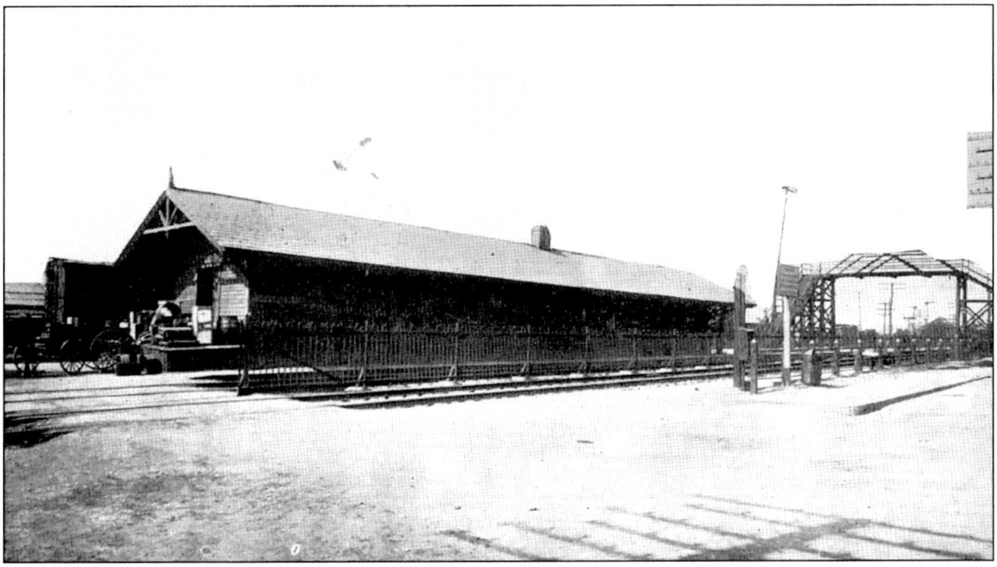

The Railroad Station. Take note of the footbridge on the right side of this photograph of the Mount Vernon Street station.

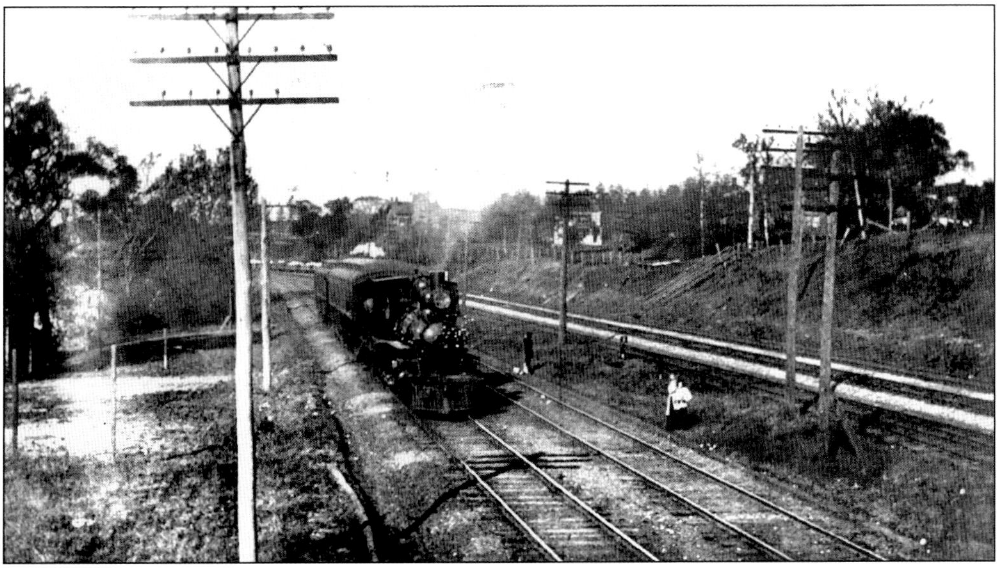

The Noon Accommodation. In 1906, trains ran regularly through Ridgefield Park. At one time, there were 68 trains running daily.

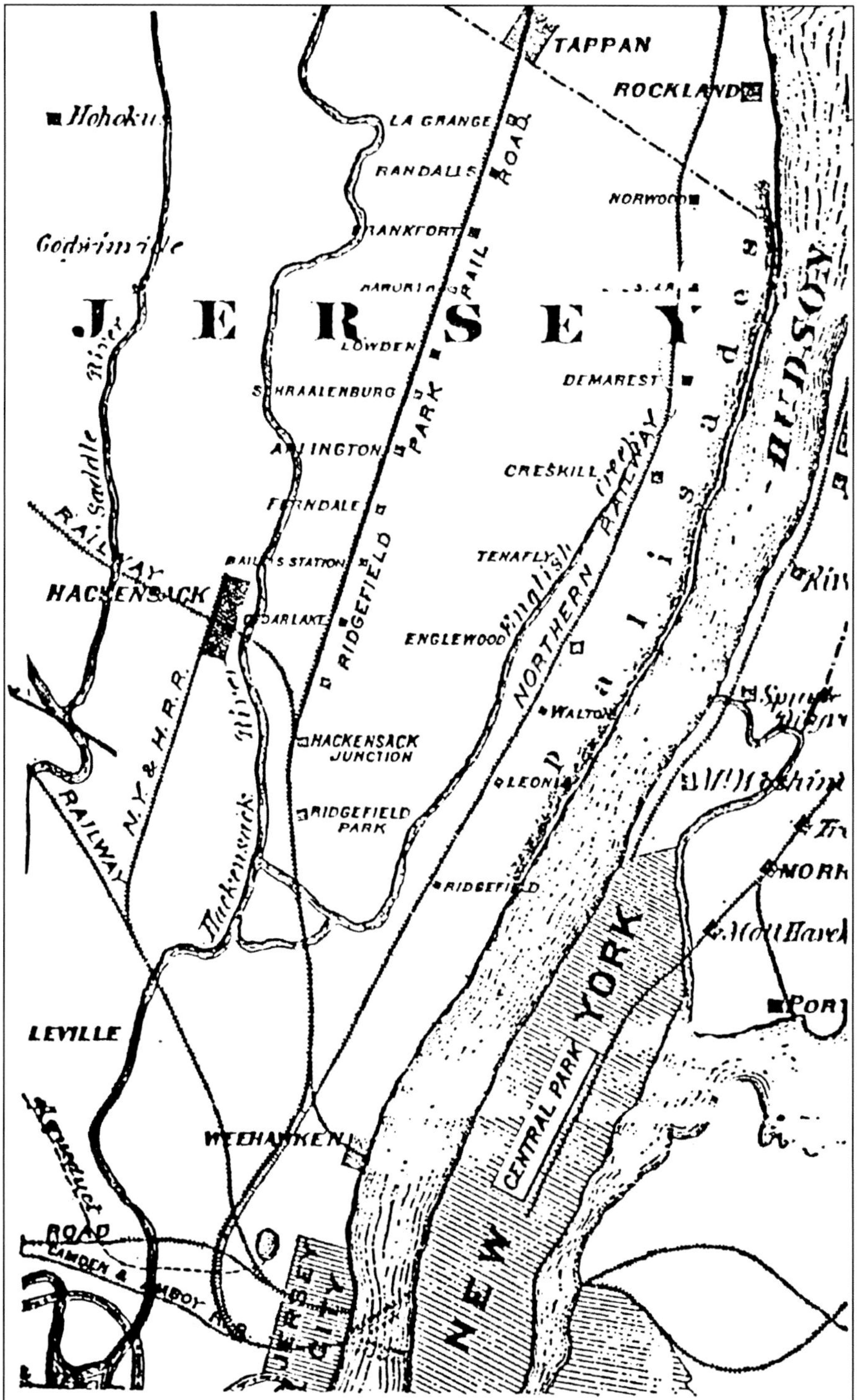

Map, Ridgefield Park Railroad. *Bergen County Historical Society.*

A MAP OF RIDGEFIELD PARK'S RAIL SERVICE. This old map shows some of the routes and stops along the railroad.

A RAILROAD PASS. In 1925, Earle Sandberg used this pass on his daily trips to New York City.

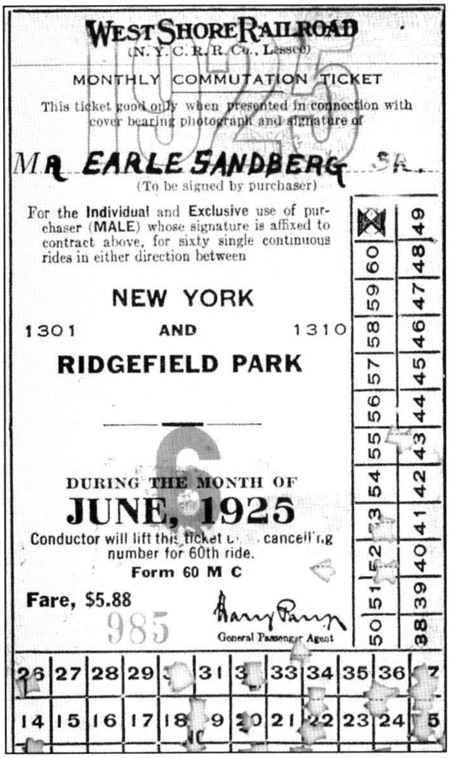

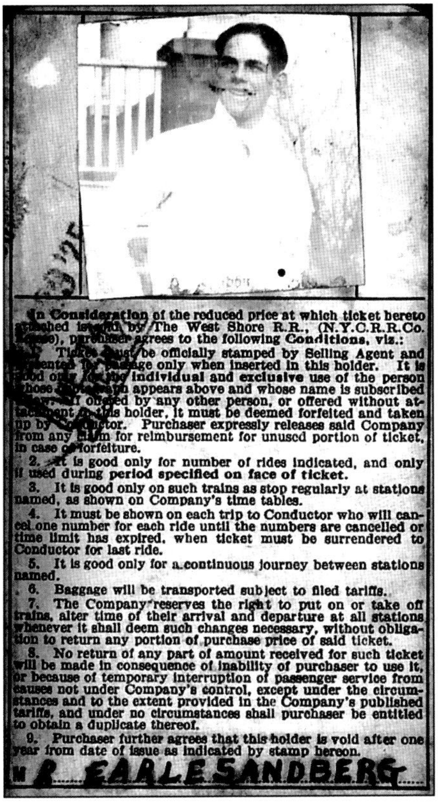
In Consideration of the reduced price at which ticket hereto attached is issued by The West Shore R.R., (N.Y.C.R.R.Co. Lessee), purchaser agrees to the following Conditions, viz.:

1. Ticket must be officially stamped by Selling Agent and presented for passage only when inserted in this holder. It is good only for the individual and exclusive use of the person whose photograph appears above and whose name is subscribed below. If offered by any other person, or offered without attachment to this holder, it must be deemed forfeited and taken up by Conductor. Purchaser expressly releases said Company from any claim for reimbursement for unused portion of ticket, in case of forfeiture.

2. It is good only for number of rides indicated, and only if used during period specified on face of ticket.

3. It is good only on such trains as stop regularly at stations named, as shown on Company's time tables.

4. It must be shown on each trip to Conductor who will cancel one number for each ride until the numbers are cancelled or time limit has expired, when ticket must be surrendered to Conductor for last ride.

5. It is good only for a continuous journey between stations named.

6. Baggage will be transported subject to filed tariffs.

7. The Company reserves the right to put on or take off trains, alter time of their arrival and departure at all stations whenever it shall deem such changes necessary, without obligation to return any portion of purchase price of said ticket.

8. No return of any part of amount received for such ticket will be made in consequence of inability of purchaser to use it, or because of temporary interruption of passenger service from causes not under Company's control, except under the circumstances and to the extent provided in the Company's published tariffs, and under no circumstances shall purchaser be entitled to obtain a duplicate thereof.

9. Purchaser further agrees that this holder is void after one year from date of issue as indicated by stamp hereon.

MR EARLE SANDBERG

A MONTHLY COMMUTATION TICKET. In 1925, commuters could purchase a monthly ticket from Ridgefield Park to New York City on the West Shore Railroad for $5.88. The conductor would punch the card for each trip.

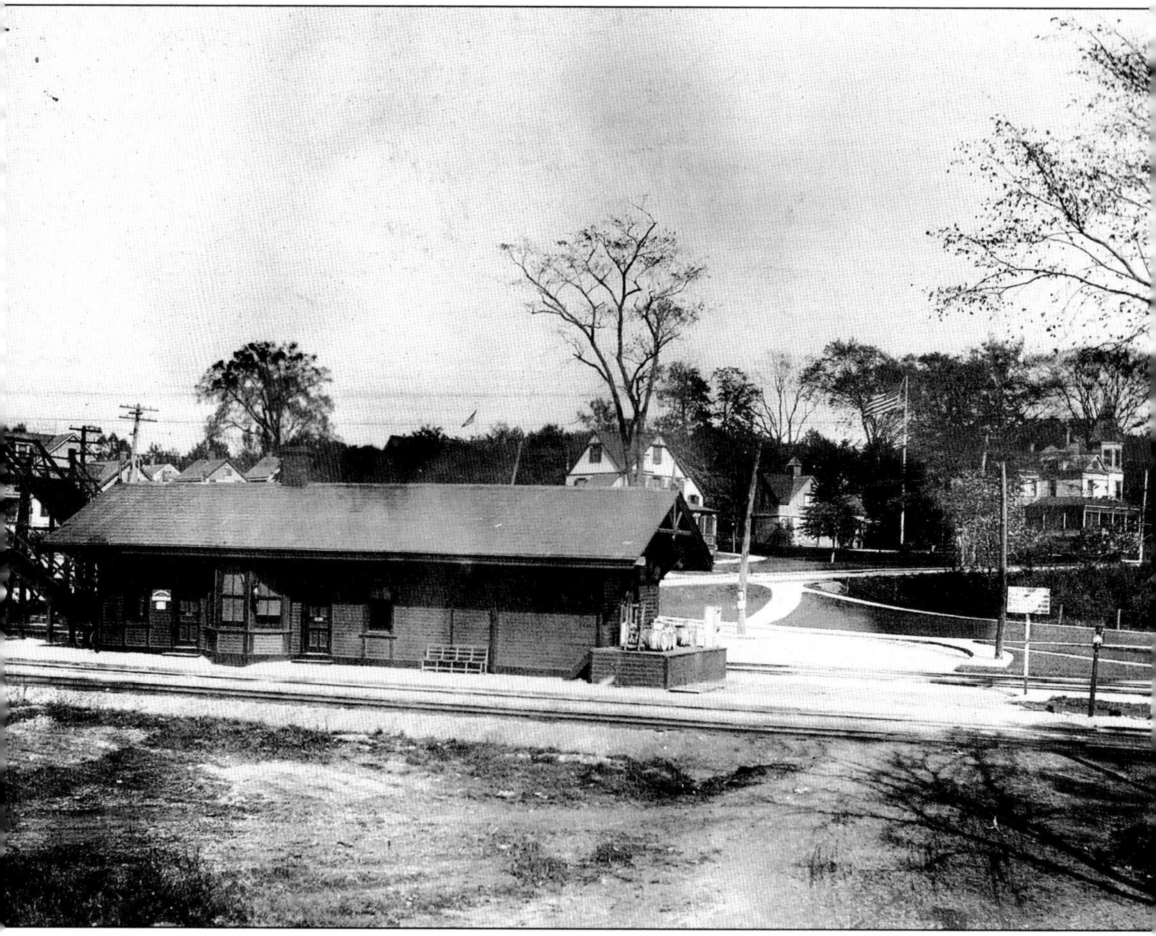

THE RAILROAD STATION IN 1910. Easy access to the railroad was very important to Ridgefield Park. Trains brought tourists to the village, which enticed people to make their homes here.

Ten

THE POLICE AND FIRE DEPARTMENTS

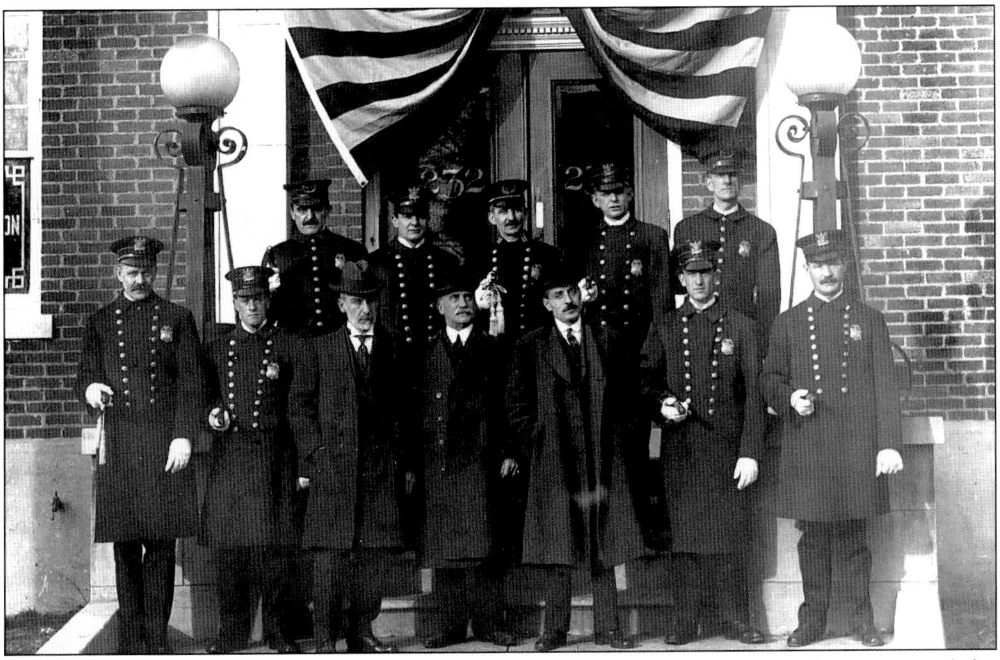

THE POLICE DEPARTMENT OF 1915. This photograph was taken on the front steps of the municipal building on Main Street. Seen here are, from left to right, (front row) Fred Larsen, Pete Wanner, Mayor Dexheimer, Commissioner Webbon, Commissioner Ayers, Jim McNeice, and John Taylor; (back row) ? Belthoff, Doc Ritter, Chief McElroy, Herman Schult, and Bill Schlag. Doc Ritter was the only village police officer to be killed in the line of duty. He was shot and killed by a prisoner while walking to headquarters.

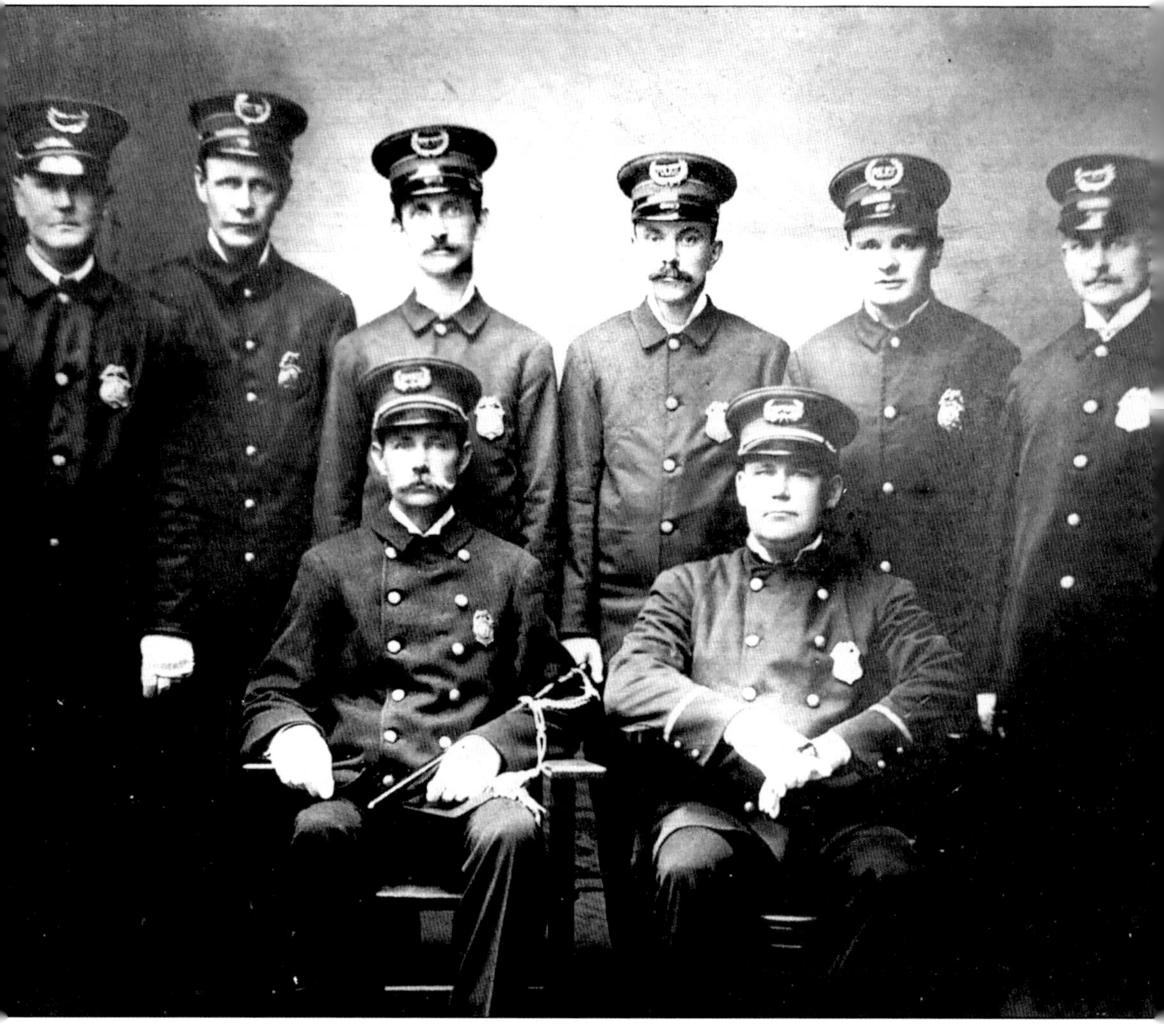

The First Uniformed Police Officers. This photograph, taken in July 1909, shows, from left to right, (seated) Louis Eucker (chief) and William Melia (captain); (standing) Harry Cole, Fred Larsen, John Britting, William Glassow, John "Doc" Ritter, and H. VanDenhben.

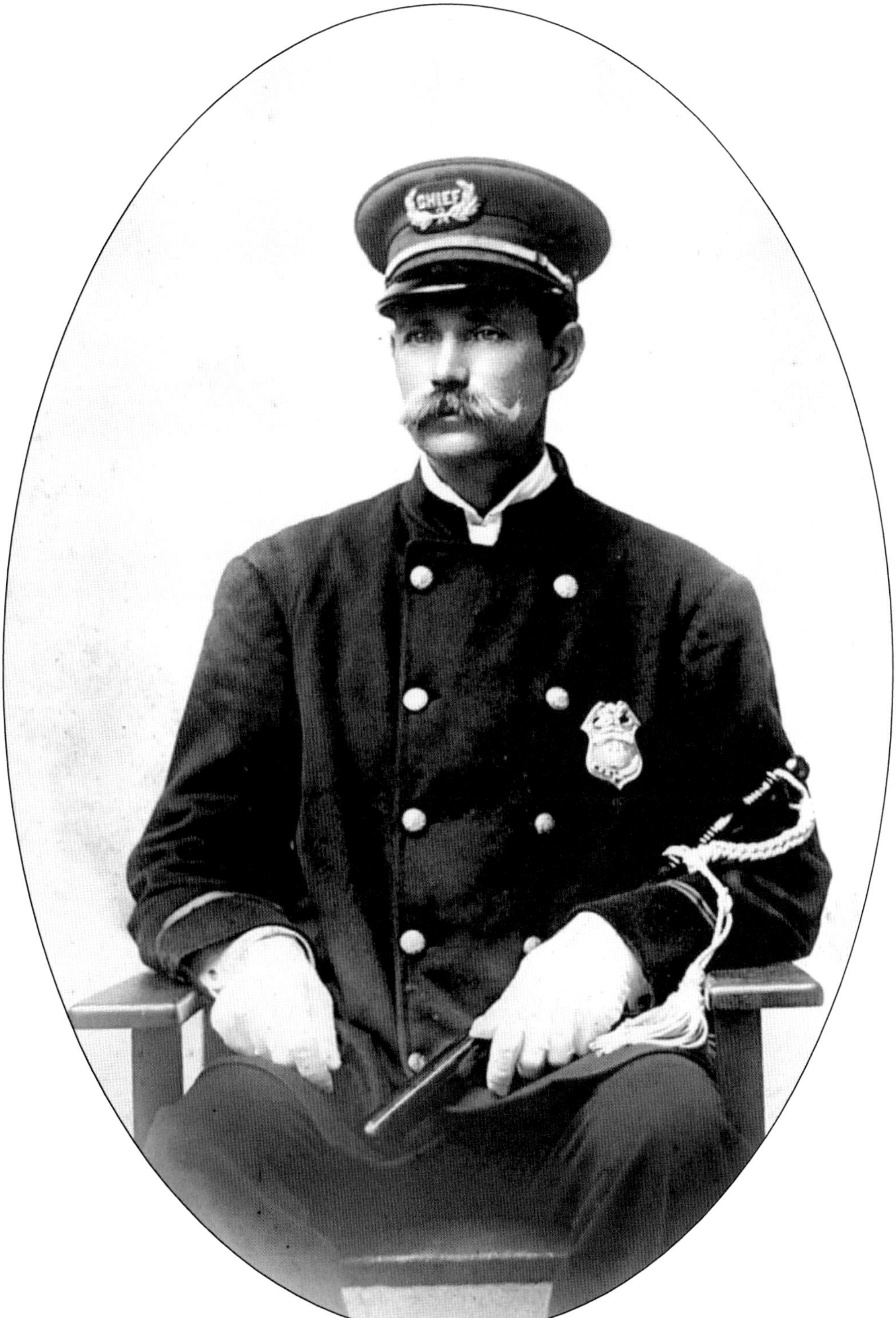

THE POLICE CHIEF. In 1909, Louis A. Eucker became the village's first chief of police.

IN CASE OF FIRE OR EMERGENCY CALL

641-6400

Ridgefield Park Volunteer Fire Department Alarm Signals

171	Grant School, Henry Street
172	St. Francis School, Mt. Vernon St.
173	Lincoln School, Lincoln Ave.
174	Roosevelt School, Teaneck Rd.
175	High School, East Grand Ave.
177	Callahan Chemical
178	Can Co., Bergen Pike & Hack. River
181	Route #80
182	N. J. Turnpike
183	Route #46 East of Teaneck Road
184	Howard Johnson's Route 46
185	Scott Ct. Apts, East End Cedar St.
186	Methodist Church, Cedar Street
187	Industrial Avenue
188	Simpkins Ind., Industrial Avenue
261	Central Ave & Second Street
262	Hackensack Ave. & Sixth Street
263	Central Ave. & Seventh Street
264	Hackensack Ave. & Fourth St.
266	Central Avenue & Fifth Street
351	Arthur St. & Roosevelt Ave.
352	Grand Ave. & Cutter Street
353	Hazelton St. & Bergen Avenue
354	Main Street & Grand Avenue
355	Teaneck Road & Grand Avenue
356	Edwin Street & Cutter Street
357	Union Place & Roosevelt Ave.
358	Gordon Street & Roosevelt Ave.
359	Arthur Street & Bergen Ave.
367	Main Street & Edwin Street
368	Teaneck Road & Hazelton Street
441	Mt. Vernon St. & Railroad Ave.
442	Main Street & Mt. Vernon Street
443	Summit St. & Lincoln Avenue
444	Park Street & Lincoln Avenue
445	Main Street & Webster Street
446	Summit Street & Fifth Street
447	Lincoln Avenue & Austin Street
448	Main Street & Preston Street
531	Mt. Vernon St. & Hudson Avenue
532	Poplar Street & Euclid Avenue
533	Park St. & Bergen Avenue
534	Mt. Vernon St. & Overpeck Ave.
535	Preston St. & Overpeck Ave.
536	Teaneck Road & Poplar Street
538	Mt. Vernon St. & Euclid Avenue
539	Preston Street & Bergen Ave.
621	Hobart St. & Euclid Avenue
622	East Winant Ave. & Hille Place
623	Brewster Ave. & Euclid Avenue
624	Teaneck Road & Brinkerhoff St.
625	Teaneck Road & Hobart Street
626	Main Street & Christie Street
711	Bergen Pike & Hackensack River
712	Oak Street & Elm Street
713	College Place & Laurel Street
714	Bergen Pike & Ridgefield Ave.
715	Bergen Pike & Teaneck Road
716	Teaneck Road & Chestnut Street
717	Route 46 & Ridgefield Avenue
718	Bergen Pike & Edison Street
719	Route 46 & Vorhees Place
111	Chief's Call
222	Schools Closed (7:20 A. M.)
333	Mutual Aid Call

Person sending alarm by call box
REMAIN AT BOX
To Direct Apparatus Upon Arrival

My Nearest Alarm Box Is No. ....

Located At..

Physicians Phone No.................................

ALARM SIGNALS. For many years, firemen and town residents were alerted to fire calls by a series of horns. This chart hung in nearly every village home. Whenever the horns sounded, villagers could look on the chart to see where the possible fire was. As a child, my favorite signal was 222, which indicated that school was closed.

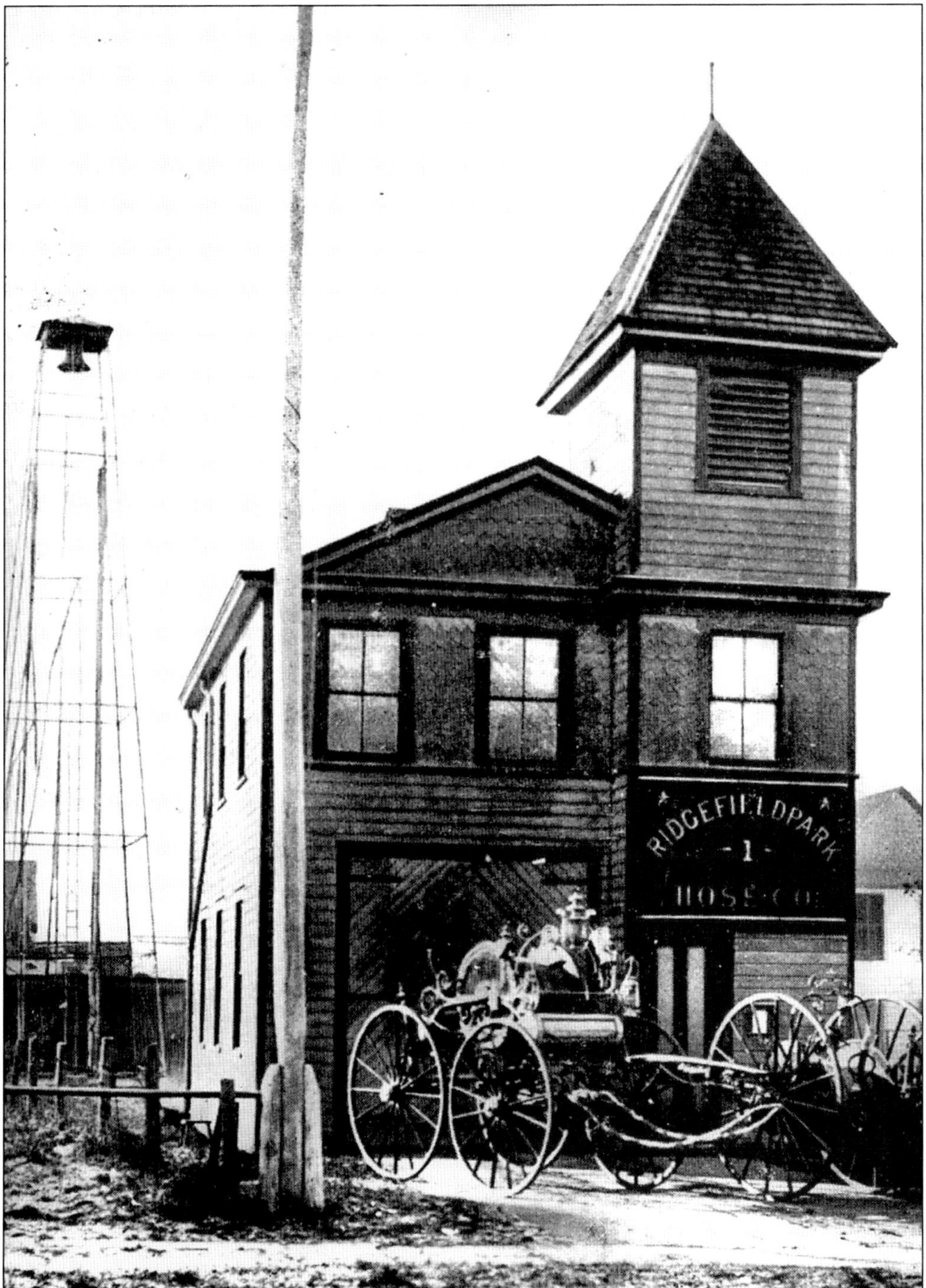

HOSE COMPANY NO. 1. Residents formed the first fire company in Ridgefield Park, and volunteers continue to serve the village today.

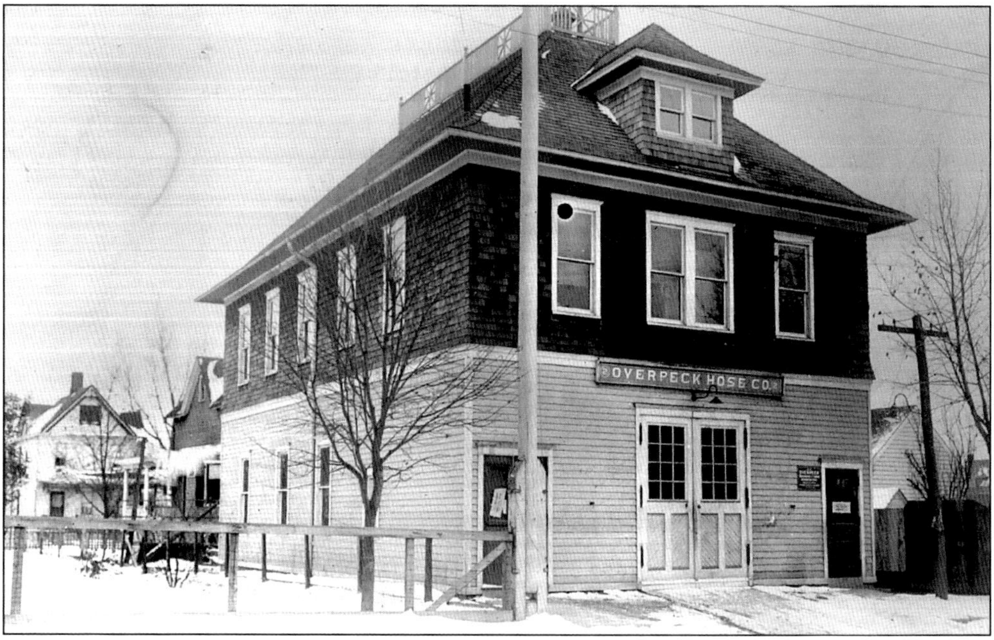

HOSE COMPANY NO. 2. Also known as the Overpeck Hose Company, this fire company was organized in 1905 and is still located on Euclid Avenue near Brinkerhoff Street. This firehouse was built as a result of a petition by residents for increased fire protection in that area of the village.

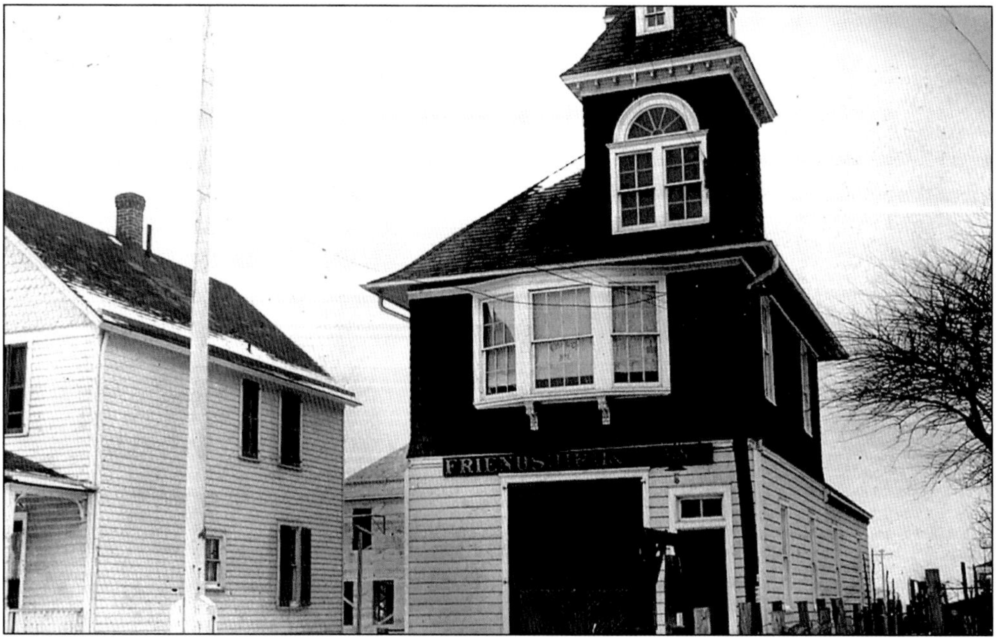

HOOK AND LADDER COMPANY NO. 1. Organized in 1892, this fire company was also known as Friendship Hook and Ladder and is located on Euclid Avenue across from Brewster Avenue. A large steel circle, seen in the foreground, still hangs in front of the Garden Street rear entrance of this firehouse. It was used to alert members of a call to duty. The original firehouse was built mainly by the members.

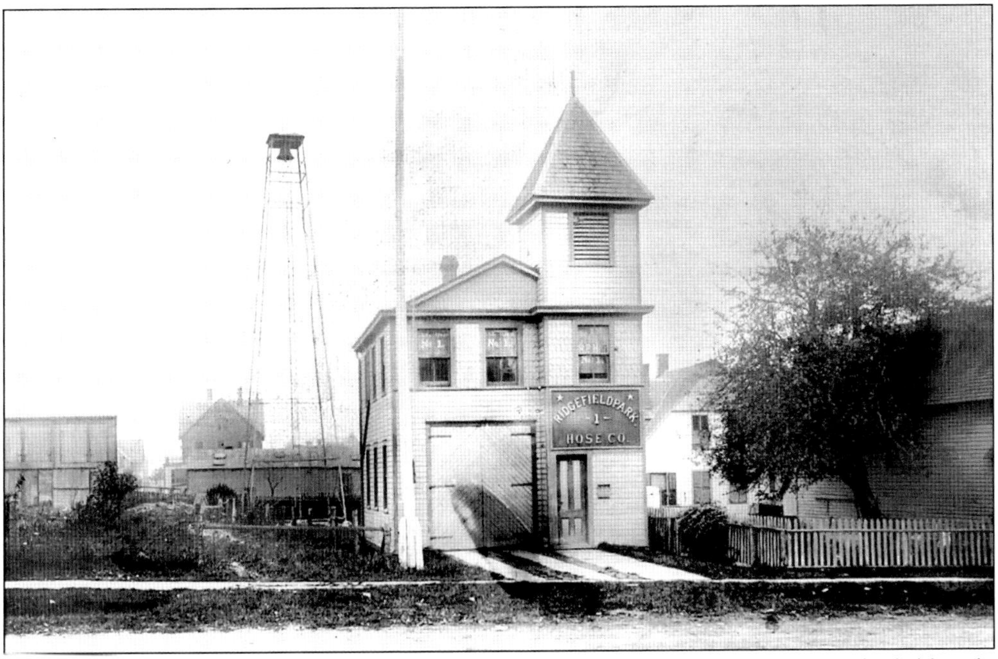

HOSE COMPANY NO. 1. Established in 1892, this was the first fire company in Ridgefield Park. It is still located on Mount Vernon Street. A large bell tower to the right of the firehouse was built in 1898 and was used to alert members of a fire call.

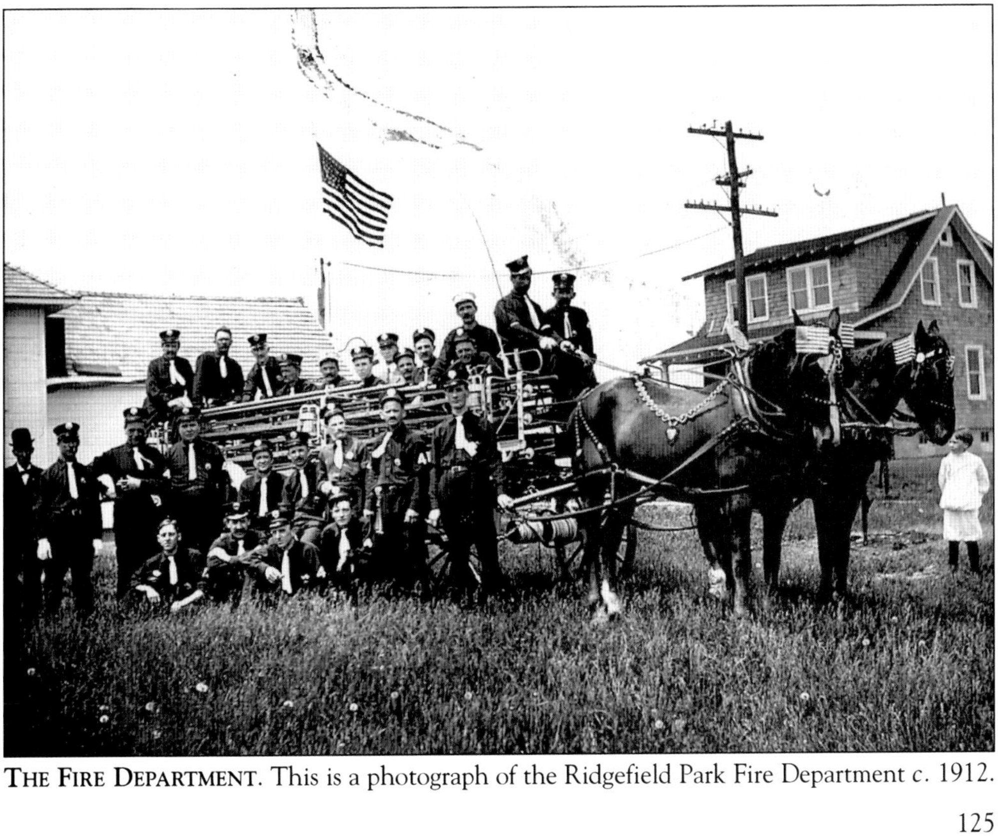

THE FIRE DEPARTMENT. This is a photograph of the Ridgefield Park Fire Department *c*. 1912.

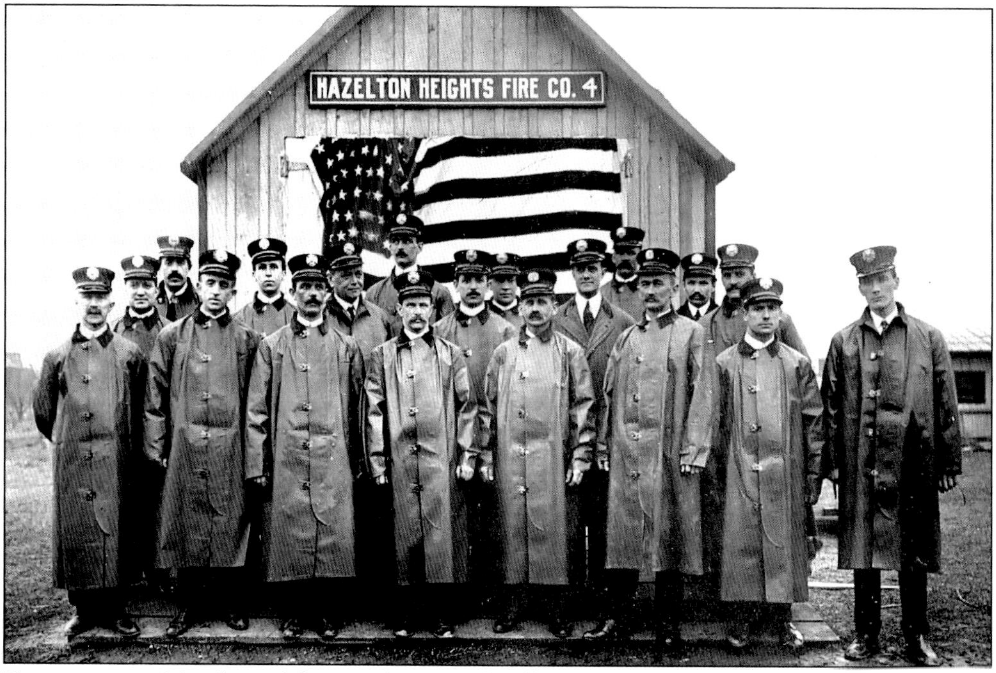

FIREFIGHTERS. Members of the Hazelton Heights Fire Company No. 4 gather for a photograph in front of the firehouse in 1911. This fire company, located on Hazelton Street near Roosevelt Avenue, was built as the result of a bad fire on Edwin Street in 1910. This fire company is now known as Truck No. 2.

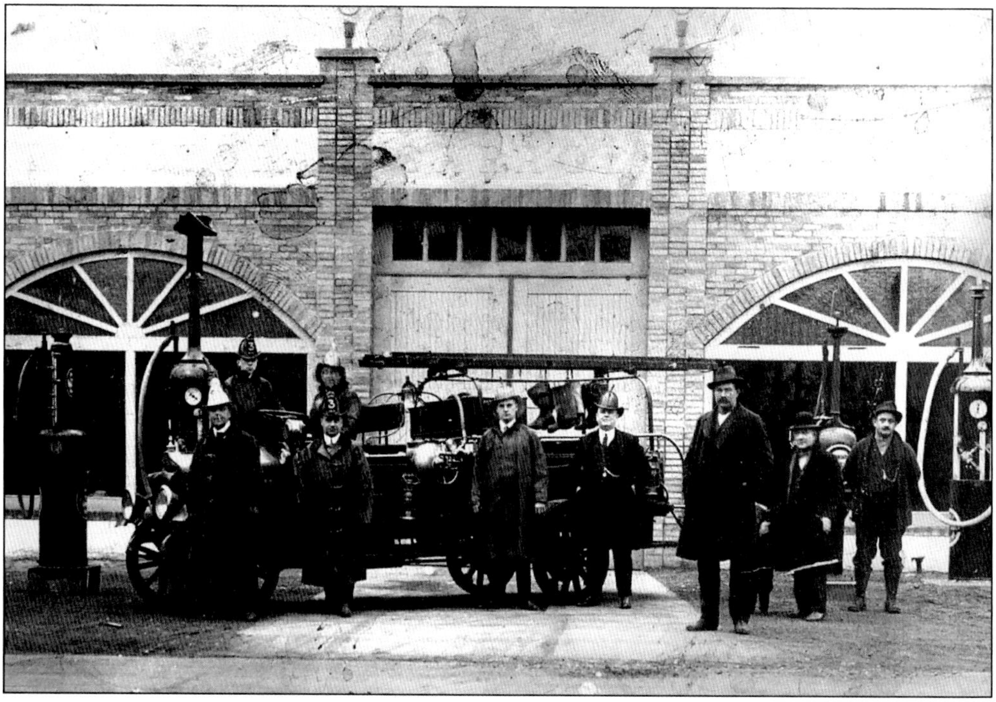

A FIRE TRUCK. Members of Hose No. 3 pose in front of Eucker's Motor and Repair Shop on Bergen Turnpike in 1920.

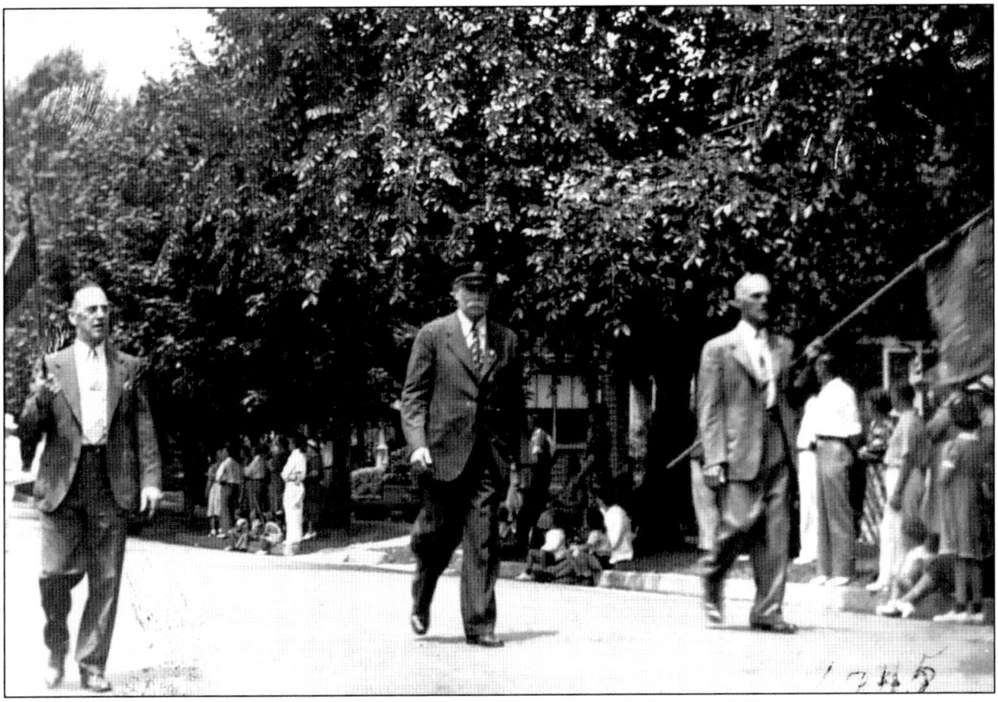

THE MEMORIAL DAY PARADE. George Alberque, Edward Eucker, and Herb Lowe represent the Exempt Firemen's Association in the Memorial Day parade on May 30, 1945.

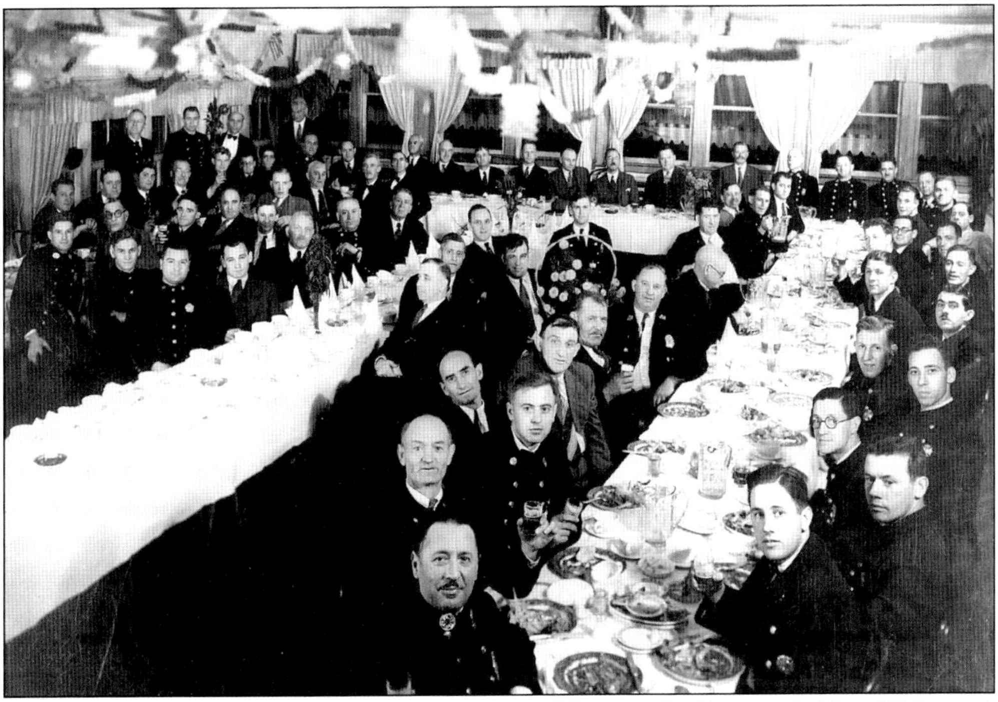

THE EXEMPT FIREMEN'S DEDICATION BANQUET. This grand affair was held at Wahrman's Overpeck Park Restaurant in Ridgefield Park on October 12, 1931. Wahrman is standing in the upper left corner of this photograph.

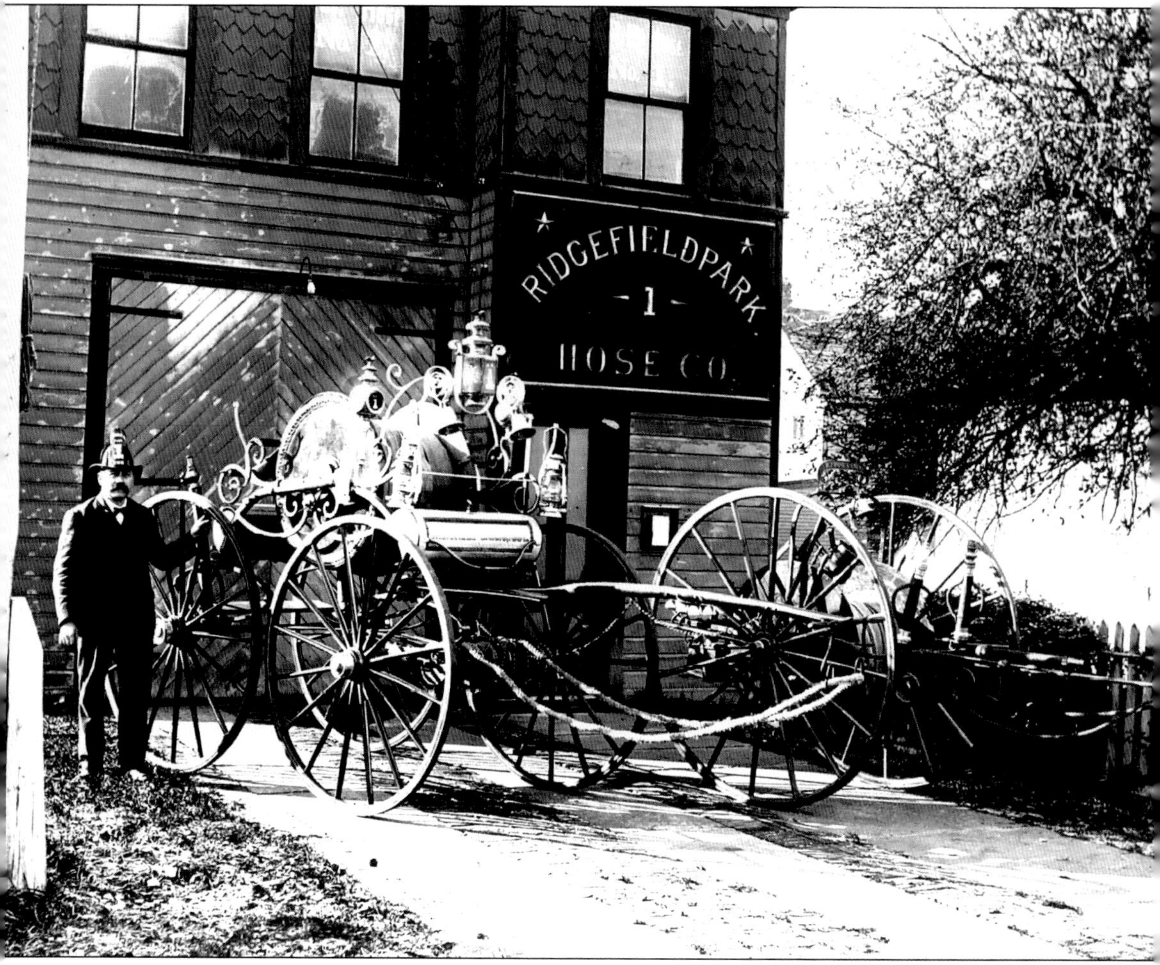

OLD HOSE NO. 1. This piece of apparatus carried hose to fire scenes. Purchased in 1895, it was pulled by the firemen if a horse was not available.